SpringerBriefs in Economics

SpringerBriefs present concise summaries of cutting-edge research and practical applications across a wide spectrum of fields. Featuring compact volumes of 50 to 125 pages, the series covers a range of content from professional to academic. Typical topics might include:

- A timely report of state-of-the art analytical techniques
- A bridge between new research results, as published in journal articles, and a contextual literature review
- A snapshot of a hot or emerging topic
- An in-depth case study or clinical example
- A presentation of core concepts that students must understand in order to make independent contributions

SpringerBriefs in Economics showcase emerging theory, empirical research, and practical application in microeconomics, macroeconomics, economic policy, public finance, econometrics, regional science, and related fields, from a global author community.

Briefs are characterized by fast, global electronic dissemination, standard publishing contracts, standardized manuscript preparation and formatting guidelines, and expedited production schedules.

Ilha Niohuru

Healthcare and Disease Burden in Africa

The Impact of Socioeconomic Factors on Public Health

Ilha Niohuru
Foundation Medicine Inc.
Cambridge, MA, USA

ISSN 2191-5504   ISSN 2191-5512   (electronic)
SpringerBriefs in Economics
ISBN 978-3-031-19718-5   ISBN 978-3-031-19719-2   (eBook)
https://doi.org/10.1007/978-3-031-19719-2

© The Author(s) 2023. This book is an open access publication.
Open Access This book is licensed under the terms of the Creative Commons Attribution 4.0 International License (http://creativecommons.org/licenses/by/4.0/), which permits use, sharing, adaptation, distribution and reproduction in any medium or format, as long as you give appropriate credit to the original author(s) and the source, provide a link to the Creative Commons license and indicate if changes were made.

The images or other third party material in this book are included in the book's Creative Commons license, unless indicated otherwise in a credit line to the material. If material is not included in the book's Creative Commons license and your intended use is not permitted by statutory regulation or exceeds the permitted use, you will need to obtain permission directly from the copyright holder.

The use of general descriptive names, registered names, trademarks, service marks, etc. in this publication does not imply, even in the absence of a specific statement, that such names are exempt from the relevant protective laws and regulations and therefore free for general use.

The publisher, the authors, and the editors are safe to assume that the advice and information in this book are believed to be true and accurate at the date of publication. Neither the publisher nor the authors or the editors give a warranty, expressed or implied, with respect to the material contained herein or for any errors or omissions that may have been made. The publisher remains neutral with regard to jurisdictional claims in published maps and institutional affiliations.

This Springer imprint is published by the registered company Springer Nature Switzerland AG
The registered company address is: Gewerbestrasse 11, 6330 Cham, Switzerland

Acknowledgements

I would like to acknowledge the contribution of my co-workers, Beatrice Birir, Abdelkader Bouregag, Fofana Daouda, Gilbert Gadzekpo, Funani Mpande, and Ademola Olokun, who contributed tremendously to the data and information collection. I would also like to acknowledge the support of the Data and Analytic Chapter of Roche, especially my supervisor Eva Xu and Gang Mu. Finally, I would like to express my gratitude to Emanuelle Mekler for her precious editorial advice.

Contents

1	**Introduction**	1
2	**Country Demographics**	7
	2.1 Country Profiles	7
	2.1.1 Algeria	7
	2.1.2 Côte d'Ivoire	8
	2.1.3 Ghana	10
	2.1.4 Kenya	10
	2.1.5 Morocco	11
	2.1.6 Nigeria	12
	2.1.7 South Africa	13
	2.1.8 Tunisia	14
	2.2 Population and Urbanization	15
	2.3 Fertility Rate and Gender	18
	2.4 Economy	21
	2.5 Education and Gender	21
	2.5.1 Literacy Rate	22
	2.5.2 School Enrollment and Gender Disparity	24
	2.5.3 Education Expenditure	31
	2.6 Summary	32
3	**Disease Burden and Mortality**	35
	3.1 Infectious Diseases	35
	3.1.1 Malaria	36
	3.1.2 HIV/AIDS	41
	3.1.3 Tuberculosis	48
	3.2 Non-communicable Diseases	49
	3.2.1 Cardiovascular Disease	51
	3.2.2 Respiratory Disorders	54
	3.2.3 Cancer	55
	3.2.4 Diabetes	58
	3.2.5 Cirrhosis and Other Liver Diseases	59

3.3　Substance Consumption 60
　　　　　3.3.1　Tobacco Consumption 60
　　　　　3.3.2　Alcohol Consumption 64
　　　3.4　Nutrition 68
　　　　　3.4.1　Nutrition 68
　　　　　3.4.2　Malnutrition 71
　　　　　3.4.3　Undernutrition 71
　　　3.5　Urbanization 75
　　　3.6　Physical Activity 77
　　　3.7　Overweight 79
　　　　　3.7.1　Obesity 82
　　　3.8　Summary 83

4　Health Resources 87
　　　4.1　Hospital Distribution 88
　　　4.2　Health Provider Distribution 89
　　　4.3　Summary 103

5　Healthcare Affordability 105
　　　5.1　Insurance Coverage 105
　　　5.2　Government Health Expenditure 108
　　　5.3　Individual Healthcare Affordability 112
　　　　　5.3.1　Hospital Costs 112
　　　　　5.3.2　Income 114
　　　　　5.3.3　Poverty 116
　　　5.4　Summary 119

6　Social Media and Technology Use 121
　　　6.1　Internet and Social Media Coverage 122
　　　6.2　Impact of COVID-19 128
　　　6.3　Summary 129

7　Conclusion 131
　　　Complete List of Works Cited 133

Chapter 1
Introduction

There is an acute scarcity of research and studies on the conditions of healthcare in African countries. According to Marincola and Kariuki (2020), 20% of the global disease burden falls on the shoulders of Africa, yet only 1% of worldwide scientific output focuses on African countries. Filling the epistemological gap is critical, for it will not only shine a light on our understanding of the realities of the continent, but also pave way for more engaged future studies. The investigation of existing healthcare conditions in Africa provides an indispensable basis for generating educated responses to the challenges that confront the continent as a whole and across its different localities. Africa also occupies a historically overlooked and underrepresented position. It is a unique continent with highly diverse cultures, societies, and economic compositions. While significantly different from the Western or more economically developed parts of the world, Africa is playing a crucial role on the global stage in a variety of aspects. Therefore, studies of Africa will not only benefit the regional communities, but also have a long-lasting impact on the rest of the world.

Africa carries the oldest and most diverse genome. Around seven billion of the world's population share a common origin in Africa. The burden of disease in Africa is also shifting from communicable to non-communicable diseases, which is also a major concern of the societies that are more economically developed. Therefore, addressing the disease burden in Africa, in parallel, means investing in the prevention and treatment of diseases in the rest of the world.

Increasing the amount of scientific research in healthcare in Africa can also benefit the cost-effectiveness of government expenditure and private sector (e.g. pharmaceutical and biotech companies) investment. For example, scientific research may constantly inspect the current healthcare system, particularly its principles, status, barriers, and vulnerabilities. This type of inspection often contributes to possible developments and modifications to the system that, in the future, will perform better for its users, governments, and other private investigators.

Theoretically, scientific output focused on African countries has great potential in terms of its natural growth. The median age in Africa is 19.7 years, making these populations the youngest and fastest-growing in the world. This implies that Africa will have a comparably higher ratio of working-age individuals to non-working-age individuals in the foreseeable future. More workers will join the healthcare field as providers, researchers, or other professional personnel. If the government provide enough resource to accept the incoming growing population in the scientific research team, the gap between the disease burden that Africa bears and the scientific output should alleviate in the future.

The number of scientific research related to the healthcare field in Africa has increased tremendously compared to the last century. However, many of them are published in the form of government reports, non-government organization reports, academic articles, or newspaper articles. This type of publication is more up-to-date with the content and the data, but the information is rather scattered due to the limitation of the publication format. The book publications provide more comprehensive and integrated information that depicts a more complete overview of the healthcare system in Africa, but the publication dates of the books are mostly from twenty or thirty years ago. Therefore, this book aims at providing an updated and integrated overview of the healthcare system in Africa, as well as compiling a list of data and report sources that updates their information on Africa annually.

In 2015, the World Health Organization (WHO) published 100 health indicators that were initially developed to ease the burden of reporting requirements of health monitoring but now serve as a tool to aid the global community in monitoring national and global progress, maintaining program support and advocating for resources and funding. The indicators include four main categories: health status, risk factors, service coverage, and health system. Some examples of the indicators are life expectancy at birth, maternal mortality ratio, children under 5 who are stunted, Immunization coverage rate, and health worker density and distribution. This book takes these 100 indicators as a crucial reference and aims at providing a brief overview of the current healthcare system in Africa along with other socio-economic factors.

A total of eight African countries are selected as samples in this book: Algeria, Côte d'Ivoire, Ghana, Kenya, Morocco, Nigeria, South Africa, and Tunisia. Three of the countries are from North Africa, three are from West Africa, one from East Africa, and one from South Africa. The diversity in the location, culture, and economic development of the countries should provide a comprehensive profile of the African continent. North Africa has a stronger public healthcare system compared to other parts of Africa.

The healthcare system of these countries is investigated in five parts: the country's demographics, disease burden, health resources, health affordability, and the use of social media and technology. These aspects are directly and indirectly related to each other as well as the performance of the healthcare system.

The country's demographics investigate the country's population, population growth, population density, urbanization rate, life expectancy, median age, fertility rate, gender equality, economy, and education. These factors play an implicit role when it comes to governments' decisions on policies and patients' decisions related to their own healthcare and well-being. For example, the current age structure is highly skewed to the younger side. This implies that the population structure will eventually be advantageous as the proportion of working-age people increases, but at the same time may be disadvantageous as the current governments and families are facing huge financial burdens due to health and education expenditures. Compared to those countries that are more economically developed and have an older population, relatively fewer health resources need to be invested in diseases related to the population. The fertility rate in many African countries, such as Nigeria, can be relevant to the fertility-related decision maker, which is usually the male, at home. The female in a traditional family usually does not have the right to decide when and how many they are going to give birth and stay at home to fulfill their domestic role. Consequently, they may less likely to seek healthcare such as breast and cervical cancer screening and HIV treatment.

In the past two decades, incidences of infectious diseases have been overtaken by NCDs as urbanization and Westernization spread across the continent. The disease burden chapter looks at the prevalence, death rate, and incidence rate of both communicable and non-communicable diseases in the eight countries in the past decade. The diseases studied in this chapter include: Malaria, HIV/AIDs, Tuberculosis, cardiovascular diseases (Ischemic heart disease, stroke, and hypertensive heart disease), respiratory disorders, cancer (breast cancer, lung cancer, cervical cancer, colorectal cancer, prostate cancer, and liver cancer), diabetes, cirrhosis and other liver diseases, This chapter also explores risk factors proved to be correlated with the increase in non-communicable disease cases, such as alcohol and cigarette consumption, nutrition, urbanization, physical activities, overweight, and obesity. Though not included in this report, a statistical model and analysis will be run using the factors and data collected in this section. Ideally, understanding the correlations between risk factors, incidence, and death rates of these diseases should provide a reliable prediction of the future disease burden in Africa.

Health resource is scarce in Africa, even though it carries over 20% of the global burden of disease. According to the target set by WHO, there should be at least two hospitals per 100,000 inhabitants, and 20 doctors per 100,000 inhabitants. Most countries studied in this book achieve the target of having at least two hospitals per 100,000 population, but only nationally not regionally. Most health resources are concentrated in the urban areas, leaving the rural areas less accessible to the resources. Furthermore, healthcare in most countries is divided into private and public. Public healthcare is often funded by the government and offered to all citizens, and private healthcare facilities are used mostly by people with more access to funds. In countries in North Africa, where the government provides a stronger healthcare budget, the healthcare facilities are mainly run publicly rendering less financial burden on patients. While in other countries, public hospitals are often less funded and more crowded, many patients with more sufficient financial ability would seek treatment through private hospitals. The loss of healthcare professional personnel is also a crucial issue existing in the healthcare system in Africa. South Africa reported an increasing resignation trend in the medical professions between 2011–2015 due to unsatisfactory salary and working conditions in the public hospitals, where they received their medical training after graduation. After resignation, these professionals often relocate themselves to private sectors, other provinces, or abroad, causing a lack of providers in the public sector.

The cost of healthcare is an enormous financial burden for the government, families, and individuals. When talking about paying medical bills, the common financial resource includes personal income and savings, as well as support from the government. Therefore, this chapter investigates insurance coverage, government expenditure on healthcare, and individual affordability, aiming at understanding the financial burden that the patient may bear when seeking medical services. Among the studied countries, only Algeria managed to provide free healthcare through insurance. The other countries tend to have a complete insurance scheme and have the choice of enrolling in private and public insurance. However, issues like public insurance are often underfunded, the claims take too long to process and the insurance is not reinforced, leaving the patients any choice but to cover the medical bills out-of-pocket upfront. Therefore, individual affordability becomes crucial when people make medical decisions. Thus, in the investigation, individual affordability is further broken down into the cost of a single hospital visit and hospitalization, the average income, and the poverty in the country, trying to understand to what extent a patient is likely to have the financial ability to cover the bills. Generally, governments are experiencing severe budget constraints, and the average cost of healthcare tends to exceed the patients' financial ability if they are earning an average or less than the average wage.

The geographic disparity in the allocation of healthcare resources can be identified in many African countries. Rural communities across the continent typically have restricted access to fewer resources. Not only are these regions faced with a limited supply of medical facilities, services, and healthcare professionals, but they are also more likely to be at a social, educational, and financial disadvantage. In addition, resources are unevenly distributed between urban and rural areas. Members of rural communities often have to travel long distances to urban areas to seek medical treatment or assistance. Given all the barriers and inequalities in real life, the Internet and social media serve as critical alternative avenues for people to access basic healthcare services regardless of their physical location. Therefore, this chapter collects data on the coverage of mobile phones, the internet, and the use of social media. All countries show a growing number in all three types of data. Some coverage is more complete than the other ones. For example, almost every citizen in Côte d'Ivoire possesses a mobile phone, which is not necessarily able to connect to the internet. Therefore, text communication may be more effective than using social media. However, considering the 50% illiterate rate in Côte d'Ivoire, using videos and photos on social media may be a better option in some circumstances. This chapter also looks at the software, website, and social media tools that people use in this country, especially during the COVID-19 pandemic. Agreed with the global trend, the internet is used more frequently during the pandemic. Meeting software, such as zoom and google meeting, gained more popularity in the workplace and in school. The user of entertainment apps, such as Tiktok, also increased during the pandemic.

To avoid potential privacy issues, all data and information presented in this book come from public sources. The most commonly used data sources include reports and open data from sites such as government health ministries, non-government organizations (e.g. World Bank and World Health Organization), and academic institutions (e.g. Washington University). The use of public data on the subject of African healthcare systems exposes and demonstrates the fact that this area is under-researched and under-attended. Some government reports only go back two to three years, and some lack continuity because the department suddenly stopped issuing reports. A similar phenomenon is also observed on the open data site. Even the World Bank, which is known for providing a consistent, reliable source, is blank in the data related to African countries. The data provided by World Bank tends to be more complete and traceable since 2014 (some from 2016 depending on the index). This implies that the data collection system has improved in recent years, and hopefully can provide stable and quality data in the near future.

Although the data sites, such as World Bank, World Bank Organization, and Global Health Data Exchange provide a lot of different types of valuable health-related data, some data on specific topics can only be retrieved from government reports or academic studies. For example, Kenya published a report named inequality trends and diagnostic in Kenya in 2020. However, the data used in the report is mainly from 1994, 2005/06, and 2015/16, leaving other years blank. The report lacks newer data and it is only published once a couple of years (sometimes there is only one report published on a certain topic.). Some less urgent topics may not even have a public report addressing them, such as insurance coverage, the average cost of hospital, the average time to call an ambulance, etc. These topics are sometimes addressed by academic research in more economically developed countries, which means they are likely to be left unaddressed and unattended in Africa.

The lack of stable and consistent data causes limitations in this book. Some data and academic sources used in this book can be dated before 2000, and some data is not sufficient enough to form a trend. There are also data from local news media and hospital websites to provide a general sense of the information. For example, the cost of the hospital varies from region to region. Therefore the data provided in this book is not sufficient to conclude all hospital costs but only to provide a rough comparison of the individual's income.

Due to the lack of data and resources on the topic, this book has its own limitation in providing precise data information. Instead of providing accurate data sources, this book intends to provide initial insights into a vast array of health-related topics in Africa. It proposes a template for assessing and understanding the healthcare system of a region. Assuming the data collection system and the science output on healthcare in Africa will continuously improve, a more comprehensive and reliable report can be produced by future studies. Theoretically, the template structure proposed by this book and the data collected can form useful information for the academic, private, public, and non-profit sectors, providing insights on possible opportunities such as data curation, digital platform formation, price referencing, partner engagement, talent attraction and leverage, public education, and innovation.

Open Access This chapter is licensed under the terms of the Creative Commons Attribution 4.0 International License (http://creativecommons.org/licenses/by/4.0/), which permits use, sharing, adaptation, distribution and reproduction in any medium or format, as long as you give appropriate credit to the original author(s) and the source, provide a link to the Creative Commons license and indicate if changes were made.

The images or other third party material in this chapter are included in the chapter's Creative Commons license, unless indicated otherwise in a credit line to the material. If material is not included in the chapter's Creative Commons license and your intended use is not permitted by statutory regulation or exceeds the permitted use, you will need to obtain permission directly from the copyright holder.

Chapter 2
Country Demographics

2.1 Country Profiles

A total of eight African countries are selected as samples in this book: Algeria, Côte d'Ivoire, Ghana, Kenya, Morocco, Nigeria, South Africa, and Tunisia. Three of the countries are from North Africa, three are from West Africa, one from East Africa, and one from South Africa. The diversity in the location, culture, and economic development of the countries should provide a comprehensive profile of the African continent. North Africa has a stronger public healthcare system compared to other parts of Africa. This chapter presents the country profiles of these countries, which includes the basic demographics (life expectancy, median age, fertility rate, population distribution), economic status (GDP and GNI), gender ratio, and education system.

2.1.1 Algeria

The People's Democratic Republic of Algeria in northern Africa has a population of 43,900,000 (World Bank, 2020) with an average life expectancy of 76.95 years (World Bank, 2020). The median age is 28.1 years (27.8 for men and 28.4 for women). The fertility rate is 2.946 (World Bank, 2020), resulting in annual population growth of 1.85% (World Bank, 2020), as shown in Fig. 2.1.

Algeria's gross national income (GNI) per capita is $3,948.3 (World Bank 2019). Spoken languages include Arabic (official), French (lingua franca), Berber or Tamazight (official), and dialects of Kabyle Berber (Taqbaylit), Shawiya Berber (Tacawit), Mzab Berber, and Tuareg Berber (Tamahaq). The main religion is Islam (99%), with Christianity and Judaism accounting for <1% (2012 est.). The northern capital, Algiers, is the most populous city (1,977,663), followed by Boumerdas (786,499), Oran (645,984), and Tebessa (634,332) (Population Data, 2021). Most

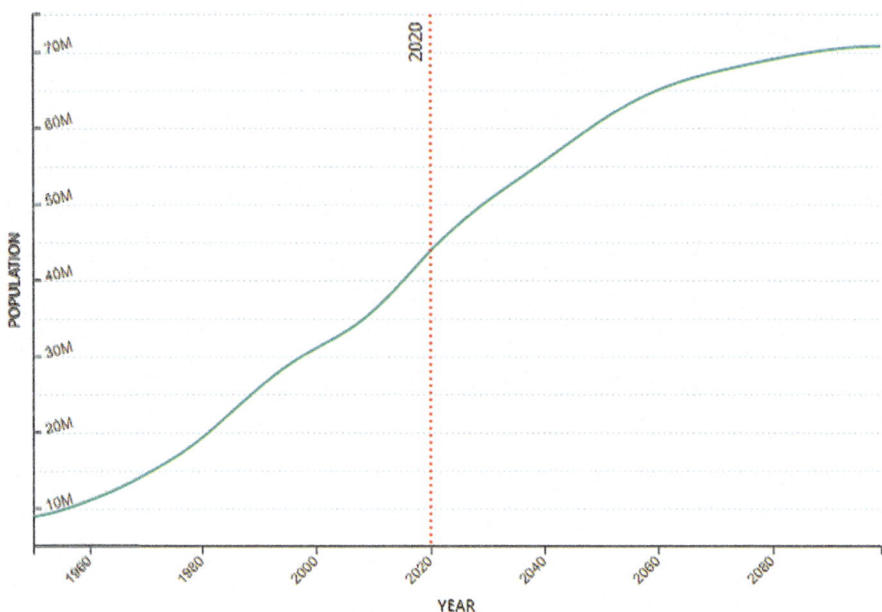

Fig. 2.1 Projected population growth in Algeria, 1960–2080 (*Data source* United Nations—World Population Prospects. *Map source* Macrotrends)

Algerians live in the northern part of the country, as the southern part is mainly a desert.

The gender ratio in Algeria fluctuates. The 2020 average was 102.10 men to 100 women, but at younger ages, there are more males than females. By age 45, the number of females surpasses that of men (Fig. 2.2).

Education in Algeria is free, starts at age six, and continues for nine consecutive years. Although mandatory, many children do not attend school, especially girls. Among girls who do attend, however, many complete secondary school and university. The government of Algeria funds a public healthcare system that is accessible and free to all Algerian citizens. This healthcare system generally favors preventative healthcare and clinics over hospitals.

2.1.2 Côte d'Ivoire

The Republic of Côte d'Ivoire is located on the southern coast of Africa along the Gulf of Guinea. It borders Guinea, Liberia, Mali, Burkina Faso, and Ghana. The population in 2020 was 26,755,519 (50.3% urban and 49.7% rural). Life expectancy is 56.6 (MICS, 2016). In 2014, Côte d'Ivoire's General Population and Housing Census projected 6,086,255 women of childbearing age by 2018, representing an annual increase of 2.6%. The total fertility rate is 4.6 (Multiple Indicator Cluster

2.1 Country Profiles 9

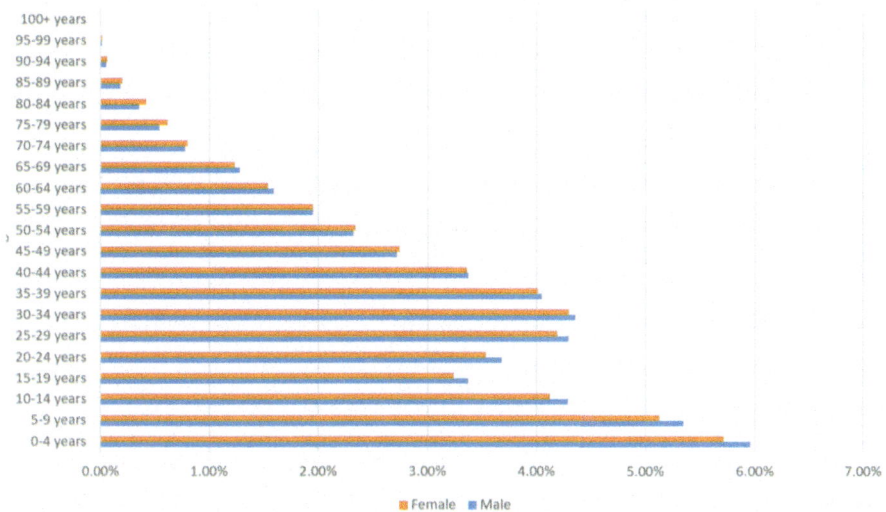

Fig. 2.2 Population distribution in Algeria, by gender and age, 2019 (*Data source* United Nations, Department of Economic and Social Affairs, Population Division. World Population Prospects: The 2019 Revision, *Graph source* Abdelkader Bouregag)

Survey 2016), resulting in annual population growth of 2.5%. The crude birth rate per 1,000 is 35.1 (Multiple Indicator Cluster Survey 2016), and the crude death mortality rate per 1,000 is 10.2 (MICS, 2018). Its most populous city is the capital, Abidjan (4,707,404). Its least populous city is Denguélé (289,779), in northwestern Kabadougou (World Population Review, 2020). Most people in Côte d'Ivoire live in the southwestern part of the country or in the capital city.

The gender ratio of Côte d'Ivoire in 2020 was 100 males to 98 females, and the overall population skews young (Fig. 2.3).

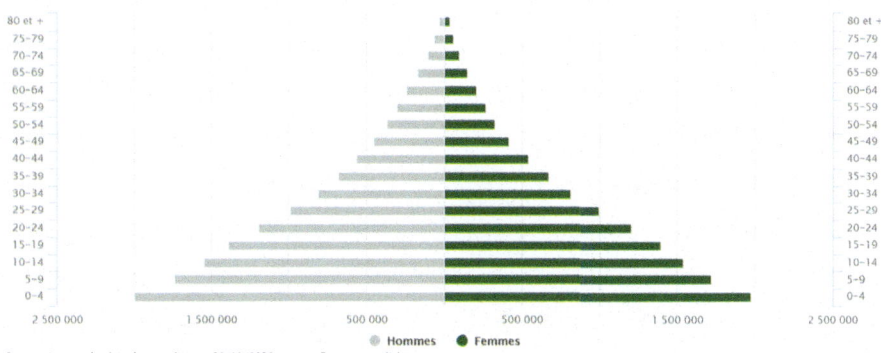

Fig. 2.3 Population distribution in Côte d'Ivoire, 2018 (*Data source* Banque Mondiale. *Graph source* Banque Mondiale)

The education system in Côte d'Ivoire is based on the French system. It was reformed in 2015 with the introduction of universal basic education to tackle a large number of out-of-school children (about 1.45 million children in 2014) and high rates of illiteracy among adolescents and adults. Students aged 3–16 years no longer pay tuition fees for most public schools, but they still pay entrance fees and purchase their own uniforms. The basic education system extends from preschool to lower secondary school. The education system also includes private, denominational, and secular schools that operate outside the public school system.

2.1.3 Ghana

The Republic of Ghana is located in western Africa along the Gulf of Guinea, bordering Togo, Burkina Faso, and Côte d'Ivoire. It has 16 administrative regions. The official language is English. The population is 76.9% Christian, 16.4%, Muslim, and 2.6% traditional faiths (Demographic Health Survey 2014). According to the World Bank (2018), the total population is 31,072,940 (Worldometer 2020), with a life expectancy of 63.78 years (62.7 for men and 64.9 for women). The total fertility rate is 3.87, resulting in 2.2% annual population growth (World Bank 2018). The unemployment rate is 4.51% among those of working age. The GDP is US$66.98 billion. In 2017, the healthcare expenditure was approximately 3.3% of GDP or $67 per capita.

The capital of Ghana is Accra, located in the Greater Accra region, which is the second most populous in Ghana (5,055,883), followed by Ashanti region. The least populous region is the northeast.

The gender ratio of Ghana is 102.79 males to 100 females (Knoema 2020), and age distribution skews heavily toward the younger end. Men outnumber women under the age of 50, but this distribution changes with advancing age (Fig. 2.4). Ghana is currently working toward universal health coverage focusing on primary healthcare and moderate investments in other sectors, such as oncology.

2.1.4 Kenya

The Republic of Kenya is located in eastern Africa along the Indian Ocean, bordering South Sudan, Ethiopia, Somalia, Uganda, and Tanzania. It is divided into 42 geographical units, referred to as counties. The official languages are English and Swahili (Kenya Law Reform Commission). The main religion is Christianity (85.5%), with only 1.8% of other religions (Index Mundi 2019). The total population is 52,573,937 with a life expectancy of 66.34 years (World Bank 2019). The total fertility rate is 3.46 births per woman (Macro Trend 2019), resulting in an annual population growth rate of 2.3% (World Bank 2019). The unemployment rate was

2.1 Country Profiles   11

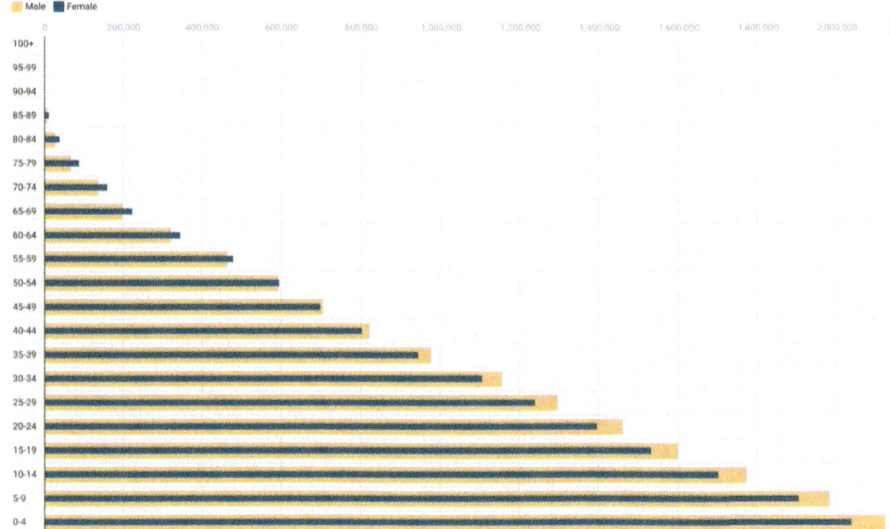

Fig. 2.4 Gender distribution in Ghana, by age, 2020 (*Data source* 2020 CIA World Factbook. *Graph source* Gilbert Gadzekpo)

2.6 in 2019, which rose to 2.98 in 2020 (World Bank). GNI per capita is US$1,750 (World Bank 2019).

The capital city of Nairobi is the most populated county, with a population of 4,397,073 (Kenya 2019 Census by Kenya National Bureau of Statistics, 2019). The least populous county is Lamu, with a population of 143,920.

The gender ratio in Kenya is 98.8 males to 100 females (Statista 2019), with more males than females until about age 10, when females surpass males. The population is very young overall (Fig. 2.5).

The government provides free primary and secondary education. Entrance into secondary school is granted by passing a national exam and obtaining the Kenyan Certificate of Primary Education. As a result, more than four-fifths of Kenyans are literate, which is extraordinarily high for sub-Saharan Africa.

2.1.5 Morocco

The Kingdom of Morocco in north Africa is home to 37,344,795 people (World Bank 2021). The average life expectancy is 77 years (World Bank 2019), with a total median age of 29.3 (World Bank 2018). The fertility rate is 2.42 (World Bank 2020), resulting in a population growth rate of 1.22% (World Bank, 2019). The GNI per capita is US $7,680 (World Bank 2019). Languages spoken include Arabic (official), Tamazight (official Berber language), Tachelhit, Tarifit, and French (often the language of business, government, and diplomacy). The capital of Morocco is

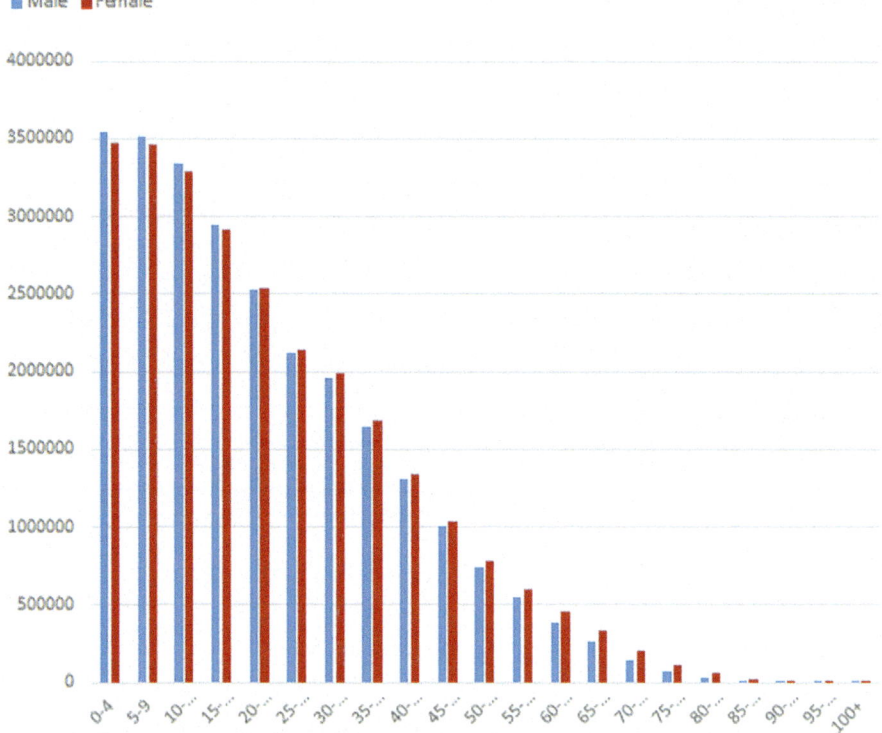

Fig. 2.5 Gender distribution in Kenya, by age (*Data source* 2020 CIA World Factbook. *Graph source* Beatrice Birir)

Rabat, but the most populous city is Casablanca (3,359,818 people as of 2014). Both cities are in northwestern Morocco, further from the desert and closer to the Atlantic Ocean (Fig. 2.6).

2.1.6 Nigeria

The Federal Republic of Nigeria is in western Africa on the Gulf of Guinea, bordering Niger, Chad, Cameroon, and Benin. It has 36 states plus the Federal Capital Territory. The official language is English. The population is almost equally split, 51.5% Muslim and 46.9% Christian, with 1.6% traditional faiths (Central Intelligence Agency World Factbook 2019). It is the most populous country in Africa with about 208.8 million people (Worldometer 2021), 52% of whom live in urban areas. Life expectancy is 54 years (53 for men and 55 for women).

The fertility rate is 5.4 (World Bank 2018), resulting in a population growth rate of 2.6 (Worldometer 2018). The median age is 18. The GDP is $442.98 million, and

2.1 Country Profiles 13

| Population by age and sex, 2015 and 2050

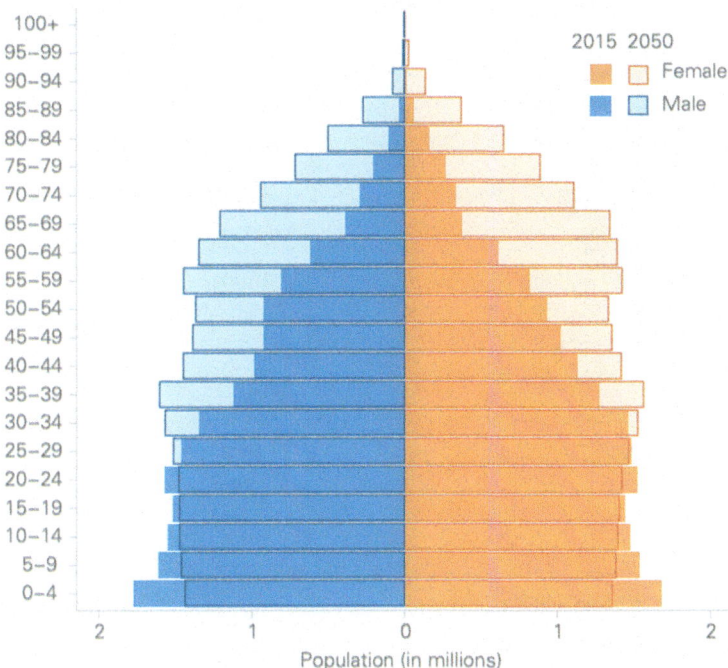

Fig. 2.6 Projected gender distribution of Morocco, 2015–2050 (*Data source* United Nations International Children's Emergency Fund, *Graph source* United Nations International Children's Emergency Fund)

the GDP per capita is US$2,150 (International Monetary Fund 2020). GNI per capita is US$5,190 PPP, and the minimum wage is 30,000 Naira (US$78.95). In 2019, 40% of the population lived in poverty. The capital of Nigeria is Abuja, located in the Federal Capital Territory. The most populous city, however, is Lagos, as it provides more economic opportunities. The least populous is Bayelsa. Kano and Lagos are Nigeria's most populous states. The gender ratio is 100 males to 97.24 females (2019), with more males than females at younger ages; however, by age 40, the number of women surpasses that of men (Fig. 2.7).

2.1.7 South Africa

South Africa, officially known as the Republic of South Africa, is located at the southernmost region of the African continent. The recorded population is 59,810,579 as of March 2021, with a life expectancy of 64.38 years. The fertility rate was

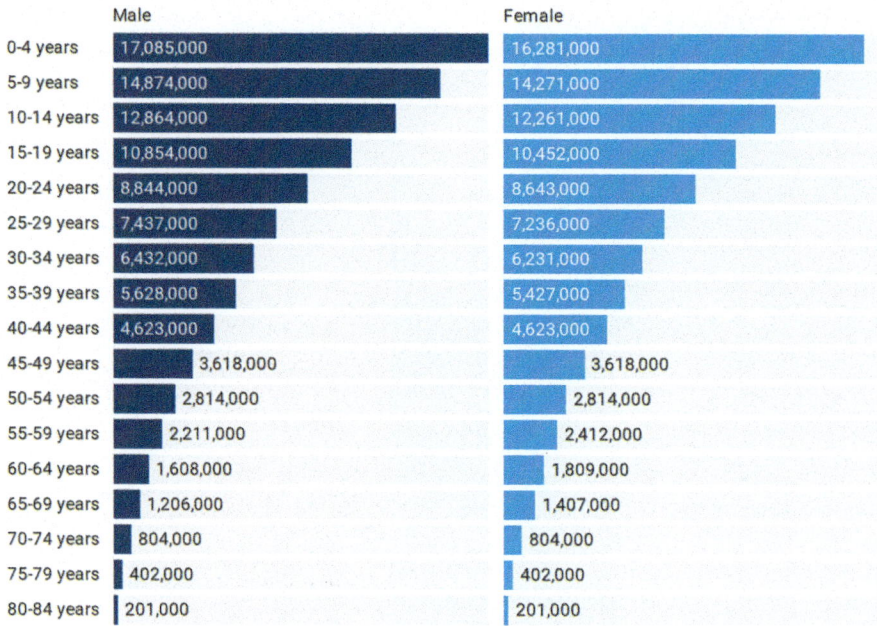

Fig. 2.7 Gender distribution in Nigeria, by age, 2019 (*Data source* 2020 CIA World Factbook. *Graph source* Ademola Olokun)

2.41 births per woman in 2018, resulting in annual population growth of 1.28% (World Bank, 2018). GNI per capita is US$12,670 PPP. The official languages are IsiZulu (23.16%), IsiXhosa (16.33%), Afrikaans (13.78%), English (9.80%), Sepedi (9.29%), Setswana (8.16%), Sesotho (7.76%), Xitsonga (4.59%), SiSwati (2.55%), Tshivenda (2.45%), and IsiNdebele (2.14%). The main religion is Christianity (86%), and others include 5.4% African religions (e.g. ancestral, tribal, and animist), 5.2% atheist, 1.9% Islamic, and 1.5% other (Central Intelligence Agency 2015). The most populated province is Gauteng, where 15 million people live. The Northern Cape is the least populated with 1 million people.

The gender ratio of South Africa is 97.09 males to 100 females. There are more males than females at younger ages, however, by the age of 40, the number of females bypasses that of males (Fig. 2.8).

2.1.8 Tunisia

The Republic of Tunisia is located in the northernmost region of the African continent. Tunisia is the 30th most populous country in Africa, with an estimated population of 11,746,695 as of 2020. Tunisians live about 77 years (World Bank, 2020). The

2.2 Population and Urbanization

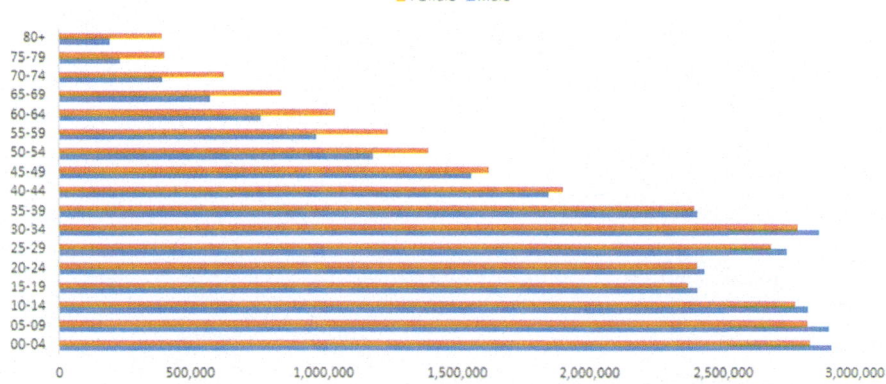

Fig. 2.8 Population distribution in South Africa, 2020 estimates (*Data source* United Nations, Department of Economic and Social Affairs, Population Division. World Population Prospects: The 2019 Revision. *Graph source* Funani Mpande)

fertility rate is 2.2 births per woman (2019), and the population growth rate is 1.06% annually.

The GNI per capita is US$10,850 PPP. Annual GDP is US$38.797 billion, and GDP per capita is US$3,317 (World Bank 2019). The poverty rate was 15.2% in 2015. Healthcare expenditure is 7.3% of GDP (World Bank 2018). The official languages are Arabic, French, and Berber. The main religion is Christianity (98%), with small numbers of people practicing Islam and Judaism. Tunisia's most populous governorate in Tunis also serves as the capital. The least populous governorate is Tozeur.

The gender ratio is 100 males to 102 females (2020). Women slightly dominate the population with life expectancies of 79 and 75 for men (Fig. 2.9).

2.2 Population and Urbanization

Africa has the fastest growing population in the world, with a 2.7% annual growth rate, which is more than twice as fast as southern Asia (1.2%) and Latin America (0.9%). Around 16.9% (1.228 billion) of the world's population (7,633 billion) lives in Africa, and the number is expected to increase to over 1.8 billion by 2030 (Fig. 2.10).

Globally, the average population density is 25 people per km^2. Most countries studied in this report have experienced increases in population density that greatly exceed the global average, according to data collected in 2018. The below-average increase in Algeria alone, as shown in Fig. 2.11, may be due to its large desert

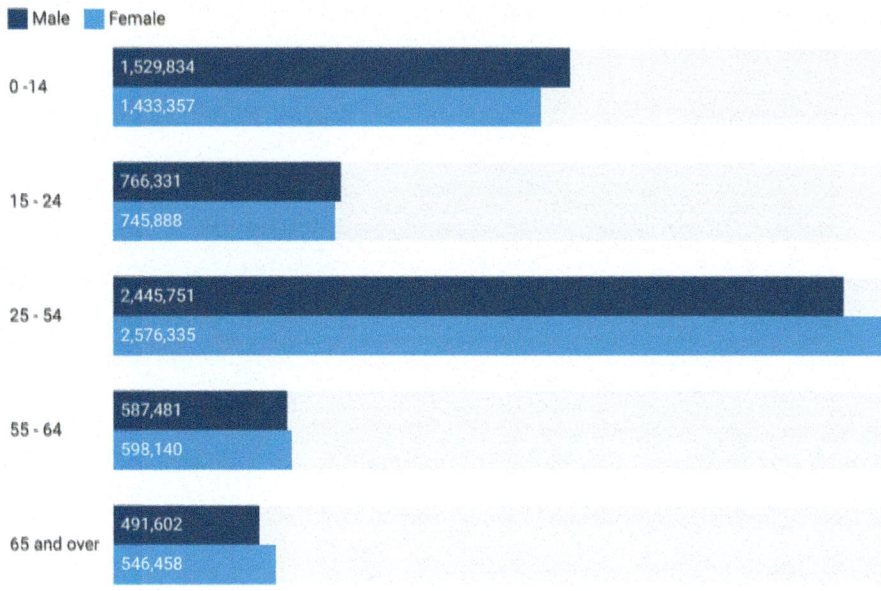

Fig. 2.9 Population in Tunisia, by age, 2020 estimates (*Data source* National Institute of Statistics (Tunisia). *Graph source* Ademola Olokun)

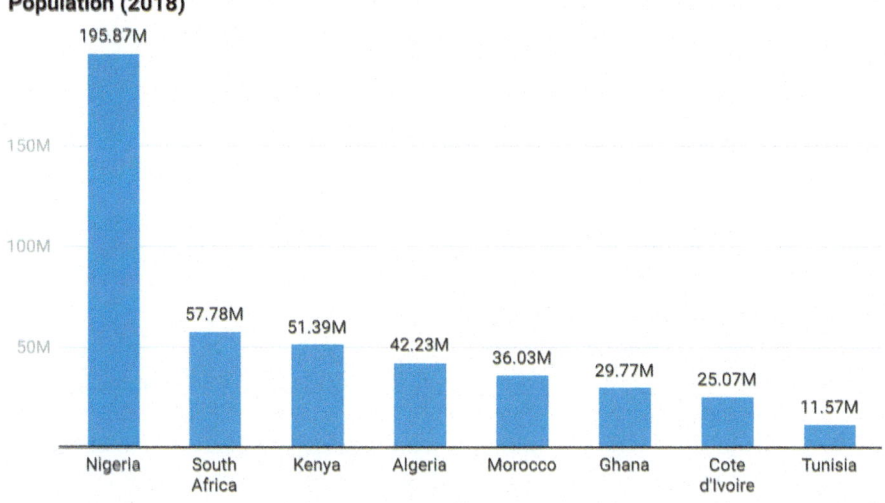

Fig. 2.10 Population in the eight studied African countries, 2018 (*Data source* World Bank. *Graph source* The author)

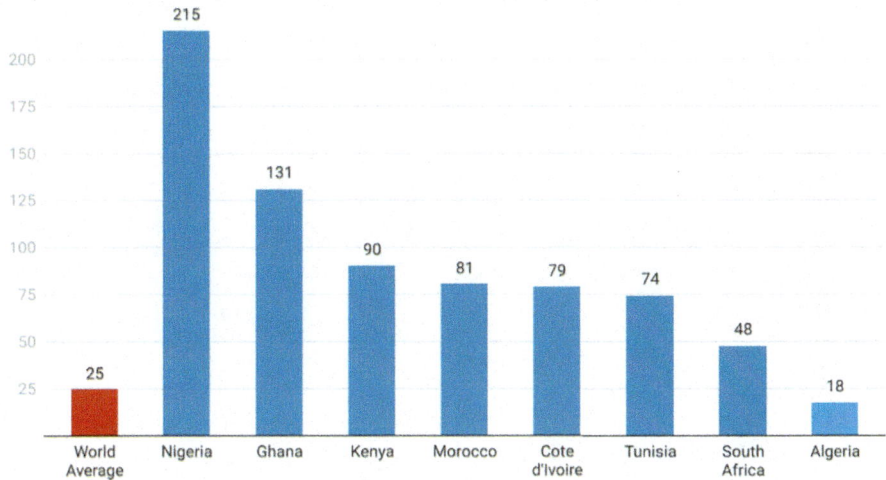

Fig. 2.11 Population density in the eight studied African countries, 2018 (*Data source* World Bank. *Graph source* The author)

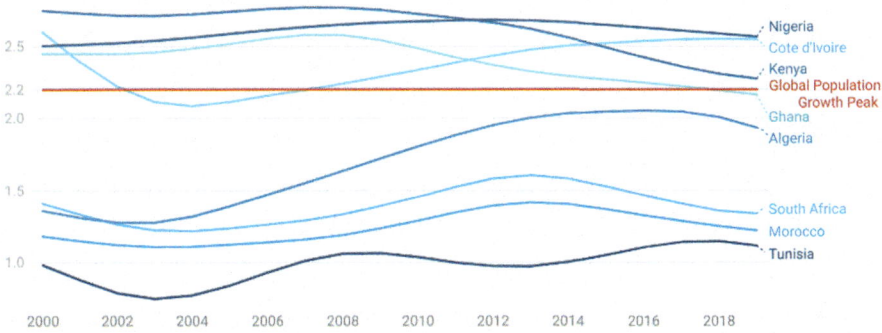

Fig. 2.12 Annual population growth in the eight studied African countries, 2000–2018 (*Data source* World Bank. *Graph source* The author)

area (Economist 2020).[1,2] This growth, as illustrated in Fig. 2.12, can be seen as a positive sign, as increased population density can indicate urbanization, rising living standards, and better quality of life.

The age range in Africa's population skews significantly young (Fig. 2.13).[3] By 2035, its population is projected to be the youngest in the world, and the ratio of working-age individuals to non-working-age individuals will increase. Another economic advantage of a younger population, compared to many developed countries such as Japan and EU countries, is reduced healthcare concerns. However, the large

---

[1] https://www.economist.com/special-report/2020/03/26/africas-population-will-double-by-2050.

[2] https://www.economicshelp.org/blog/20614/economics/population-density/.

[3] https://www.cia.gov/the-world-factbook/field/median-age/country-comparison.

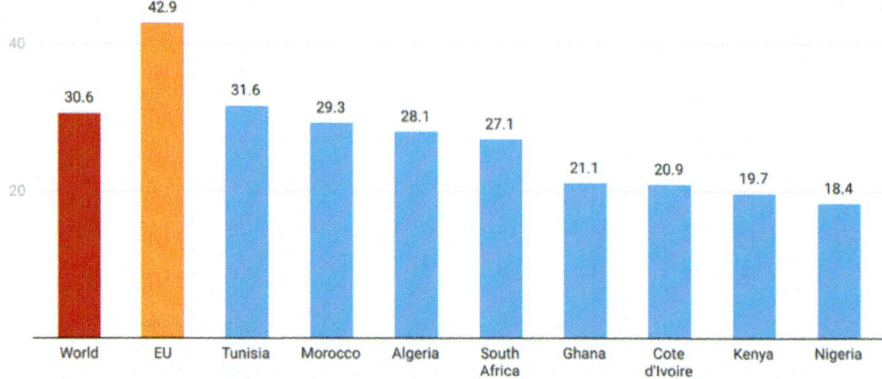

Fig. 2.13 Average ages in the eight studied African countries, compared to the world and EU, 2018 (*Data source* World Bank. *Graph source* The author)

share of children and young adults below age 29 means that governments will face large healthcare and education expenditures. It is thus important to prepare youths with job skills and to create jobs for people as they reach working age.

Some countries, mostly in western and central Africa, are experiencing demographic transitions, with shifts from high birth and death rates to older and more stable populations characterized by lower birth rates and higher life expectancies. This *demographic dividend* process occurs when the share of working-age people increases, thus creating an economic boost. Expansion of the labor force also can increase production capacity, as well as savings and investment. However, this transition can be jeopardized if fertility rates remain high and life expectancy increases, as is the case in many sub-Saharan African countries. For example, Nigeria is on the verge of such a demographic transition. It has the highest fertility rate (5.4) and population growth rate among all countries in this report, yet its life expectancy (54.3) is the lowest. Life expectancy at birth reflects overall mortality across all age groups. It has steadily risen by 26 years, from 38 in 1950 to 64 in 2021 (Fig. 2.14). The difference in life expectancy between men and women also has widened and is expected to continue widening as deaths from HIV/AIDS decrease.

A subregional variation on the continent indicates that the average life expectancy for northern African countries rose by more than 50% from 1960 to 2011, compared to 10% or less in almost all southern African countries. Eastern Africa had the most rapid increase in life expectancy, whereas southern Africa experienced declines due to HIV/AIDS (Fig. 2.15).

2.3 Fertility Rate and Gender

Fertility rate refers to the number of children born to each woman if she lives to the end of her childbearing years. If the fertility rate reaches 2.1, the replacement level,

2.3 Fertility Rate and Gender

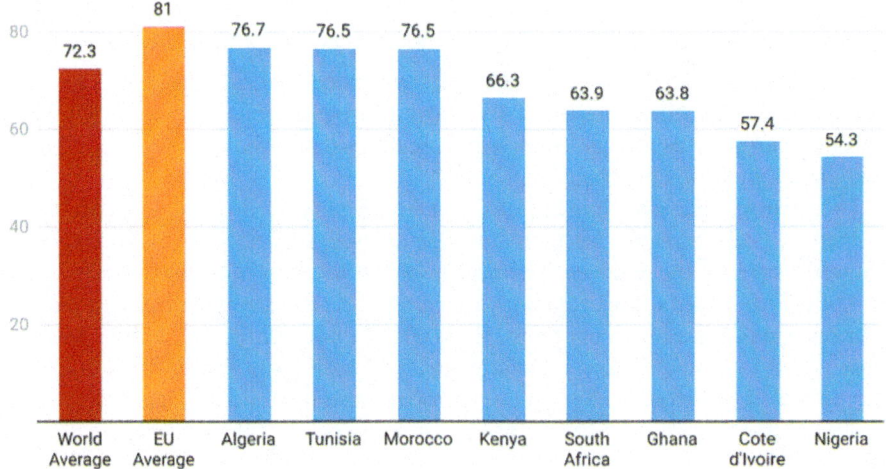

Fig. 2.14 Life expectancy in the eight studied countries, compared to the world and EU (*Data source* World Bank. *Graph source* The author)

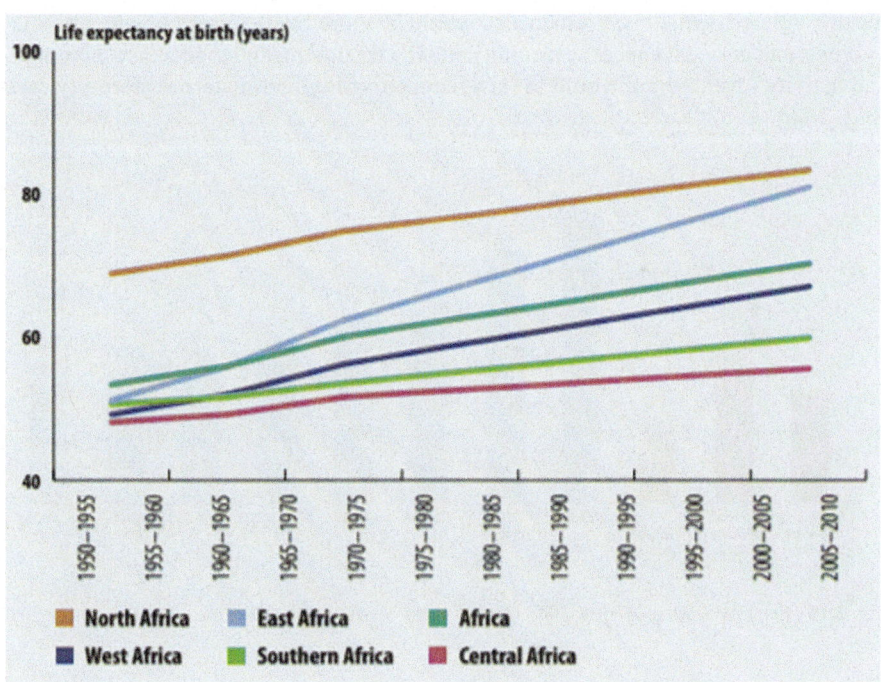

Fig. 2.15 Life expectancies in Africa, 1950–2010, adapted from AfDBm (2011)

the population will exactly replace itself from one generation to the next. The global fertility rate is 2.4. In 2018, the EU average fertility rate was 1.6. All eight countries in this study have a fertility rate that exceeds the replacement rate, and five exceed the global average. Fertility rates often decreases as urbanization and income increases and child mortality decreases.[4] Developed countries tend to have lower fertility rates but much higher life expectancies.

The fertility rate may indicate the gender equality of a country. Historically, husbands make decisions for their families in most traditional African societies, and wives care for the children. The burden of fertility thus falls almost exclusively on women. In Nigeria, for example, women tend to have many children to prevent their husbands from divorcing them. High fertility rates in these countries become closely tied to women's low societal status.[5] Reducing the fertility rate could be interpreted as an increase in gender equality because it would indicate that women are less restricted by their domestic roles as housewives and mothers and are gaining autonomy.

Women's autonomy is significant to the healthcare system. Being viewed as an individual, rather than solely as a mother, gives women a better chance at education and job training, more control over their own bodies, and the power to make fertility-related decisions. Women also would be more likely to seek healthcare, such as breast and cervical cancer screening and HIV treatment, and to increase their physical activity level, which would in turn reduce fertility and maternal mortality rates (Fig. 2.16).

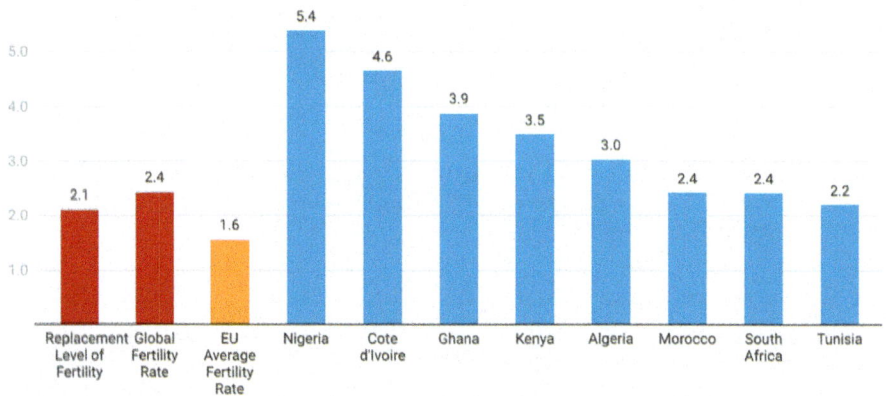

Fig. 2.16 Fertility rates in Africa, 2018 (*Data source* World Bank. *Graph source* The author)

---

[4] https://www.wri.org/research/achieving-replacement-level-fertility#:~:text=%E2%80%9CRepl acement%20level%20fertility%E2%80%9D%20is%20the,modestly%20vary%20with%20mort ality%20rates.

[5] https://epc2012.princeton.edu/papers/120061.

2.4 Economy

The healthcare system in the African region is weak compared to many developed countries. It is underfunded, overstretched, and understaffed. The underlying reason for the current poor state of health is the failure to alleviate extreme poverty.[6] Overseas aid and debt relief are not sufficient to address core issues in the African healthcare system. Most of this aid goes to general budget support and is lost to inefficiencies in the system. For example, relief funds aimed at healthcare are spent on expensive tertiary hospitals that do not reach most people seeking medical help. Diseases like HIV/AIDS rely heavily on primary care rather than tertiary care. Furthermore, foreign aid from traditional international donors to Africa is declining. Therefore, African countries will need to shift their focus to greater domestic ownership of health systems and the involvement of new international aid players.

According to *Health in Africa over the Next 50 Years*, published by the African Development Bank Group in 2013, even though the overall wealth of Africa has increased, the poorest sectors of the population remain out of reach of the healthcare system due to governance and income inequality. Weak institutions make some governments vulnerable to corruption and conflict. Thus, although the poverty level has declined from 9% since 1995, 47% of Africa's population (excluding northern Africa) still earns $1.25 or less a day.

All eight countries studied in this report had an annual GDP lower than the average annual GDP of low-income countries in 2018. However, all had a higher GDP per capita than the average low-income country, especially South Africa (Figs. 2.17 and 2.18). For example, the local currency in Ghana has consistently depreciated (GHC 5.74 to US$1), and it has experienced relatively low economic growth (1.6% increase between 2018 and 2019). Increased public debt and government expenditures continue to generate negative fiscal and trade balances.

2.5 Education and Gender

Education and healthcare have a bidirectional relationship, each playing an important and direct role in the other. Higher education typically leads to higher income, which means more options for investing in healthcare, more knowledge about medicine, greater self-awareness and emotional regulation, and better physical fitness. Lack of education in developing countries can lead to poor health, unequal gender roles, child labor, poverty, and so on.

---

[6] https://www.ncbi.nlm.nih.gov/pmc/articles/PMC1239980/.

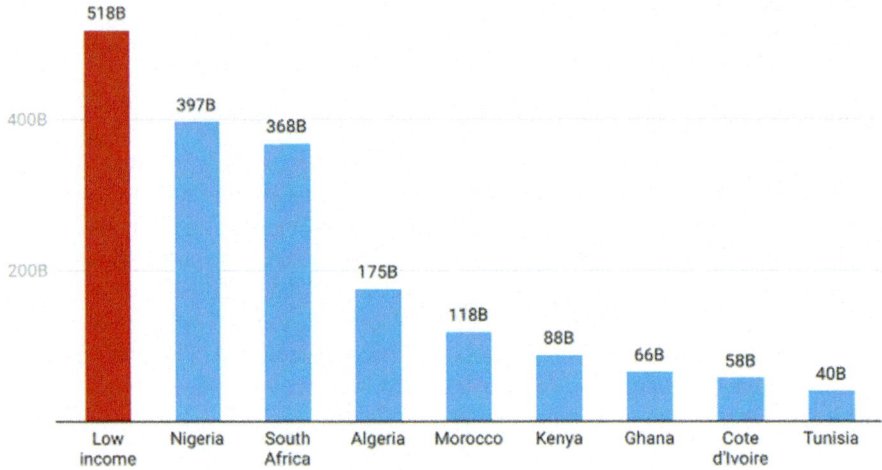

Fig. 2.17 GDP (USD) in the eight studied countries, 2018 estimates (*Data source* World Bank. *Graph source* The author)

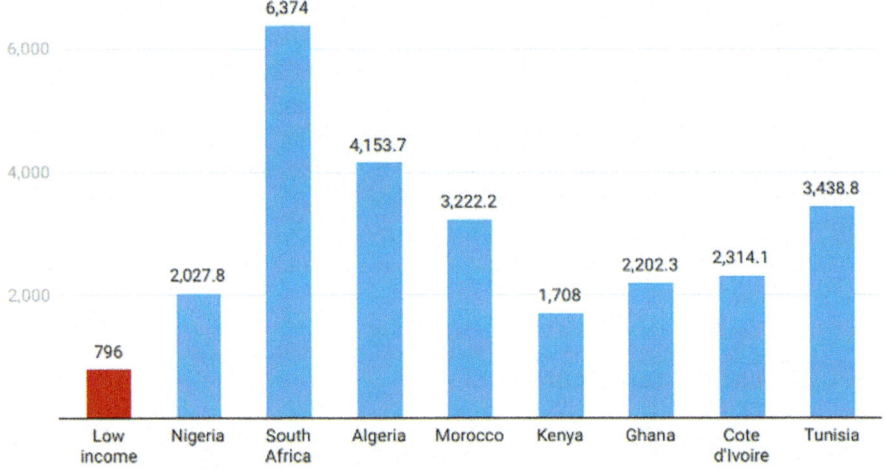

Fig. 2.18 GDP per capita in the eight studied countries (*Data source* World Bank. *Graph source* The author)

2.5.1 Literacy Rate

Literacy refers to the ability to read and write and has been shown to be complementary to health services. The cost of increasing the literacy rate, particularly education expenditure, outweighs the cost of mortality and reduces direct healthcare costs. Patients who are literate can act on health information and better advocate for their individual, family, and community health. The general literacy rate also affects the health literacy rate, which is the degree to which people can access, understand, appraise, and communicate information to engage with the demands of different health contexts and promote and maintain good health across the life course.[7] Being health literate implies an increased ability to take responsibility for one's health and to adhere to treatment. However, low literacy is not always associated with low health literacy. People who cannot read but have excellent verbal communication skills can still acquire knowledge and understanding from medical providers, just as people with high overall literacy may fail to interpret certain medical information. Nevertheless, people with low health literacy generally have less access to healthcare, higher medical costs, and increased emergency care visits and hospital admissions. It is, therefore, crucial to present and communicate health-related information in an accessible way. Due to data limitations, this report will not look at health literacy directly but instead draw conclusions based on overall literacy data.

According to the World Bank, Côte d'Ivoire had the lowest literacy rate in 2018 among the eight studied countries, with only 47% of the population aged 15 and older able to read and write. Nigeria ranked second lowest (62%), then Ghana (79%), Algeria (81%), and Kenya (82%). In South Africa, 87% of the adult population aged 15 or older was considered literate in 2017. Literacy rates vary by region, gender, and income quartile. For example, the highest literacy rates in Nigeria were registered in the southern regions of the country, where 89% of males and 81% of females were considered literate in 2018. The southern zones of Nigeria also reflect the smallest gender discrepancies in literacy: female literacy in Nigeria is among the highest in western Africa. The primarily Muslim northern region has lower rates because most Muslim students pursue Islamic education after completing some elementary education.

In most of the studied countries, fewer women than men are literate. The Ministry of Education reported 60 million Nigerians (~30%) as illiterate in 2017, 60% of whom were female. In South Africa, women with lower incomes than men also have lower literacy rates. Literacy is directly proportional to income in other countries as well. In Nigeria, the literacy rate in urban areas (80.2%) is much larger than that in rural areas (47.45%), as shown in Fig. 2.19.

In South Africa, literacy also has a direct proportional relationship to the income quintile. As income increases, so does literacy among all genders (Fig. 2.20).

In 2017, Ghana introduced a free senior high school policy to eliminate some of the financial burdens parents face in educating their children. Ghana's literacy rate has since increased to 79.04%. The literacy rate of Tunisia, as measured by the percentage of people aged 15 and above who can read and write was around 79.04% in 2014. Literacy among males has decreased since 2012, but literacy among females has continued to increase (Fig. 2.21).

---

[7] Health literacy as a metric was introduced in 1974. For more information, see https://www.cdc.gov/healthliteracy/learn/index.html.

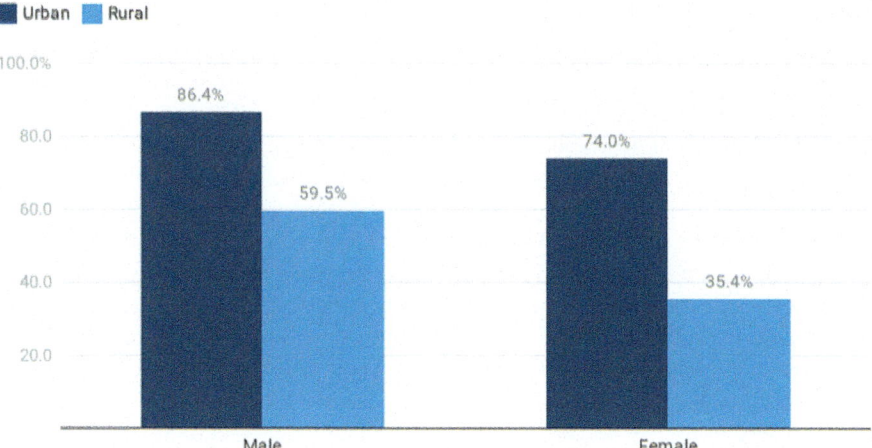

Fig. 2.19 Literacy rate in Nigeria, by area and gender, 2018 (*Data source* World Bank. *Graph source* The author)

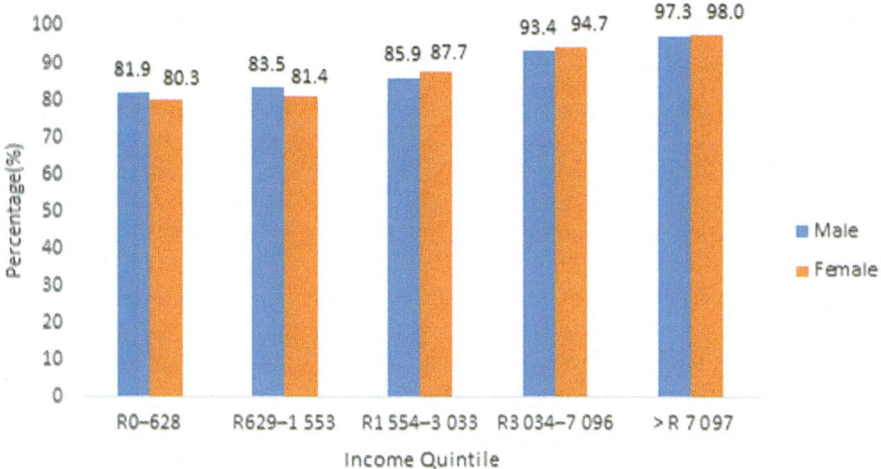

Fig. 2.20 Literacy among people aged 15 years and older, by gender and by monthly per capita income quintile, 2018 (*Data source* World Bank. *Graph source* The author)

2.5.2 School Enrollment and Gender Disparity

Individuals with higher levels of education tend to have higher incomes and are more likely to consume preventative medical care, purchase healthy food, and exercise regularly. Their employers also may offer health insurance, paid leave, and retirement

2.5 Education and Gender

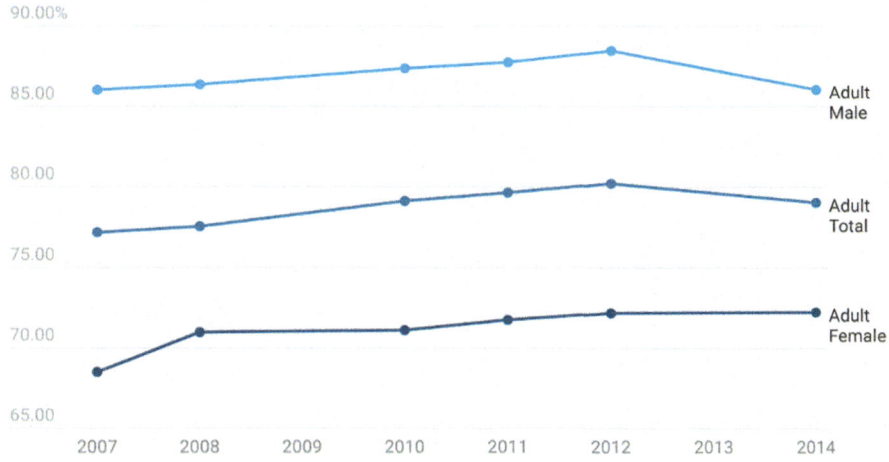

Fig. 2.21 Literacy rate in Tunisia, 2007–2014 (*Data source* World Bank. *Graph source* The author)

plans.[8] However, school enrollment in African countries is complicated. In 2012, only about half of the children in sub-Saharan Africa attended school, mainly due to barriers caused by poverty. UNICEF has identified 13 barriers to education in developing countries, including direct and indirect costs; lack of national budgets for education, health, and nutrition; and local attitudes and traditions.[9] These barriers affect girls, children with disabilities, ethnic minorities, and poor and rural children most acutely.

The Social Progress Index[10] (Fig. 2.22) measures the capacity of a society to meet the environmental and social needs of its citizens through various indicators, such as basic human needs (nutrition, sanitation, shelter, and personal safety), wellbeing (education, health, technology access, and environmental quality), and opportunities (personal rights, freedom and choice, inclusiveness, and access to advanced education).

According to the index, five of the eight studied countries (Algeria, Côte d'Ivoire, Nigeria, Morocco, and Tunisia) rated poorly for educating women, and three of those (Morocco, Côte d'Ivoire, and Tunisia) also rated low in gender parity in secondary school, indicating the alarming lack of school attendance and participation among girls, and Côte d'Ivoire rated low in access to knowledge in general.

Algeria has the highest social index due to its high primary and secondary school enrollment. It provides free and mandatory nine years of education to children from age six. According to 2018 data, fewer girls were enrolled in primary and middle school, but more girls than boys were enrolled in advanced education. Although not

---

[8] https://www.ifc.org/wps/wcm/connect/REGION__EXT_Content/IFC_External_Corporate_Site/Sub-Saharan+Africa/Priorities/Health+and+Education/.

[9] https://www.unicef.org/sowc06/pdfs/sge_English_Version_B.pdf.

[10] https://www.socialprogress.org/index/global/results.

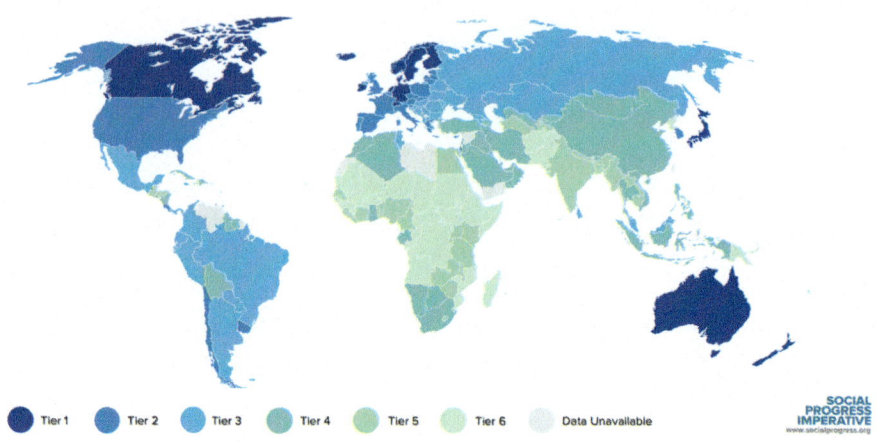

Fig. 2.22 Social Progress Index, 2020 (*Data source* Social Progress Index, 2020. *Graph source* The author)

investigated in this paper, the graph indicates that more boys drop out of school after completing middle school (Figs. 2.23 and 2.24).

In Côte d'Ivoire, the difference in school enrollment in urban and rural areas is more evident. Preschools and students in urban areas outnumber those in rural areas, as urban residents have enough money to send their children to school and less time to take care of them when they are at work (Figs. 2.25 and 2.26). To balance the proportion of students across zones, the government has taken actions to bring schools to remote areas of the country.

Ghana introduced the Education Reform Program in 1987 and the Free Compulsory Universal Basic Education Program in 1996 requiring six years of primary education followed by three years of secondary school, three years of senior high education, and four years of tertiary education. These two programs have contributed immensely to the country's basic education achievements (Fig. 2.27).

The national educational system of Kenya consists of three main levels: eight years of compulsory primary education beginning at age six, four years of secondary school, and four years of higher education. This "8-4-4" education system, which started in 1985, is being replaced by Kenya's new 2-6-6-3 (2-6-3-3-3) curriculum, which includes two years of pre-primary, six years of primary, three years of junior secondary, three years of senior secondary, and at least three years of higher education. See Fig. 2.28.

In Nigeria, the gross enrollment rate in elementary schools was 68.3% in 2018. The northwestern and southwestern states have the highest enrollment rates (70.3% for boys and 73% for girls). The gross enrollment rate in middle schools in Nigeria is 54.4%, with the highest numbers in the southeastern states (52.5% for boys and 59.8% for girls). Figures 2.29 and 2.30 illustrate these statistics.

2.5 Education and Gender

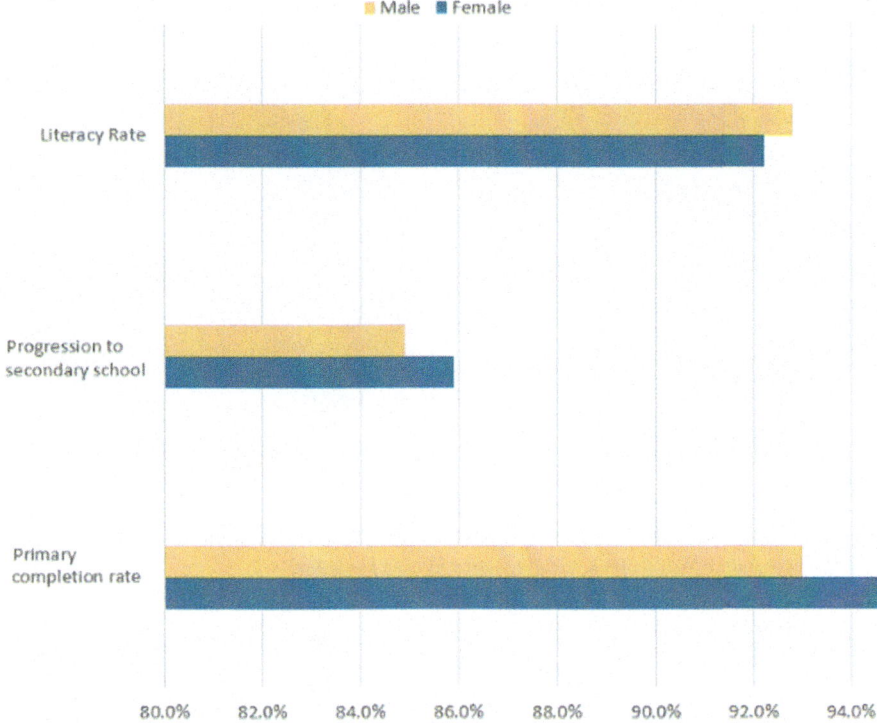

Fig. 2.23 Literacy and education in Algeria, by gender (*Data source* World Bank. *Graph source* The author)

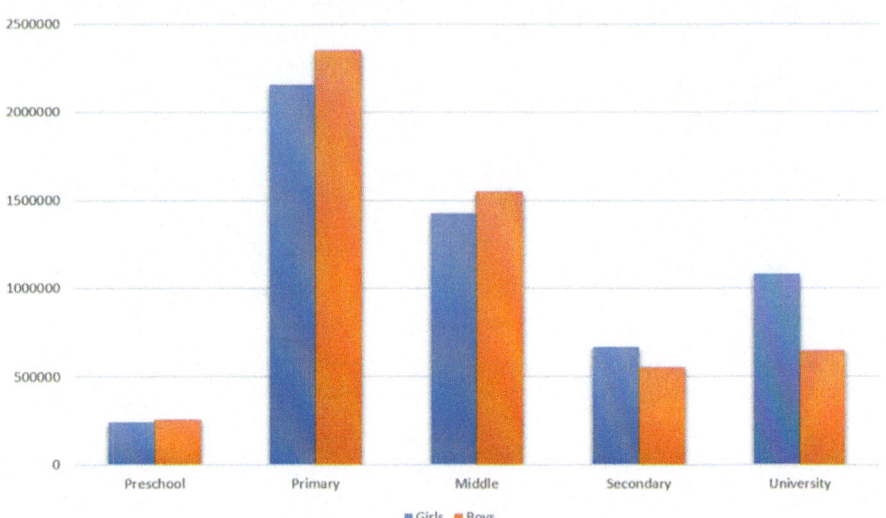

Fig. 2.24 Education level in Algeria, by gender, 2018 (*Data source* World Bank. *Graph source* The author)

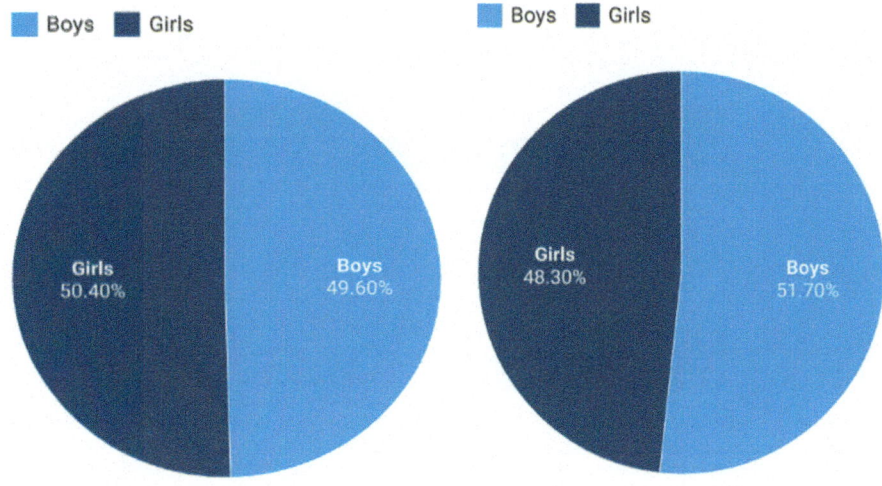

Fig. 2.25 Preschool attendance (left) and primary school attendance (right) in Côte d'Ivoire, by gender (*Data source* World Bank. *Graph source* Fofana Daouda)

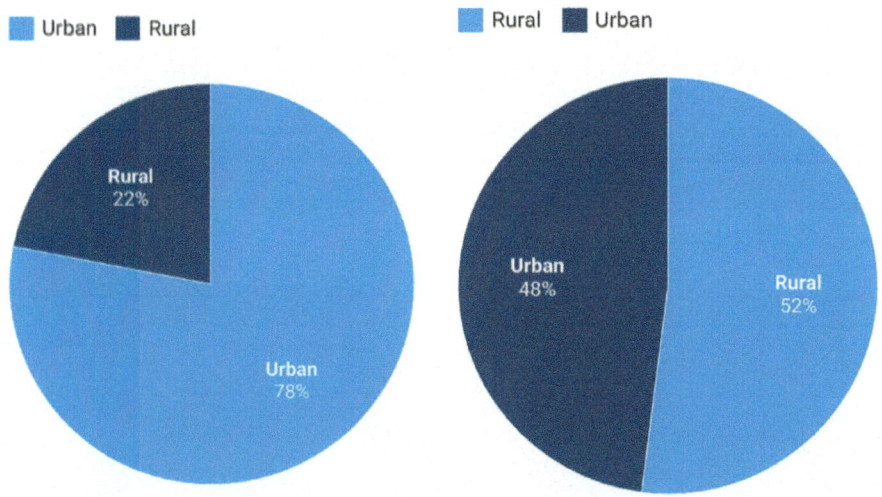

Fig. 2.26 Proportion of students in preschool (left) and primary school (right) in Côte d'Ivoire, rural and urban (*Data source* World Bank. *Graph source* Fofana Daouda)

South Africa has struggled to provide quality and affordable education. It is one of the few countries studied in this report that does not offer any free education. Primary school enrollment rates are much lower than in the other seven studied countries. School attendance varies by province and gender. In Gauteng, more boys than girls attend grades 10–12, but boys drop out more often than girls in both primary and

2.5 Education and Gender

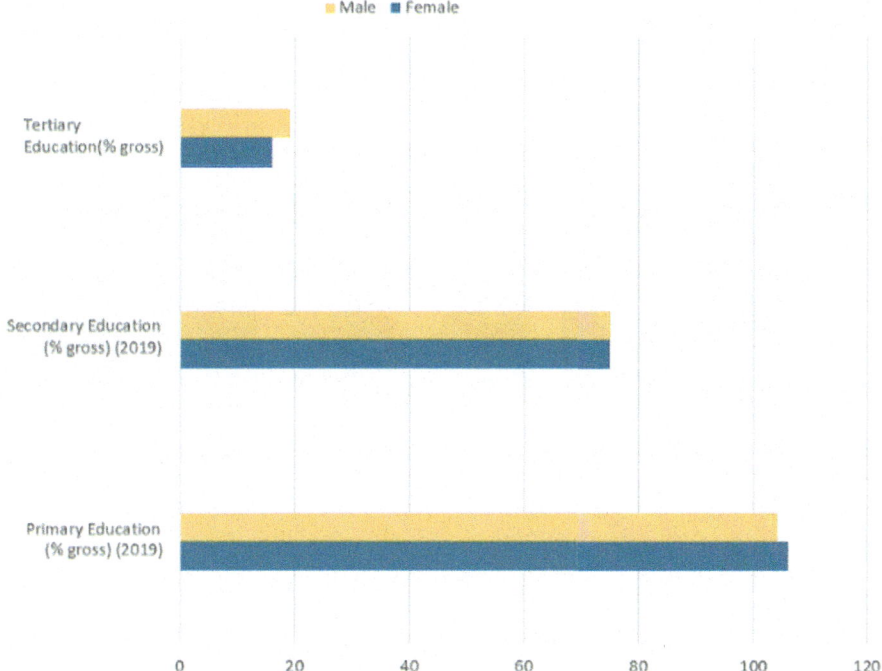

Fig. 2.27 Education in Ghana, 2019 (*Data source* World Bank. *Graph source* The author)

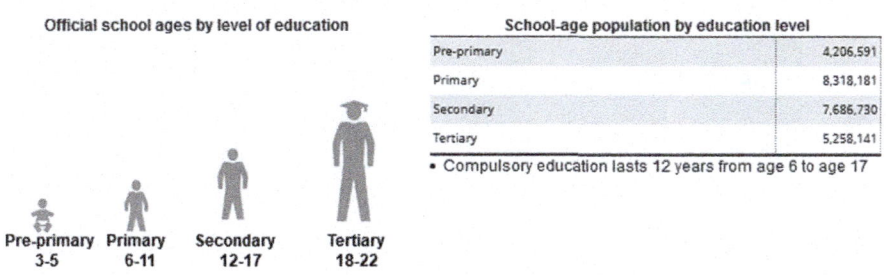

Fig. 28 Number of children enrolled in Kenyan education system, by level (*Data source* Kenya National Bureau of Statistics. *Graph source* Beatrice Birir)

secondary school. Most adults in South Africa have not completed grade 12, and less than 20% of the population has any schooling beyond grade 12 (Figs. 2.31 and 2.32).

In 2017, science, engineering, and technology were the most pursued (29.2%) major fields of study at public higher education institutions, and humanities and social sciences were the least pursued (22.3%) in South Africa. Among graduates of these institutions, most were women, though many men pursued science, engineering, and technology fields of study.

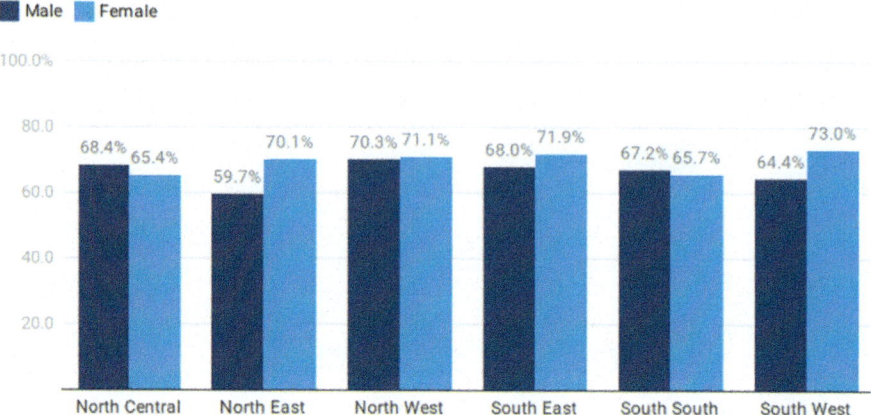

Fig. 2.29 Gross enrollment in elementary school in Nigeria, by zone and gender, 2018 (*Data source* World Bank. *Graph source* The author)

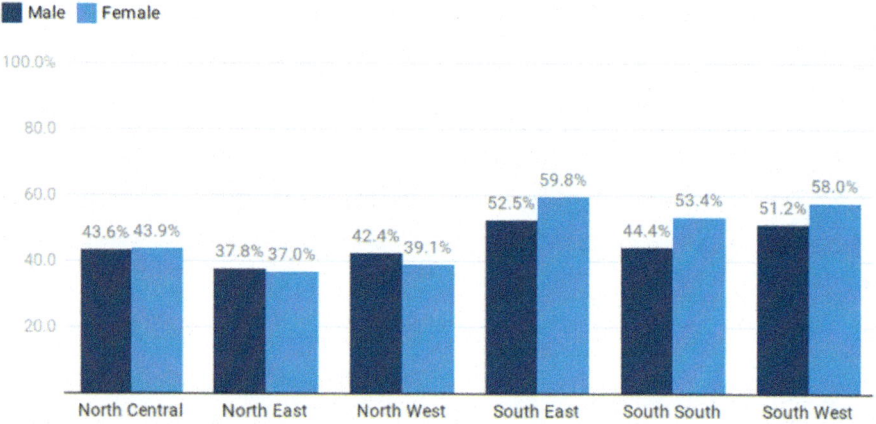

Fig. 2.30 Gross enrollment in lower secondary school in Nigeria, by zone and gender, 2018 (*Data source* World Bank. *Graph source* The author)

In Tunisia, the education system is built on the French model, as it was a French protectorate before gaining independence. The education system comprises early childhood (preschool for ages 3–6), basic (six years of primary plus three years of lower secondary), upper secondary (four years of pre-university education), and higher education (three years for a bachelor's, two more years for a master's; and up to five more years for a doctoral degree). It incorporated Arabic teachings into primary and secondary education, though French remains the language of university-level instruction and is mandatory for students in years 6–16. The Tunisian government has a goal to integrate information and communications technology at all levels of

2.5 Education and Gender

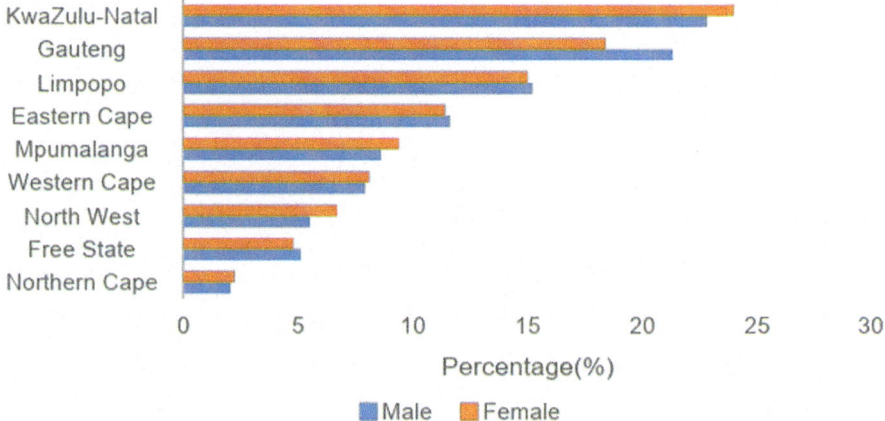

Fig. 2.31 School attendance in South Africa, grades 10–12, by gender and province, 2018 (*Data source* Department of Statistics South Africa. *Graph source* Funani Mpande)

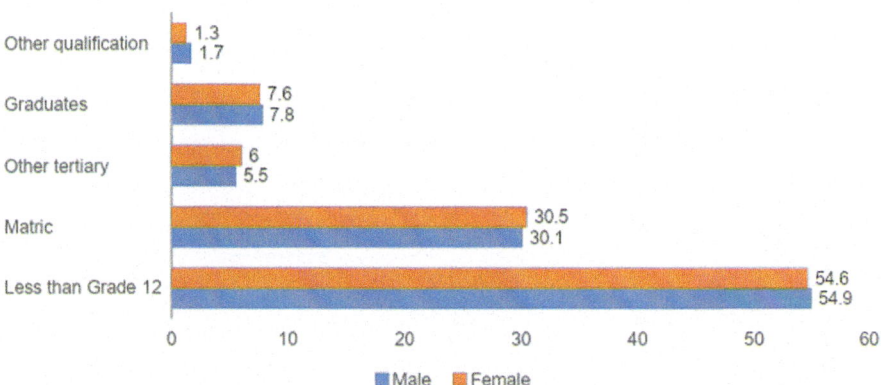

Fig. 2.32 Education level of South Africans aged 18 and older, 2018 (*Data source* Department of Statistics South Africa. *Graph source* Funani Mpande)

education, and these efforts are supported by organizations like Microsoft, Apple, and the World Bank.

2.5.3 Education Expenditure

Funding for education in Nigeria is low, with only 5.68% of the 2021 budget allocated to the education sector, far below the 15–20% benchmark set by UNESCO (Fig. 2.33).

The last year of recorded data for public spending on education in Tunisia was 2015, indicating only 6.6% of the GDP allocated for education (Fig. 2.34).

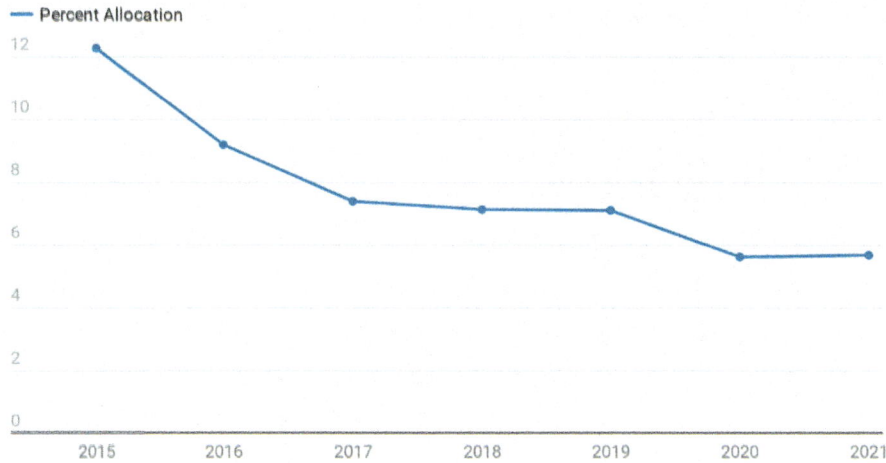

Fig. 2.33 Budget allocation to education in Nigeria, 2021 (*Data source* World Bank. *Graph source* The author)

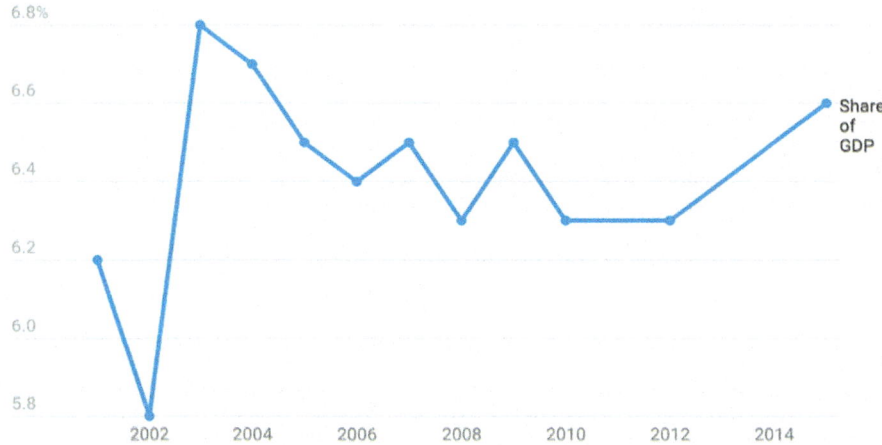

Fig. 2.34 Public spending on education as a percentage of GDP in Tunisia, 2002–2014 (*Data source* World Bank. *Graph source* The author)

2.6 Summary

Africa has the youngest and fastest growing population in the world. Although this population structure will eventually be advantageous as the proportion of working-age people increases, current governments and families are facing huge financial burdens due to health and education expenditures. Life expectancy in Africa is also far below the average of developed countries (79 years for males and 82 years for females in 2020, analyzed by Statista), and maternal and infant deaths remain high. As these countries continue to undergo demographic transitions, child and infant mortality are important areas for research. The higher-than-average fertility rate in Africa has declined in recent years, indicating improved gender equality. Theoretically, gender equality could help predict the burden of certain diseases, as well as fertility, infant mortality, and maternal mortality rates. Understanding these outcomes could identify ways to give women a better chance at receiving education and individual incomes.

Poverty and gender inequality in Africa negatively affect the literacy rate, which in turn affects the healthcare system. As previously mentioned, less than half (47%) of people in Côte d'Ivoire are literate, which can be an obstacle when providing information to patients. Applying technological advances, such as video and photos, could improve the accessibility of this information. Although many countries are trying to at least partially subsidize primary school, coverage is inconsistent. Children increasingly drop out of school as they age. The decline in the number of female students is especially alarming because it leads to fewer career opportunities, limited income, and less access to preventive and medical treatment such as screening for HIV and cancer. Providing long-term and stable education to women is thus crucial.

The lack of students in higher education means a scarcity of professionals in the healthcare sector. Even among students who attend medical school, many choose to study and work overseas or change careers upon graduation. This "brain drain" worsens the challenges the healthcare system is facing and enlarges the gap in healthcare resources between urban and rural areas. Education coverage and gender equality in education should improve in the future as governments become more aware of the situation and create plans and policies to support it. However, considering the lack of financial capacity in most countries, there is a long way to go.

Open Access This chapter is licensed under the terms of the Creative Commons Attribution 4.0 International License (http://creativecommons.org/licenses/by/4.0/), which permits use, sharing, adaptation, distribution and reproduction in any medium or format, as long as you give appropriate credit to the original author(s) and the source, provide a link to the Creative Commons license and indicate if changes were made.

The images or other third party material in this chapter are included in the chapter's Creative Commons license, unless indicated otherwise in a credit line to the material. If material is not included in the chapter's Creative Commons license and your intended use is not permitted by statutory regulation or exceeds the permitted use, you will need to obtain permission directly from the copyright holder.

Chapter 3
Disease Burden and Mortality

Africa carries over 20% of the global burden of disease. A lack of local academic research and resources along with recurring natural disasters, military conflicts, and poor economic performance creates unique and formidable challenges for Africa's healthcare systems. The disease burden in Africa accounted for the loss of 629,603,271 disability-adjusted life years in 2015. This number represents about US$243 billion in income loss, of which 59.1% (US$144 billion) was from communicable, maternal, perinatal, and nutritional conditions; 30.7% (US$74.6 billion) from non-communicable diseases (NCDs); and 10.2% (US$24.8 billion) from injuries. The structure of Africa's disease burden also has changed in recent years. In the past two decades, incidences of infectious diseases have been overtaken by NCDs as urbanization and Westernization spread across the continent.

This section focuses on changes in the incidence and death rate of selected infectious diseases and NCDs over the past decade, as well as risk factors proved to be correlated with such changes. Though not included in this report, a statistical model and analysis will be run using the factors and data collected in this section. Ideally, understanding the correlations between risk factors, incidence, and death rates of these diseases should provide a reliable prediction of the future disease burden in Africa.

3.1 Infectious Diseases

The three most prevalent infectious diseases in Africa are malaria, HIV/AIDS, and tuberculosis. This section assesses the incidence and death rate of each, as well as relevant policies and treatments.

3.1.1 Malaria

According to the *World Malaria Report 2020*, an estimated 229 million cases of malaria occurred globally in 2019. About 94% (215 million) of these cases occurred in Africa (27% in Nigeria, 12% in Congo, 5% in Uganda, 4% in Mozambique, and 3% in Niger). However, the overall trend for malaria incidence cases per 1,000 people in Africa declined from 363 in 2010 to 225 in 2019. Among those exposed to malaria, 12 million were pregnant women in 33 moderate-to-high transmission countries in Africa (40% in central Africa, 39% in western Africa, and 24% in eastern and southern Africa). Malaria infection during pregnancy can cause low birth weight.

Figure 3.1 shows the incidence of malaria in five of the eight studied countries, and Fig. 3.2 shows the mortality rates. Malaria is fully eliminated in Algeria, Morocco, and Tunisia, so these three countries are excluded from this section.

Understanding the factors behind the eradication in these three countries is essential to address the malaria situation in the remaining five countries. Algeria reported its last indigenous case in 2010 after a successful eradication led by well-trained healthcare workers who responded quickly to new cases, provided free diagnosis and treatment, and applied indoor residual insecticide spray in homes.[1] Morocco was certified malaria-free by WHO in 2010.[2] It achieved this goal mainly by following WHO guidelines, including surveillance of malariogenic risk factors.[3] Reducing malaria requires daily sanitation and rapid diagnosis and treatment. However, the financial

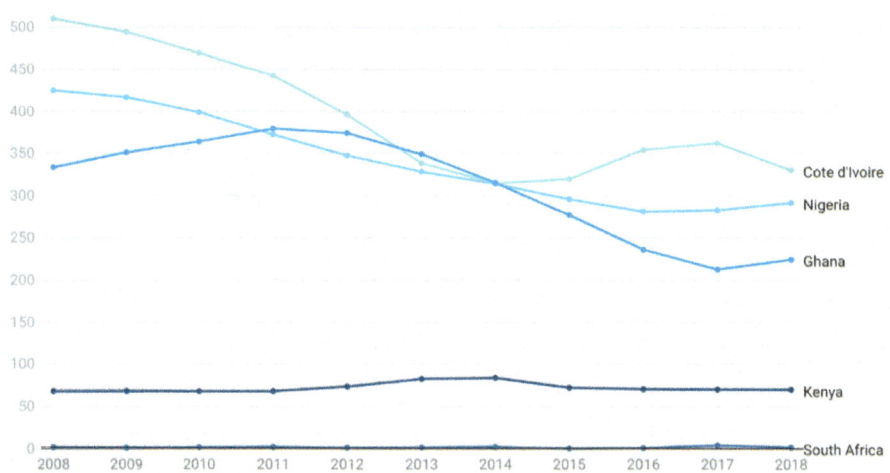

Fig. 3.1 Incidence of malaria in five of the studied countries, per 1,000 population at risk. (*Data source* World Bank. *Graph source* the author)

---

[1] https://www.who.int/news/item/22-05-2019-algeria-and-argentina-certified-malaria-free-by-who.

[2] http://apps.who.int/iris/bitstream/handle/10665/205565/WHO_HTM_GMP_2016.3_eng.pdf.

[3] https://www.hindawi.com/journals/mrt/2011/391463/.

3.1 Infectious Diseases

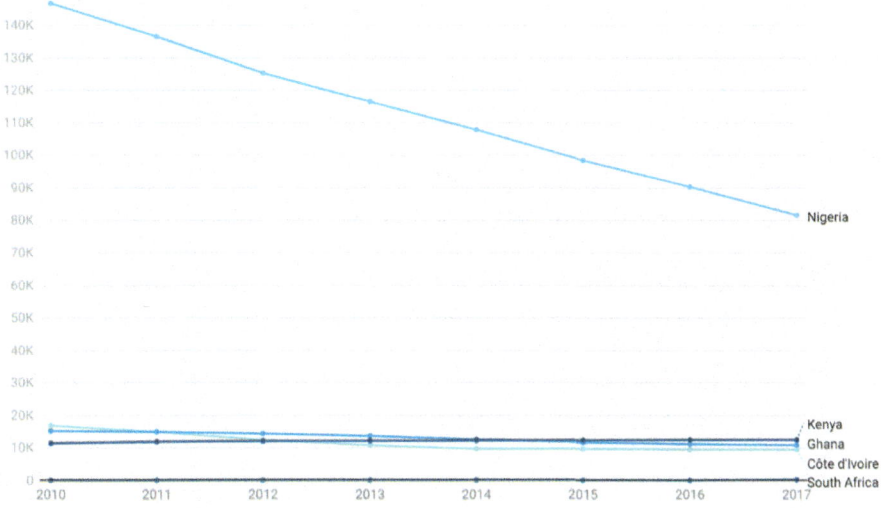

Fig. 3.2 Estimated deaths from malaria in five of the studied countries, 2010–2017. (*Data source* World Bank. *Graph source* the author)

burden to achieve the goal can be a hardship. For example, the 2012 budget of the National Malaria Control Programme in Tunisia was US$145,500. Tunisia finally eliminated malaria in 1979 after first implementing controls in 1935. From 1935–1967, its control measures included active case detection, treatment, quarantine, seasonal chemoprophylaxis with quinine, larval control, sanitation, and drainage, which reduced monthly mortality from five to two cases per 1,000 inhabitants (incidence reverted back to five cases during the Second World War). From 1967–1979, malaria was successfully eradicated via indoor residual spraying, intensive active case detection by health workers, efficient laboratory diagnosis, regular reporting, publication, and notification of malaria cases, and radical treatment. Since 1980, Tunisia has focused more on controlling the importation of plasmodium species (the type of mosquito that causes malaria) by monitoring and managing travelers and foreign students.[4]

Though malaria deaths in Africa have dropped by nearly 30% from 533,000 in 2010 to 384,000 in 2019 (about 10 per 100,000 at risk), most (94%) of the world's malaria deaths (409,000 cases globally in 2019) occur in Africa (23% in Nigeria, 11% in the Democratic Republic of the Congo, 5% in the United Republic of Tanzania, and 4% in Niger, Mozambique, and Burkina Faso combined). Out of all malaria deaths among children under five, 84% in 2000 and 67% in 2019 were in Africa.[5]

In Côte d'Ivoire, the incidence of malaria in the general population skyrocketed 21% from 189.9% in 2018 to 229.8% in 2019. At the national level, 15 out of 20

---

[4] WHO. *Eliminating Malaria Case Study 10*.

[5] For more information, see https://apps.who.int/gho/data/view.main.14117?lang=en.

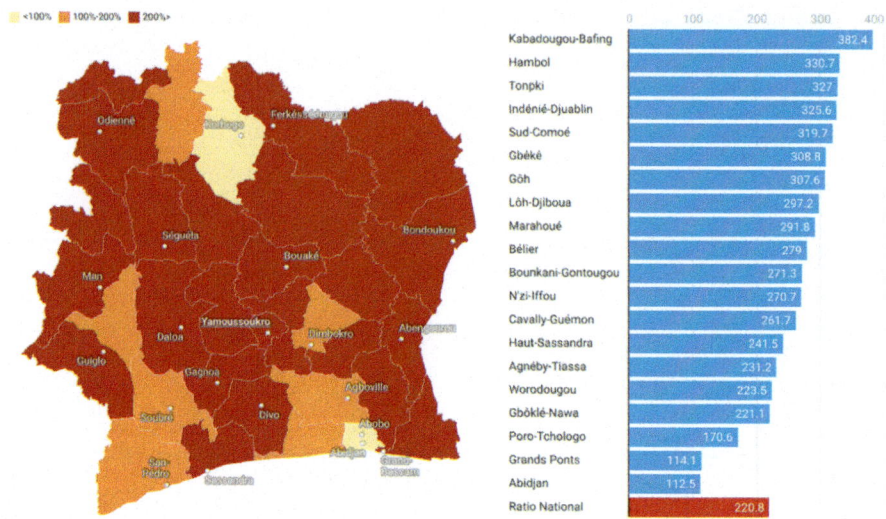

Fig. 3.3 Incidence of malaria in Côte d'Ivoire, by region and population, 2019. (*Data source* World Bank. *Map and graph source* the author)

health regions have an incidence rate above the national value (229.8%), as shown in Fig. 3.3.

Over the past decade, Ghana has witnessed an overall decrease in the incidence of 5.61% annually from over 320 cases per 100,000 people in 2008 to 224.3 cases per 100,000. The recently adopted 2015–2020 Ghana Malaria Strategic Plan aims to reduce the malaria burden by 75%. The number of deaths from malaria in Ghana has steadily declined, but deaths remain most prevalent among children under age five.

In Kenya, about 3.5 million new clinical malaria cases and 10,700 deaths occur each year. Malaria cases in Kenya fell gradually from 166.2 cases per 100,000 people in 2004 to 70.1 cases per 100,000 people in 2018. Western Kenya has the highest risk of malaria. Moreover, patients often seek treatment in the private sector, self-medicate, or forego treatment, which can lead to over-diagnosis or uncontrolled laboratory cases (Fig. 3.4).

In Nigeria, malaria poses a risk for 97% of its population. Case numbers plateaued at 292–296 per 1,000 inhabitants at risk between 2015 and 2018, but 76% of Nigerian live in high-transmission areas. The burden of malaria is three times greater among rural dwellers in comparison to urban dwellers. According to the 2015 *Malaria Indicator Survey*, malaria prevalence among children under five years of age was 27% (Fig. 3.5).

In South Africa, malaria cases mainly occur in three provinces: Limpopo, Mpumalanga, and KwaZulu-Natal, due to their low altitudes and the bordering regions of Zimbabwe and Mozambique (Fig. 3.6).

During 2008–2018, malaria deaths showed a cumulative percentage change of 5.77%, which increases and decreases throughout the decade (Fig. 3.7).

3.1 Infectious Diseases

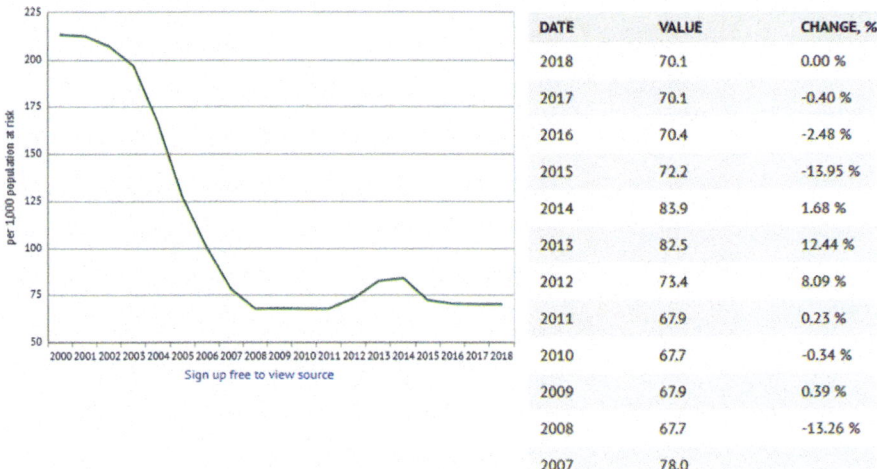

Fig. 3.4 Malaria in Kenya

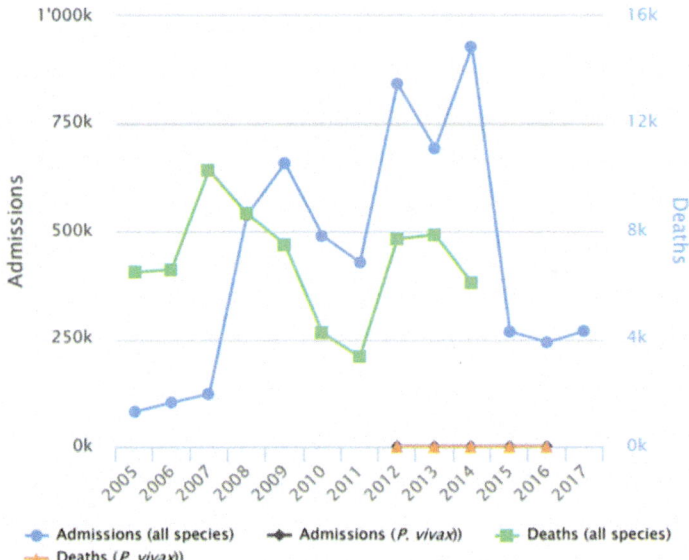

Fig. 3.5 Malaria admissions and deaths in Nigeria, 2005–2017

Insecticide-treated bed nets (ITNs) effectively reduce parasite prevalence and malaria mortality and morbidity in children under five and pregnant women.[6] WHO considers ITNs a major, inexpensive malaria prevention method. In 2019, the total funding for malaria control and elimination was estimated at US$3 billion, about

---

[6] https://pubmed.ncbi.nlm.nih.gov/30398672/.

	Medium		Low		Very Low	
	Greater than 1 per 1,000 population at risk		Between 1 and 0.1 per 1,000 population at risk		Less than 0.1 per 1,000 population at risk	
Province	District	Rate	District	Rate	District	Rate
Limpopo	Mopani	2.51	Greater Sekhukhune	0.06		
			Capricorn	0.12		
	Vhembe	3.79	Waterberg	0.18		
Mpumalanga			Ehlanzeni	0.69		
Kwa-Zulu Natal					Umkhanyakude	0.21
					King Cetshwayo	0.00
					Zululand	0.01
Local and unclassified cases for 2018, population figures from mid-year 2018 population estimates (Stats SA)						
Unclassified = unknown + untraceable						

Fig. 3.6 Malaria incidence rates along the elimination continuum, 2018

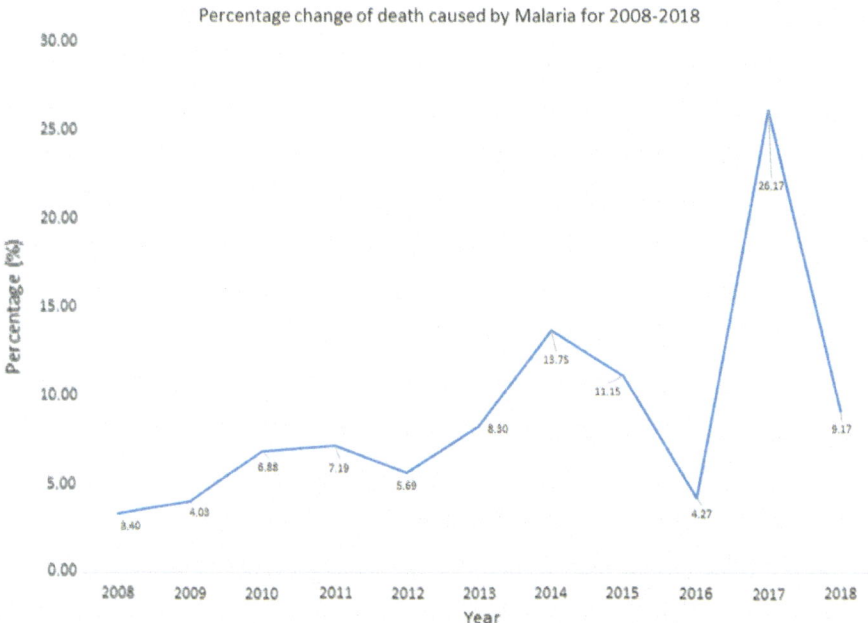

Fig. 3.7 Percentage change in deaths caused by malaria, 2008–2018

31% of which was contributed by governments in malaria-endemic countries. Of the US$3 billion invested in 2019, 73% (US$2.19 billion) benefited the WHO African Region. As a result, about 213 million ITNs were delivered to malaria-endemic countries in sub-Saharan Africa (64.4 million to Nigeria, 49 million to the Democratic Republic of the Congo, 26.1 million to Ethiopia, 10.4 million to Mali, and 10.2 million

3.1 Infectious Diseases 41

to Mozambique). In 2019, about 68% of households in sub-Saharan Africa had at least one ITN, an astounding increase from 5% in 2000, which means 52% of the population has access to an ITN.

Ghana implemented mass ITN distribution in 2006–2008, 2011–2012, 2014–2015, and 2018, resulting in increases in both the proportion of households with access to an ITN and the percentage who slept under an ITN. The percentages of children under five and pregnant women aged 15–49 who slept under an ITN also have steadily increased. The Government of Kenya received support from USAID to procure and distribute ITNs through mass campaigns and at antenatal and child welfare clinics. During 2020–2021, Kenya conducted a mass distribution aimed at universal coverage, defined as one net for every two people in malaria-endemic and endemic-prone counties.

3.1.2 HIV/AIDS

The HIV epidemic is disproportionately concentrated in Africa. In 2018, approximately 37.9 million people were living with HIV, 25.7 million (68%) of whom lived in Africa. Africa further accounted for 1.1 out of 1.7 million newly infected people in 2018. In 2019, 20.7 million people were living with AIDS in eastern and southern Africa, 4.9 million in western and central Africa, and 0.24 million in northern Africa and the Middle East. The adult prevalence was 6.7% in eastern and southern Africa, 1.4% in western and central Africa, and less than 0.1% in northern Africa and the Middle East. There were 730,000 new infections and 30,000 HIV-related deaths in eastern and southern Africa, 24,000 new infections and 140,000 deaths in western and central Africa, and 20,000 new infections and 8,000 deaths in northern Africa and the Middle East.[7]

As the heatmap figures demonstrate, southern and eastern Africa are most affected by HIV. Western and central Africa have comparatively low incidence rates and prevalence but higher death rates. This difference may indicate poor treatment of HIV, despite effective control of the disease. Northern Africa (and the Middle East) generally have lower HIV rates, possibly due to religious rules against premarital sex.

According to the *2020 AIDS Data Book* published by UNAID, key populations vulnerable to HIV include men who have sex with men, people in closed settings (e.g. prison), sex workers and their clients, transgender people, and people who inject drugs. In 2019 in western and central Africa, these populations accounted for 69% of new infections (27% in clients of sex workers, 21% in men who have sex with men, and 19% in sex workers). Overall, 60% of the newly infected were female. In eastern and southern Africa, only 28% of cases occurred in the key populations (15% in clients of sex workers, 6% in men who have sex with men, and 5% in sex workers) and again, 60% of the newly infected were female. In both regions, people who inject

---

[7] https://www.avert.org/professionals/hiv-around-world/middle-east-north-africa-mena.

drugs accounted for only 2% of newly infected cases, and females in general have higher HIV incidence rates.

Northern Africa is a unique case in the region. Data from this region are gathered collectively with the Middle East region and thus may not be of representative northern Africa alone. Religious prohibition on premarital sex also may explain the significantly lower infection rate in the general population. However, the distribution of infections in key populations reveals important information. For example, same-sex relationships are outlawed in this region, yet the percentage of new infections due to sex between men is 23%. The percentage of people who inject drugs is a surprising 43%, even though drugs such as marijuana are illegal in northern African and Middle Eastern countries (Fig. 3.8).

In eastern and southern Africa, 87% of people living with HIV know their status (with no significant gender difference), 72% are on treatment, and 65% are virally suppressed. Women tend to have a higher prevalence than men and are slightly more active in receiving ART than men, yet slightly more men are virally suppressed. The gender difference in AIDS-related deaths is also small. However, considering the difference in the number of women and men living with HIV, a bigger portion of infected men have lost their lives to AIDS than women (Fig. 3.9).

In western and central Africa, 68% of people living with HIV know their status, 58% are on treatment, and 45% are virally suppressed (Fig. 3.10).

Among the eight countries studied in this report, South Africa has the highest HIV burden based on incidence, prevalence, and death rates. Most countries show a downward trend in all three indicators; in South Africa, despite a significant decrease in the death rate, the prevalence of HIV has increased. Nigeria also shows an increase in HIV prevalence, along with a slightly increased death rate (Fig. 3.11).

In 2019, more than 90% of people living with HIV knew their status in Kenya and South Africa, compared to about 70% in Côte d'Ivoire, Nigeria, Algeria, and Morocco, about 50% in Ghana, and only 20% in Tunisia. Among those who knew their HIV status, 98% were on treatment in Tunisia, followed by more than 80% in Kenya, Côte d'Ivoire, Nigeria, and Algeria, more than 70% in South Africa and Ghana, and only 64% in Morocco. These data indicate that fewer people know their HIV status in Côte d'Ivoire, Ghana, Nigeria, Algeria, and especially Tunisia, where HIV treatment is encouraged and covered. Countries like Morocco and South Africa have high acknowledgement of the disease, but treatment coverage may be a concern. Among those who knew their status and were receiving treatment, more than 90% were virally suppressed in Morocco, Kenya, and South Africa, and more than 70% were virally suppressed in Algeria and Côte d'Ivoire, indicating the effectiveness of HIV treatment. However, a large percentage of people who were virally suppressed did not necessarily receive treatment, which can make it difficult to accurately assess the effectiveness of HIV treatment. Therefore, further research could be done in this area.

In Kenya, 1.4 million people aged 15 and over are living with HIV (0.88 million females and 0.51 million males), and 0.11 million children aged 0 to 14 are living with HIV. Prevalence is 5.8 among women and girls aged 15–49, 3.2 among men and boys aged 15–49, 2.4 among girls up to age 15, and 1.3 among boys up to age 15.

3.1 Infectious Diseases

Distribution of newly HIV infections by population (aged 15-49), Eastern and Southern Africa, 2019

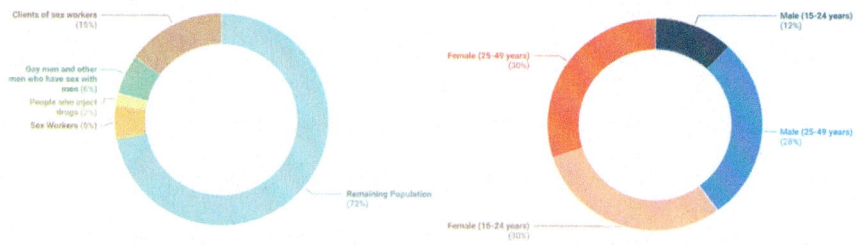

Distribution of newly HIV infections by population (aged 15-49), Western and Central Africa, 2019

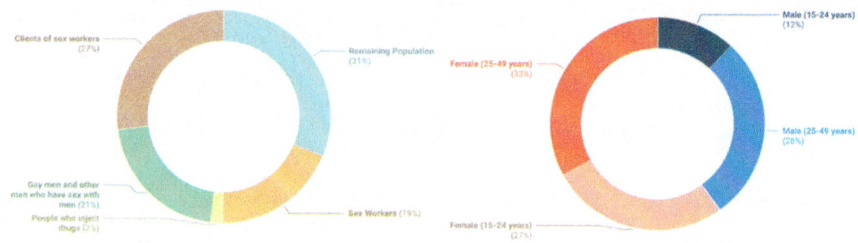

Distribution of newly HIV infections by population (aged 15-49), North Africa and Middle East, 2019

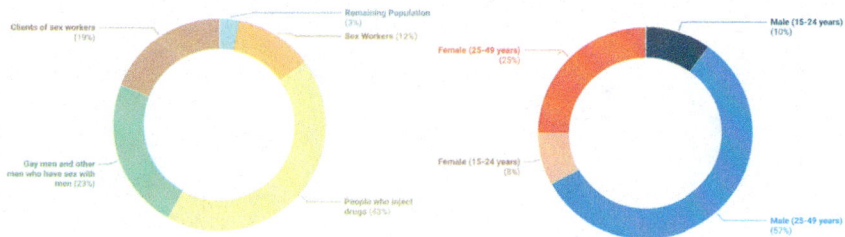

Fig. 3.8 HIV infections in Africa. (*Data source* UNAIDS DATA 2020. *Map source* UNAIDS DATA 2020)

Among 35,000 newly infected people aged 15 and over, 22,000 were female. In 2018, the number of people living with HIV reached 1.6 million, making Kenya the third-largest HIV epidemic in the world (alongside Tanzania). In the same year, 25,000 people died from AIDS-related illnesses, a steady decline from 64,000 in 2010. Kenya's HIV epidemic is driven by sexual transmission and affects all populations and genders, including children, young people, and adults. As of 2015, 660,000 children were orphaned by AIDS. A disproportionate number of new infections in Kenya occur among key populations. In 2014, about 30% of new HIV infections were among these populations.

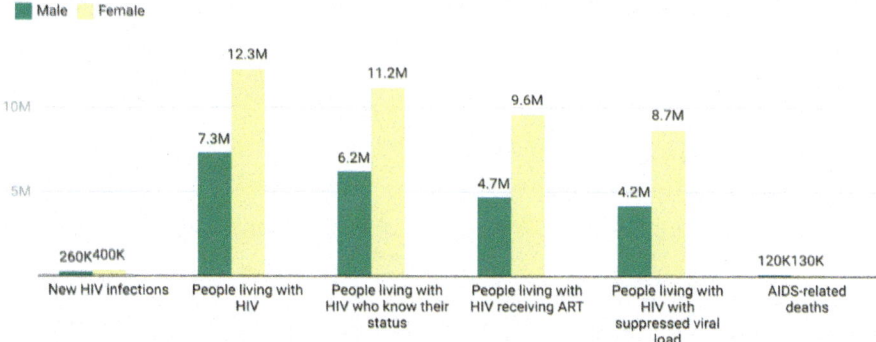

Fig. 3.9 Gender differences in HIV status among adults in eastern and southern Africa, 2019. (*Data source* UNAIDS DATA 2020. *Map source* UNAIDS DATA 2020)

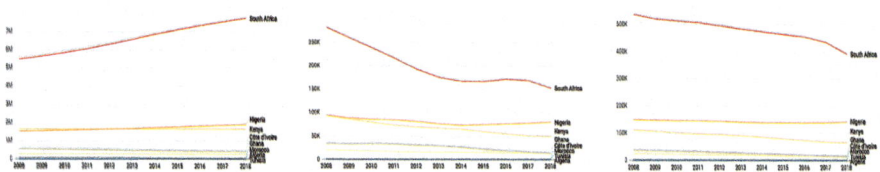

Fig. 3.10 Prevalence (left), incidence (middle) and number of death (right) of HIV. (*Data source* Institution for Health Metrics and Evaluation. *Graph source* The author)

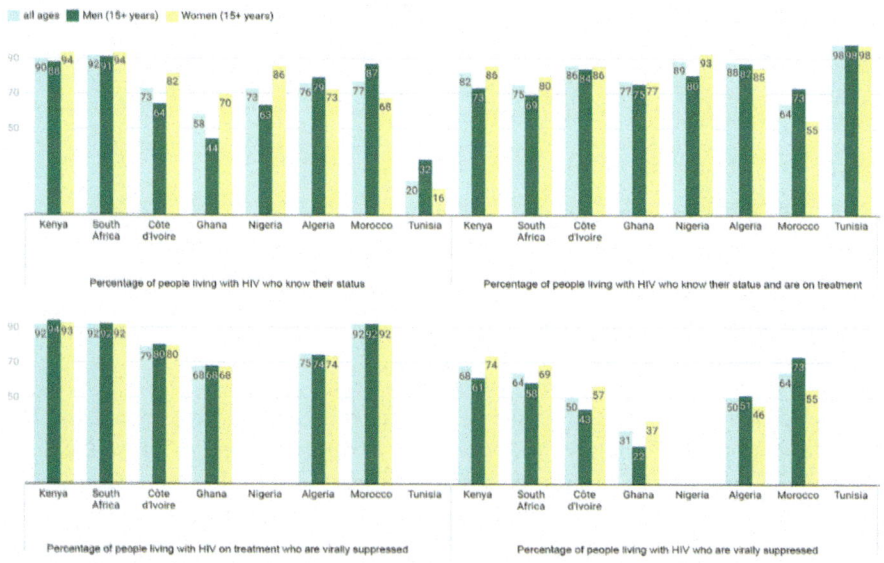

Fig. 3.11 Knowledge of status, treatment, and viral suppression, 2019. (*Data source* UNAIDS DATA 2020. *Map source*: UNAIDS DATA 2020)

3.1 Infectious Diseases   45

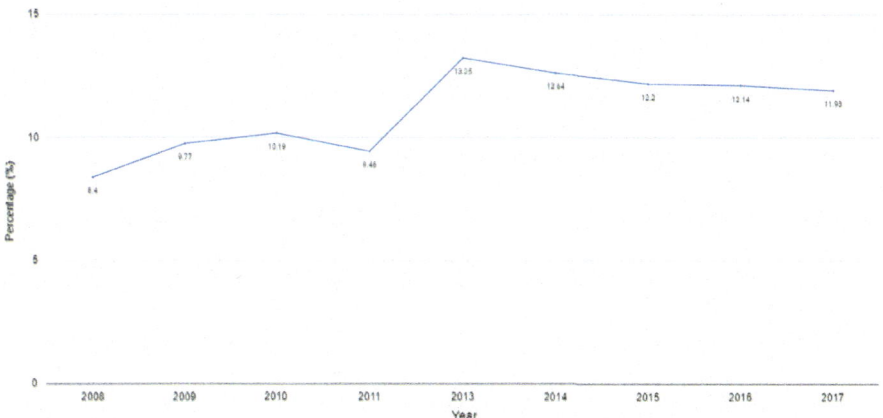

Fig. 3.12 Percentage of deaths caused by HIV, 2008–2017. (*Data source* World Bank. *Graph source* The author)

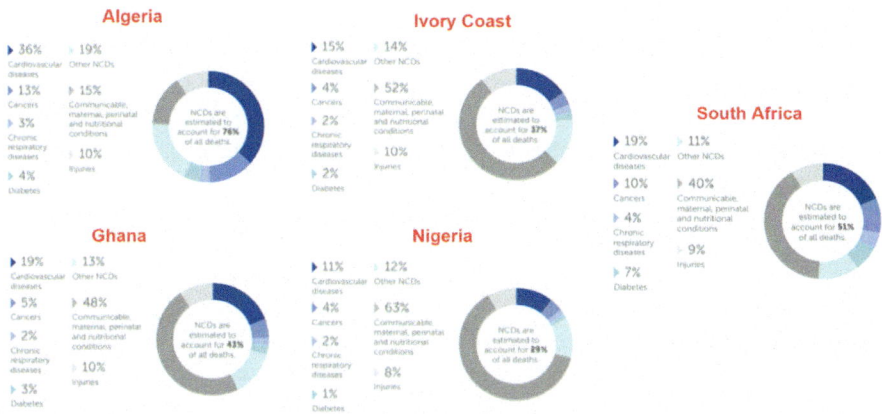

Fig. 3.13 Total number of deaths estimated over time versus AIDS-related deaths, 2002–2020. (*Data source* Department of Statistics South Africa. *Graph source* Department of Statistics South Africa)

South Africa has made serious efforts to prevent, treat, and control HIV, as it is the second-leading underlying natural cause of death for males. During 2008–2017, deaths caused by HIV increased by 3.53% (Statistics South Africa 2017), as shown in Figs. 3.12 and 3.13.

3.1.2.1 ART Treatment

Antiretroviral therapy (ART) treatment is the main treatment to control HIV. This combination of daily HIV antiretrovirals (ARVs) does not cure HIV but helps those living with HIV to live longer. Measuring the coverage of ARV treatment in one country provides insights into the status of the disease and associated death rates. Some of the studied countries provide free ARV treatment to citizens. This report studies the coverage rate of ARV and costs incurred by the patients and the government. For example, in Nigeria, the average unit cost for ARV was US$157 ($1 = NGN363) in 2018, and 65% of people with HIV received treatment in 2019. In Kenya, the average unit cost of one year of adult ART is Ksh 12,032.4 (US$ 115.7). The unit costs vary by regimen type: an adult first-line regimen is Ksh 9,501.44 (US$91.4) per year, a second-line adult regimen is Ksh 26,499.20 (US$254.8) per year, and a pediatric ARV regimen is 17,800.64 (US$171.2) per year.

Under the National AIDS & STI Control Program, the estimated cost of implementing the new guidelines was Ksh 53.4 billion (US$513 million) in FY 2019/20, up from Ksh 47.2 billion (US$ 454 million) in FY 2016/17 (Table 1). Under this scenario, coverage of people living with HIV grew from 80% in 2016 to 95% in 2019, with a projected 5% increase each year.

The Government of Ghana has a current HIV testing target of 100% of all pregnant women. About 1.2 million pregnancies occur per year in Ghana, which accounts for a large percentage (39–44%) of HIV tests. The government aims to provide ARV therapy to all pregnant women who test positive, and all infants born to HIV-positive women will receive two early infant diagnosis tests with baseline yields at 9.7%. The revised ART targets based on the Ghana Health Service/National AIDS Control Programme's 90–90-90 roadmap (Fig. 3.14) were entered into the 2016 Spectrum AIDS Impact Model for Ghana.

The average annual unit cost is US$128 for adult first-line ART and US$1,021 for second-line ART. Laboratory fees for patients on ART are US$58 (Figs. 3.15 and 3.16).

In South Africa, the provincial government and Médecins Sans Frontières in the Cape Town township of Khayelitsha formed a partnership in 2001 to provide ART district-wide. When the program launched in April 2004, 2,327 patients received

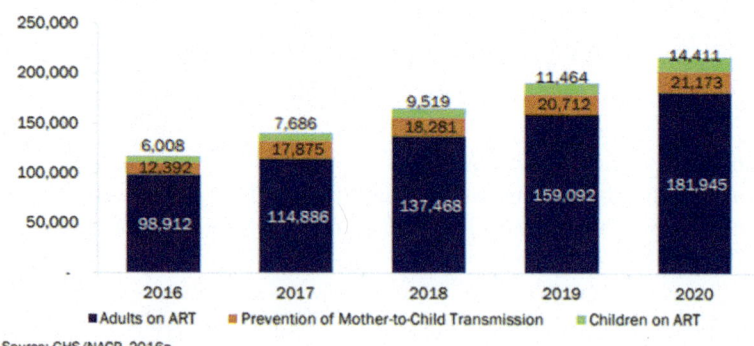

Fig. 3.14 Oadmap 90–90-90 roadmap ART enrollment targets for people living with HIV, by subcategory. (*Data source* Ghana Health Service/National AIDS control Programme. Table source: Ghana Health Service/National AIDS control Programme)

3.1 Infectious Diseases

Service	US$ per person year
Adult ART, first line	128
Adult ART, second line	1,021
Laboratory tests for patients on ART	58
Cotrimoxazole	31
Nutritional support	79
HTC	6.5
Condom, male	0.031 each
FSW service package (x6 contacts)	17.8 per contact
MSM service package (x4 contacts)	21 per contact
PMTCT (all costs excluding ART)	42

Fig. 3.15 HIV service costs per person per year. (*Data source* Ghana Health Service/National AIDS control Programme. *Table source* Ghana Health Service/National AIDS control Programme)

Healthcare sector	Supplier	South Africa (ZAR)	US($)	Euro
Public	Macleods Pharmaceuticals SA	R75.13	5.21	4.32
	Adcock Ingram Healthcare	R98.61	6.84	5.67
Private		R616	42.72	35.45

Fig. 3.16 HIV treatment monthly costs per month per person (exchange rate for May 3, 2021). (*Data source* UNAIDS AND MÉDECINS SANS FRONTIÈRES. *Table source* Funani Mpande)

treatment. By the end of March 2006, 16,324 had received treatment, mostly limited to a small population in Khayelitsha. Therapy outcomes were reported up to four years after treatment initiation and indicated a peak in AIDS in South Africa in 2006 (demonstrating the large scale of the ART program). Since the national roll-out in April 2004, treatment has been available at public health facilities in every district. In July 2019, a new class of antiretrovirals called integrase inhibitors (e.g. dolutegravir, lamivudine, and tenofovir) was introduced. Integrase inhibitors suppress HIV quickly and effectively with fewer side effects.

3.1.2.2 Discrimination Related to HIV

The stigma, discrimination, and violence toward HIV patients is a key factor that decreases treatment compliance, especially in western and central Africa, where 51.6% of people aged 15–49 will not buy vegetables from HIV-infected shopkeepers, compared to 32.2% in eastern and southern Africa (Fig. 3.17).

According to Kenya's Act No. 14 law of 2006, parliament must provide measures for the prevention, management, and control of HIV and AIDS and promote public health via appropriate treatment, counseling, support, and care of persons infected or at risk of HIV and AIDS infection. Yet, laws in Kenya and Côte d'Ivoire criminalize the transmission of, nondisclosure of, or exposure to HIV transmission. Kenya and

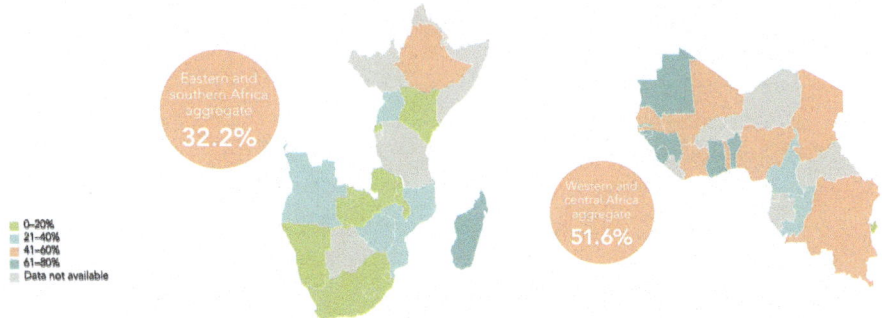

Fig. 3.17 Percentage of people aged 15–49 years in eastern and southern (left), and western and central (right) Africa who would not purchase vegetables from a shopkeeper living with HIV, 2014–2019. (*Data source* UNAIDS DATA 2020. *Map source* UNAIDS DATA 2020)

Tunisia criminalize same-gender sexual acts with imprisonment of up to 14 years. Tunisia also criminalizes transgender people; prohibits the entry, stay, and residence of people living with HIV; and requires HIV testing or disclosure for some permits. Kenya and Tunisia require parental consent for adolescents under 18 to access HIV testing. In Côte d'Ivoire, that age limit is 16.

3.1.3 Tuberculosis

Tuberculosis (TB) mainly occurs in Asia and Africa. In 2016, 2.5 million people were affected by TB in Africa, which is 25% of new cases worldwide. Nigeria, South Africa, China, India, Indonesia, and Pakistan account for 60% of TB cases worldwide. TB was the leading underlying cause of death from 2008–2017 in South Africa, especially among males, though the death rate has since declined by about 10.65% (Statistics South Africa 2017). In 2018, TB deaths in Nigeria reached 115,420 or 5.95% of total deaths, with an age-adjusted death rate of 128.71 per 100,000 people. Globally, TB incidence is declining by roughly 2% per year (Fig. 3.18). However, it remains a leading cause of death worldwide, ranking above HIV/AIDS.

According to WHO, people living with HIV are 20 to 30 times more likely to develop TB than those who do not have HIV. In 2016, 34% of people living with HIV in Africa also had TB.

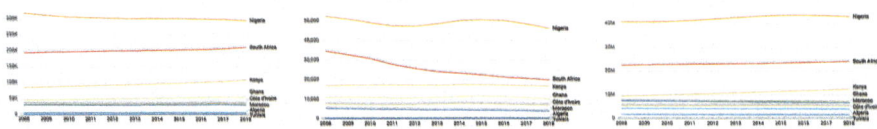

Fig. 3.18 Prevalence (left), incidence (middle) and number of death (right) of TB. (*Data source* Institution for Health Metrics and Evaluation. *Graph source* The author)

3.2 Non-communicable Diseases

In addition to infectious diseases, which continue to be a severe issue in sub-Saharan Africa, there has been an increase in the prevalence of non-communicable diseases (NCDs) over the past two decades. NCDs are diseases that are not directly transmissible between humans, such as coronary, oncological, diabetic, and respiratory diseases. Many of these NCDs are due to cardiovascular risk factors, such as unhealthy diets, reduced physical activity, and air pollution (Bigna 2019). WHO predicts that NCDs will be the leading cause of death in sub-Saharan Africa by 2030 (Fig. 3.19).

In 2018, WHO published a set of country profiles regarding NCDs. Sub-Saharan countries (Kenya, Ghana, South Africa, Nigeria, and Côte d'Ivoire) showed an average 20.2% increase in NCD-related mortality between 2010 and 2016. South Africa had the fastest increase (76%), followed by Côte d'Ivoire (12%), Ghana (10%), and Nigeria (7%). Kenya showed a 4% decrease in NCDs. In northern Africa, NCDs increased about 15.7% on average, including 21% in Algeria, 19% in Tunisia, and 7% in Morocco. In 2010, NCD rates in northern African countries (about 70%) were higher than in sub-Saharan countries (31%).

This report investigates several predominant NCDs, including cardiovascular, respiratory disorders, cancer, diabetes, stroke, asthma, hypertension, chronic hepatic diseases, and chronic renal diseases. For diseases with various subtypes, such as cancer, the specific type investigated depends on each country's situation. Overall, this section focuses on the most concerning NCDs of each country (Fig. 3.20).

In Kenya during 2000–2017, deaths due to NCDs (mainly cardiovascular diseases, cancer, and digestive diseases) increased by 72% (Fig. 3.21).

Kenya's National Strategy for the Prevention and Control of Non-communicable Diseases 2015–2020 indicates that 26% of Kenyan men smoke tobacco and more

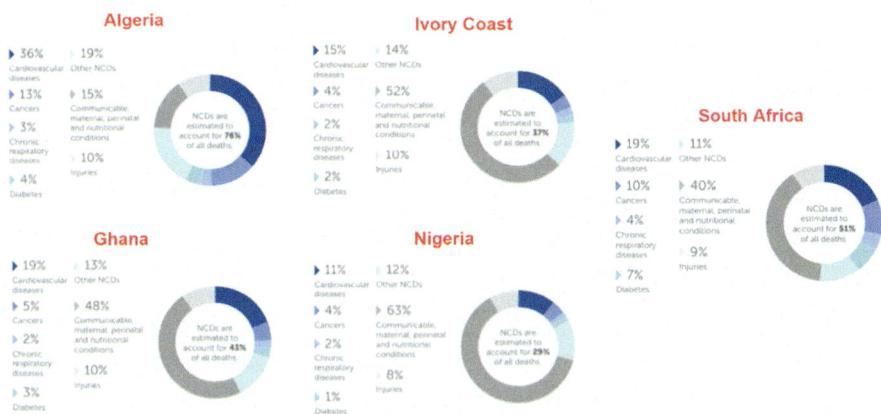

Fig. 3.19 Non-communicable diseases in five African countries. (*Data source* World Health Organization. *Graph source* World Health Organization)

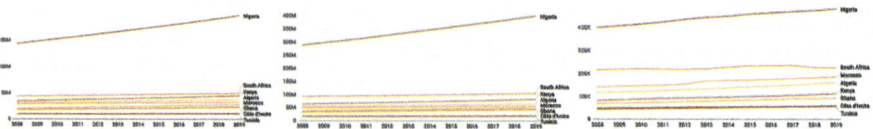

Fig. 3.20 Prevalence (left), incidence (middle) and number of death (right) of non-communicable disease. (*Data source* Institution for Health Metrics and Evaluation. *Graph source* The author)

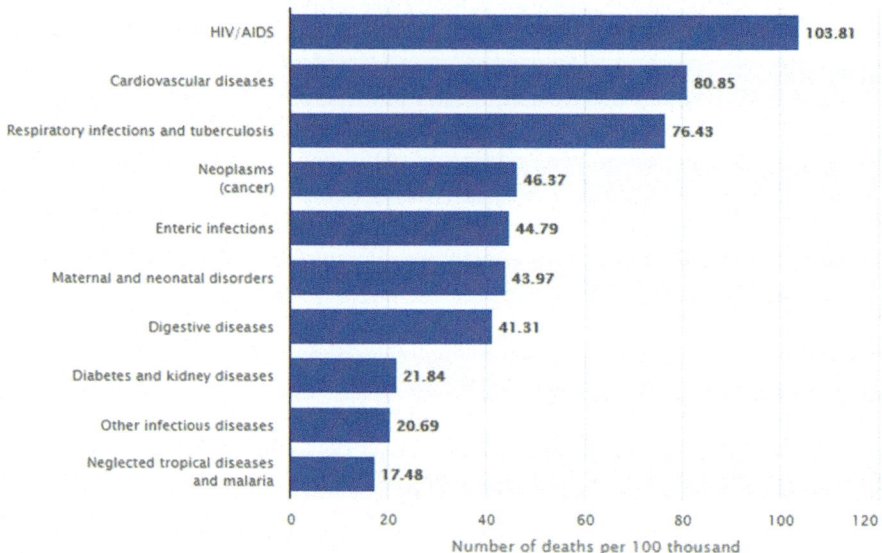

Fig. 3.21 Number of deaths per 1,000, by disease. (*Data source* World Health Organization. *Graph source* World Health Organization)

than 25% of children are exposed to second-hand tobacco smoke at home. Prevalence of insufficient physical activity for adults aged 18 and over was estimated to be 10% for men and 14% for women in 2010. Around 30% of Kenyan adults are overweight, and around 9% are obese. The total annual estimated consumption of pure alcohol in Kenya is 4.3 L per person aged 15 years and older.

In Nigeria during 2009–2019, six non-communicable diseases were the top causes of deaths: ischemic heart disease, stroke, congenital defects, cirrhosis, diabetes, and chronic kidney disease (Fig. 3.22).

In South Africa during 2008–2017, deaths caused by NCDs increased by 14%. Overall mortality cause is categorized as natural and non-natural. Natural causes (e.g. circulatory system and respiratory diseases) account for 88% of deaths. The leading underlying NCD causes of death in 2017 were diabetes mellitus (mostly among women), cerebrovascular diseases, and other heart diseases (Fig. 3.23).

3.2 Non-communicable Diseases

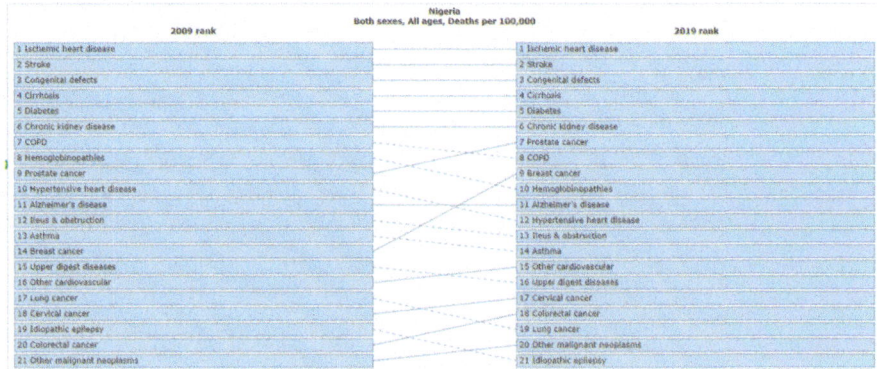

Fig. 3.22 Comparison of causes of deaths in Nigeria, 2009 versus 2019. (*Data source* World Health Organization. *Graph source* World Health Organization)

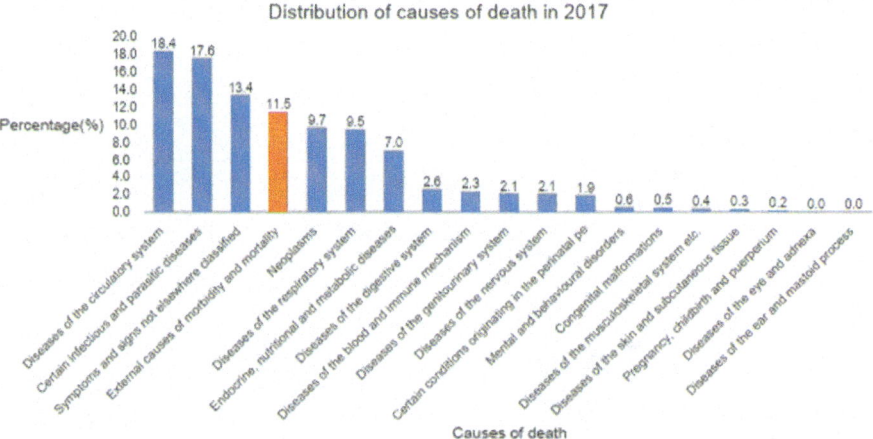

Fig. 3.23 Causes of death in South Africa, 2017. (*Data source* World Health Organization. *Graph source* Funani Mpande)

In Tunisia in 2018, NCDs (mainly cardiovascular) accounted for 86% of total deaths. Between 2009 and 2019, the top three causes of deaths were cardiovascular disease, cancer, and diabetes or chronic kidney disease (Figs. 3.24 and 3.25).

3.2.1 Cardiovascular Disease

Cardiovascular disease is the leading cause of death globally. Over three-quarters of cardiovascular disease deaths occur in low- and middle-income countries, where people often do not have access to an integrated primary and preventive healthcare

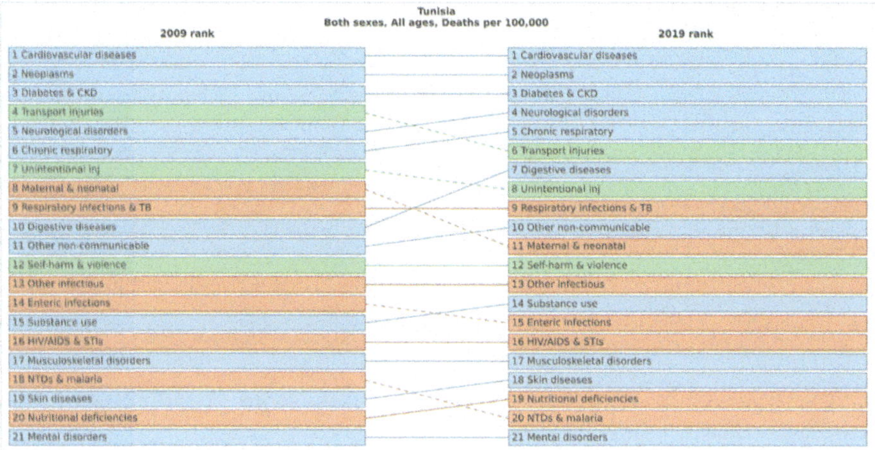

Fig. 3.24 Comparison of causes of deaths in Tunisia, 2009 versus 2019. (*Data source* World Health Organization. *Graph source* World Health Organization)

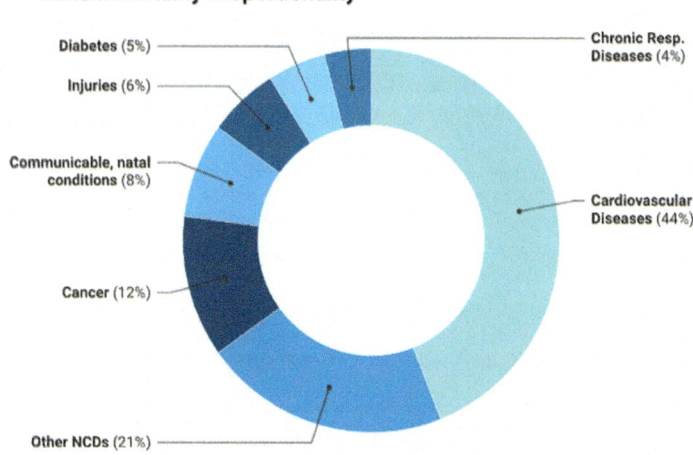

Fig. 3.25 Total mortality in Tunisia. (*Data source* World Health Organization. *Graph source* World Health Organization)

system. Without adequate treatment, patients have less access to effective and equitable healthcare, and they often lack the financial capacity to support health spending and out-of-pocket expenditure. The cardiovascular disease thus is often detected at later stages, causing many patients to die younger than they would from other NCDs (Fig. 3.26). The high financial expenditure and death rate also causes heavy burdens for families and governments.

3.2 Non-communicable Diseases

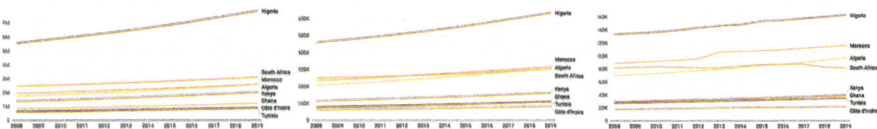

Fig. 3.26 Prevalence (left), incidence (middle) and number of death (right) of cardiovascular disease. (*Data source* Institution for Health Metrics and Evaluation. *Graph source* The author)

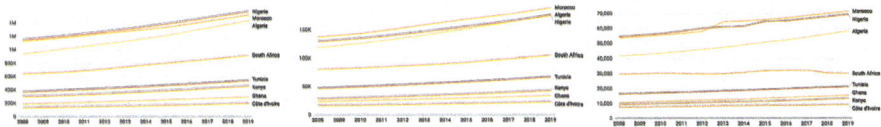

Fig. 3.27 Prevalence (left), incidence (middle) and number of death (right) of ischemic heart disease. (*Data source* Institution for Health Metrics and Evaluation. *Graph source* The author)

According to WHO data published in 2018, coronary heart disease deaths in Nigeria reached 108,578, or 5.60%, of total deaths. The age-adjusted death rate is 197.37 per 100,000 of population, ranking Nigeria as 31st in the world for such deaths, compared to Tunisia, which reached 20,968, or 31.65%, of total deaths for an age-adjusted death rate of 182.62 per 100,000 of the population (ranking 40th in the world). Other forms of heart disease (e.g. cardiac arrest and heart failure) are the 4th-leading cause of underlying deaths in 2017 (Statistics South Africa 2017), though rates decreased by 1.78% from 2008–2017.

3.2.1.1 Ischemic Heart Disease

Ischemic heart disease is a subtype of cardiovascular disease that was previously considered rare in sub-Saharan Africa, but ranked eighth among the leading causes of death in 2008 and first in Algeria and Nigeria in 2009 and 2019 (Fig. 3.27).

In South Africa, ischemic heart disease was the ninth leading cause of death in 2017 (Statistics South Africa 2017), increasing by about 0.68% from 2008 to 2017.

3.2.1.2 Hypertensive Heart Disease

Hypertension (blood pressure ≥ 140 mmHg) is a risk factor for cardiovascular disease and stroke. Globally, an estimated 1.13 billion people have hypertension, two-thirds of whom live in low- and middle-income countries. Africa has the highest prevalence of hypertension (27%). Reducing tobacco and alcohol consumption, increasing physical activity, and consuming a low-fat, low-salt diet can help prevent and control hypertension. Hypertension-related diseases from 2008 to 2017 by 3.3% (Statistics South Africa 2017). See Fig. 3.28.

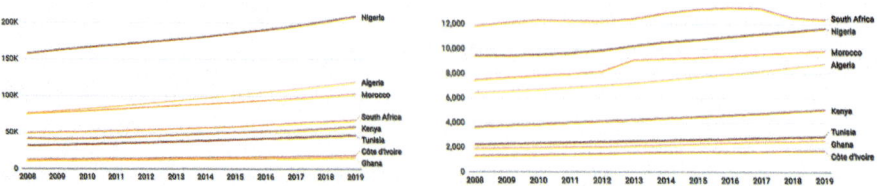

Fig. 3.28 Prevalence (left) and number of death (right) of hypertensive heart disease. (*Data source* Institution for Health Metrics and Evaluation. *Graph source* The author)

3.2.1.3 Stroke

Strokes occur when the blood supply to the brain is interrupted or reduced. A study by Sarfo et al. states that sub-Saharan Africa bears the highest burden of stroke, with an incidence rate of 316 per 100,000, a prevalence rate of 0.14%, and a 1-month fatality rate of 40% (Fig. 3.29).

According to the Heart and Stroke Foundation of South Africa, strokes are a leading cause of death in the country, though rates declined by 0.92% from 2008 to 2017 (Statistics South Africa 2017).

3.2.2 Respiratory Disorders

Chronic obstructive pulmonary disease was the fourth leading cause of death in 2005, and by 2025 it is predicted to become the third, surpassing AIDS/HIV in Africa. Risk factors include smoking, air pollution, occupational exposure, and tuberculosis, all challenges for urbanizing African countries. Chronic lower respiratory diseases (e.g. bronchitis) were ranked as the eighth leading underlying natural causes of death in 2017 (Statistics South Africa 2017), though the rate declined by 0.89% from 2008 to 2017 (Fig. 3.30).

Asthma rates have significantly increased due to rapid urbanization. Both incidence and prevalence rates are increasing in most African countries, especially the eight sampled in this study. Death rates are declining or stabilizing, however. In South Africa, asthma rates drastically declined by 6.77% from 2008 to 2017 (Statistics South Africa 2017), though according to the *South African Medical Journal*,

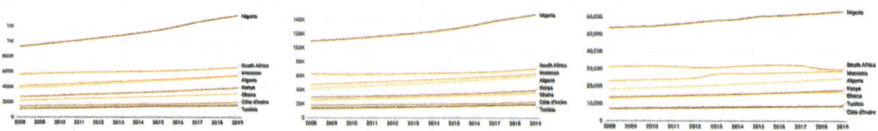

Fig. 3.29 Prevalence (left), incidence (middle) and number of death (right) of stroke. (*Data source* Institution for Health Metrics and Evaluation. *Graph source* The author)

3.2 Non-communicable Diseases

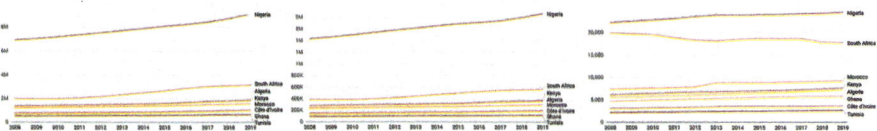

Fig. 3.30 Prevalence (left), incidence (middle) and number of death (right) of chronic respiratory diseases. (*Data source* Institution for Health Metrics and Evaluation. *Graph source* The author)

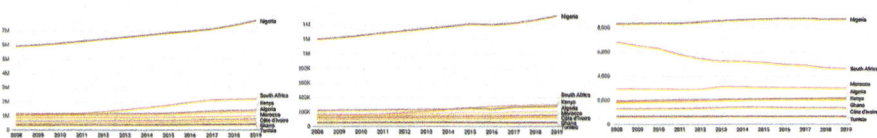

Fig. 3.31 Prevalence (left), incidence (middle) and number of death (right) of asthma. (*Data source* Institution for Health Metrics and Evaluation. *Graph source* The author)

asthma continues to be a burden to children in both rural and urban populations (2018).[8] Children in urban areas experience severe symptoms, and most lack formal diagnoses and access to treatment (Fig. 3.31).

3.2.3 Cancer

Cancer has been a low priority in African countries due to the heavy burden of communicable diseases. As of 2006, few facilities were available to provide treatment for cancer.[9] Cancer incidence, prevalence, and death rates are rapidly increasing in our sample countries, implying that cancer may be the next main focus of Africa's public health system (Fig. 3.32). Increases in tobacco and alcohol consumption, as well as HIV-related immunosuppression, are key risk factors for cancer.

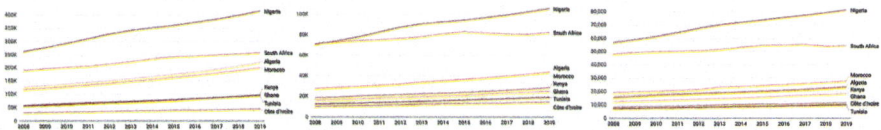

Fig. 3.32 Prevalence (left), incidence (middle) and number of death (right) of cancers. (*Data source* Institution for Health Metrics and Evaluation. *Graph source* The author)

---

[8] http://www.samj.org.za/index.php/samj/article/view/12337.

[9] Sitas F, Parkin M, Chirenje Z, et al. "Cancers." *Disease and Mortality in Sub-Saharan Africa*. 2nd ed., edited by Jamison DT, Feachem RG, Makgoba MW, et al. International Bank for Reconstruction and Development and the World Bank, 2006, https://www.ncbi.nlm.nih.gov/books/NBK2293. Accessed 13 Dec. 2021.

3.2.3.1 Breast Cancer

Breast cancer represents the most (27.7%) cancer cases in African countries and is the leading cause of cancer-related death in women according to the Cancer Association of South Africa. Incidence increased by more than 23% between 2012 and 2018 from 1.7 million to 2.1 million (Ferlay et al. 2018).[10] From 2008 to 2019, breast cancer rates increased 3.6% (Statistics South Africa 2017). See Fig. 3.33.

The five-year survival rate is less than 40% due to financial barriers to mammography screening and a lack of well-trained radiologists and technicians. Most countries in sub-Saharan Africa do not have mammography, and if they do, it is mainly available only in urban areas. Furthermore, the peak age of incidence in breast cancer is lower in sub-Saharan Africa, compared to other regions, which means later diagnoses. Many women are already at an advanced stage when the cancer is detected.

3.2.3.2 Lung Cancer

Lung cancer is the fifth-leading cause of cancer deaths for women and third for men, according to the Cancer Association of South Africa. From 2008 to 2017, lung cancer increased by 2.97% (Statistics South Africa 2017). Prevalence is related to HIV, tobacco consumption, poor economic circumstances, low standard of living, inaccessible and inadequate medical care, urbanization, and air pollution (Fig. 3.34).

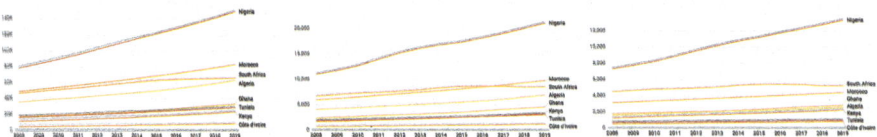

Fig. 3.33 Prevalence (left), incidence (middle) and number of death (right) of breast cancer. (*Data source* Institution for Health Metrics and Evaluation. *Graph source* The author)

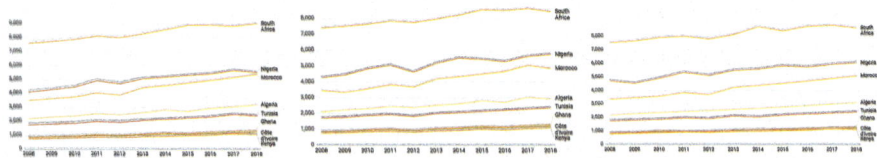

Fig. 3.34 Prevalence (left), incidence (middle) and number of death (right) of tracheal, bronchus, and lung cancer. (*Data source* Institution for Health Metrics and Evaluation. *Graph source* The author)

---

[10] Ferlay J, Ervik M, Lam F, et al. *Cancer Today*. International Agency for Research on Cancer, Lyon, 2018, https://gco.iarc.fr/today. Accessed 13 Dec. 2021.

3.2 Non-communicable Diseases

3.2.3.3 Cervical Cancer

Cervical cancer represents 19.6% of total cancer cases in African countries. It is the second-leading cause of cancer-related deaths in women according to the Cancer Association of South Africa. From 2008 to 2017, deaths caused by cervical cancer increased by 5.3% (Statistics South Africa 2017). See Fig. 3.35.

Human papillomavirus (HPV) and lack of HPV vaccines are the most common factors responsible for cervical cancer in Africa. HPV infection usually resolves in immunocompetent women, but it increases their risk of developing cervical cancer. Nevertheless, two-thirds of cervical cancer cases caused by HIV and HPV could be prevented by HPV vaccination. However lack of knowledge about cervical cancer and HPV and a lack of screening centers contribute to the late diagnoses and poor survival rates.

3.2.3.4 Colorectal Cancer

Colorectal cancer is the second-most common cancer among men and third-most common among women, according to the Cancer Association of South Africa. From 2008 to 2017, colorectal cancer deaths increased by 1.73% (Statistics South Africa 2017). See Figs. 3.36.

3.2.3.5 Prostate Cancer

Prostate cancer represents 18.1% of total cancer cases in African countries, and it is the leading cause of cancer-related deaths in men. From 2008 to 2017, deaths

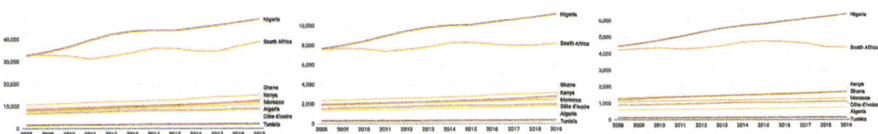

Fig. 3.35 Prevalence (left), incidence (middle) and number of death (right) of cervical cancer. (*Data source* Institution for Health Metrics and Evaluation. *Graph source* The author)

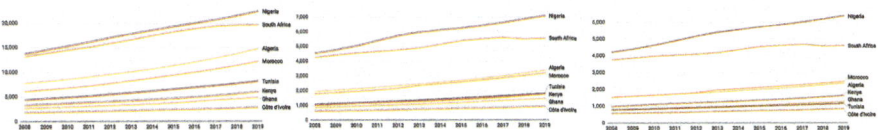

Fig. 3.36 Prevalence (left), incidence (middle) and number of death (right) of colorectal cancers. (*Data source* Institution for Health Metrics and Evaluation. *Graph source* The author)

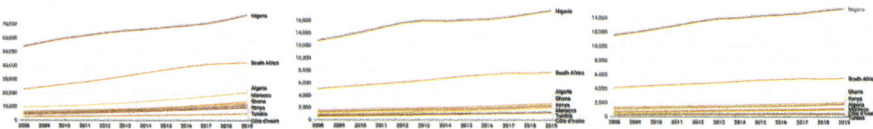

Fig. 3.37 Prevalence (left), incidence (middle) and number of death (right) of prostate cancer. (*Data source* Institution for Health Metrics and Evaluation. *Graph source* The author)

caused by prostate cancer increased by 4.78% (Statistics South Africa 2017).[11] See Fig. 3.37.

Race plays an important role in the incidence of prostate cancer. Around 30–43% of black men develop preclinical prostate cancer by the age of 85 years, which is 28–56% higher than in non-black populations. Just like other types of cancers, the lack of screening (such as prostate-specific antigen testing and transrectal ultrasound biopsy), lack of access to healthcare, genetics, lifestyle, and environmental factors result in late diagnoses and low survival rates.

3.2.3.6 Liver Cancer

Liver cancer is the third-leading cause of cancer-related deaths in Africa. Apart from the challenges mentioned previously, such as lack of screening and lack of knowledge, the absence of comprehensive surveillance programs for liver cancer, inaccessible expert medical care, and socioeconomic and sociocultural factors that affect treatment decision-making also make this type of cancer difficult to control (Fig. 3.38).

3.2.4 Diabetes

Diabetes is a key risk factor for developing cardiovascular diseases. In 2019, 19 million adults were living with diabetes in Africa, which is estimated to increase to 47 million by 2045, and 45 million adults have impaired glucose tolerance. Around 60% of adults living with diabetes are undiagnosed. Despite spending US$9.5 billion

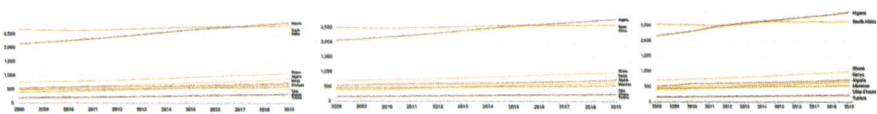

Fig. 3.38 Prevalence (left), incidence (middle) and number of death (right) of liver cancer. (*Data source* Institution for Health Metrics and Evaluation. *Graph source* The author)

---

[11] https://www.frontiersin.org/articles/10.3389/fonc.2020.604214/full#h3.

3.2 Non-communicable Diseases

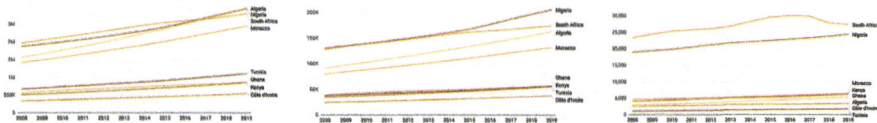

Fig. 3.39 Prevalence (left), incidence (middle) and number of death (right) of diabetes. (*Data source* Institution for Health Metrics and Evaluation. *Graph source* The author)

on diabetes in 2019, rates are still increasing. South Africa has the largest diabetic population, followed by Nigeria. Diabetes mellitus was the second-leading cause of death among men and women and the leading cause of death among women from 2015–2017 in South Africa (Statistics South Africa 2017). Rates have increased by 2.53% from 2008 to 2017. In Kenya, more men than women are affected by diabetes (Fig. 3.39).

3.2.5 Cirrhosis and Other Liver Diseases

Between 1980 and 2010, cirrhosis-related deaths doubled in sub-Saharan Africa. Chronic alcoholism is the most common cause, followed by lifestyle, sexual partners, and obesity. Nonetheless, from 2008 to 2017, rates of liver disease declined by 4.57% (Statistics South Africa 2017; Fig. 3.40). Currently, the treatment of liver cirrhosis is inaccessible in most of sub-Saharan Africa due to shortages of hepatologists, gastroenterologists, interventional radiologists, hepatobiliary surgeons, and pathologists. Liver transplants are available only in South Africa and considered a rare and expensive treatment that may be further prohibited by the government. Prevention of liver disease requires screening, improved hygiene in health facilities, training or retraining of healthcare workers on safe injection practices, vaccination of hepatitis carriers, reduced alcohol consumption, weight control, and diabetes management.

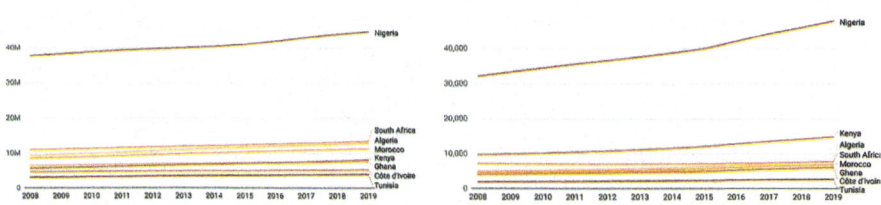

Fig. 3.40 Prevalence (left) and incidence (right) of cirrhosis and other liver diseases. (*Data source* Institution for Health Metrics and Evaluation. *Graph source* The author)

3.3 Substance Consumption

NCDs have many underlying risk factors. Understanding these risk factors can help predict future issues and identify possible treatments. Three main risk factors are covered here: substance consumption (tobacco and alcohol), nutrition, and physical activity. Tobacco causes over 8 million deaths each year, including 1.2 million due to second-hand smoke exposure. Smoking during pregnancy can cause birth defects. Alcohol consumption contributes to 3 million deaths annually and is responsible for 5.1% of the global burden of disease, particularly affecting premature mortality and disability among those aged 15 to 49 years. Both tobacco and alcohol are known risk factors for NCDs, and they are heavily associated with social aspects in many countries. Their harm may be easily overlooked or discounted, and consumers tend to find it challenging to quit.

3.3.1 Tobacco Consumption

In Côte d'Ivoire, where tobacco is the most consumed, men's consumption far exceeds that of women, though it has not increased in recent years (Fig. 3.41).

In Ghana, the 2014 Demographic and Health Survey indicates a 4.8% prevalence of cigarette smoking among males and 0.1% among females. The sale of tobacco products is prohibited for persons under the age of 18. The percentage of people aged 15 years and older who use any tobacco product (smoked or smokeless) on a daily or non-daily basis is 3.1%, which is decreasing and expected to fall further in the next decade. Regional differences in smoking prevalence also exist, with several studies demonstrating higher use among those living in the remote northern areas (31.2% in the northeast, 22.5% in the north, and 7.9% in the northwestern regions). In

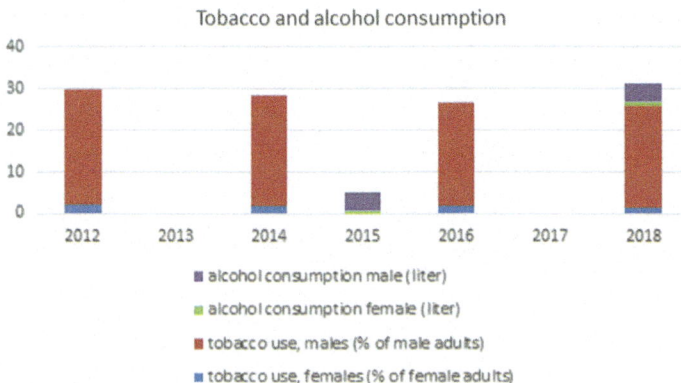

Fig. 3.41 Tobacco and alcohol consumption. (*Data Source* World Bank. *Graph Source* Fofana Daouda)

3.3 Substance Consumption

terms of age groups, 25–34 and 35–59 year-olds have a higher prevalence of cigarette smoking than 15–24 year-olds.

Kenya's National Strategy for the Prevention and Control of Non-communicable Diseases 2015–2020 indicates that 26% of Kenyan men use tobacco and more than 25% of youth are exposed to second-hand tobacco smoke at home. In 2018, smoking prevalence among adult women was 2.8% and 20.8% among men, both of which decreased from 2005 (Fig. 3.42).

Nigeria has made considerable progress in controlling tobacco consumption. In 2016, 246 men and 64 women died every week from tobacco consumption, which is low in comparison to other low-Human Development Index countries (Figs. 3.43 and 3.44). Smoking in Nigeria is prohibited in public places. A 2018 report by the United Nations Office on Drug and Crime revealed marijuana to be the most consumed substance in Nigeria (about 10.8% of the population, or 10.6 million Nigerians). Possession of cannabis carries a minimum sentence of 12 years in prison.

In South Africa, tobacco consumption has declined overall but remains more prevalent among males. The overall percentage of smokers exceeded 5% in 2012 and 2016. For women, it drastically declined in 2016, with an overall percentage of less than 2% for all age groups. Between 2008 and 2017, smoking among men decreased by about 3.5% and by 1.6% among women in South Africa (Fig. 3.45).

From 2012 to 2016, the population of women who smoked cigarettes declined with age, whereas it increased among men (Fig. 3.46).

Only pure tobacco was recorded in 2016 (vaping was excluded), and men consumed about three times as many cigarettes as similarly aged women (Fig. 3.47).

After 2010, deaths reported or associated with smoking declined or the cause of death was listed as "unknown or unspecified," indicating poor reporting on death notification forms (World Bank 2017). See Figs. 3.48 and 3.49.

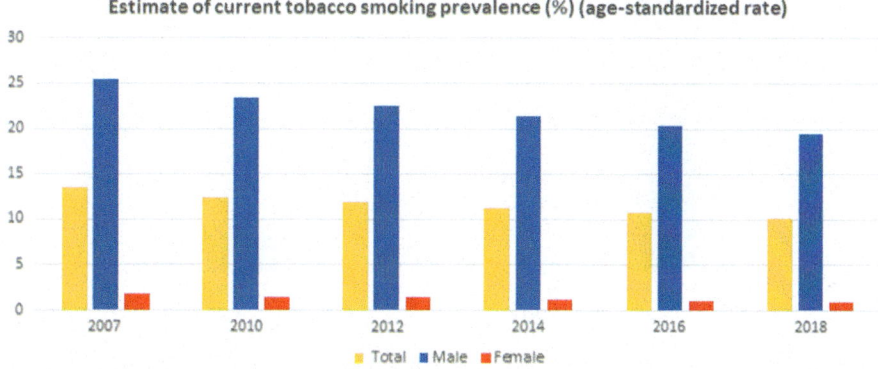

Fig. 3.42 Tobacco smoking prevalence. (*Data Source* National Strategy for the Prevention and Control of Non-communicable Diseases 2015–2020. *Graph Source* National Strategy for the Prevention and Control of Non-communicable Diseases 2015–2020)

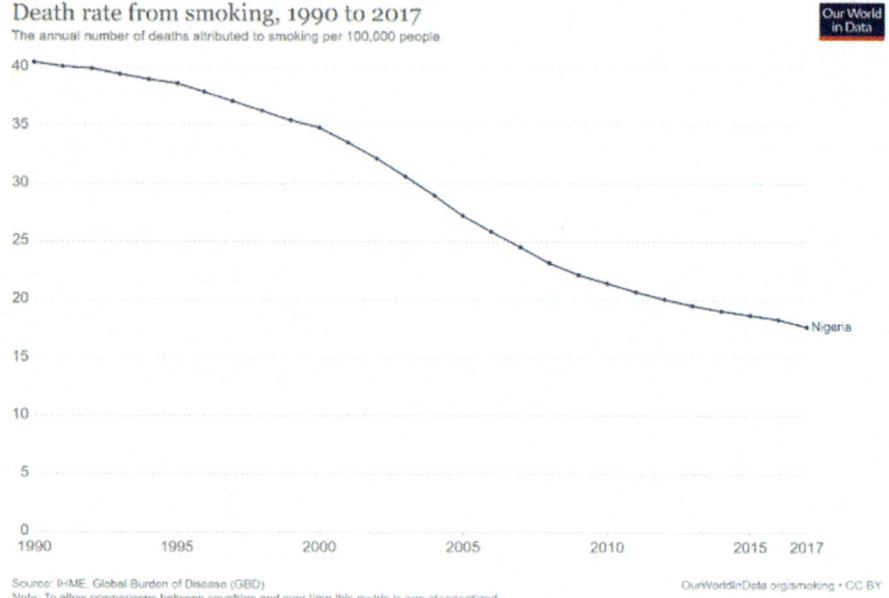

Fig. 3.43 Deaths from smoking, 1990–2017. (*Data source* Institution for Health Metrics and Evaluation. *Graph source* Our World in Data)

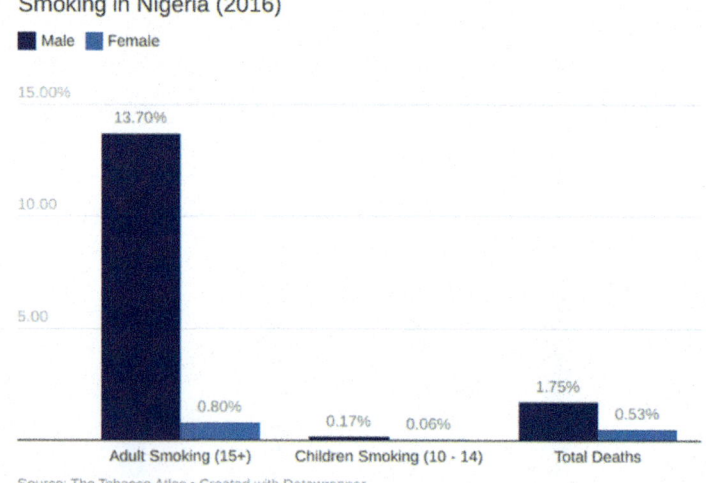

Fig. 3.44 Smoking in Nigeria, 2016. (*Data source* Institution for Health Metrics and Evaluation. *Graph source* Ademola Olokun)

3.3 Substance Consumption   63

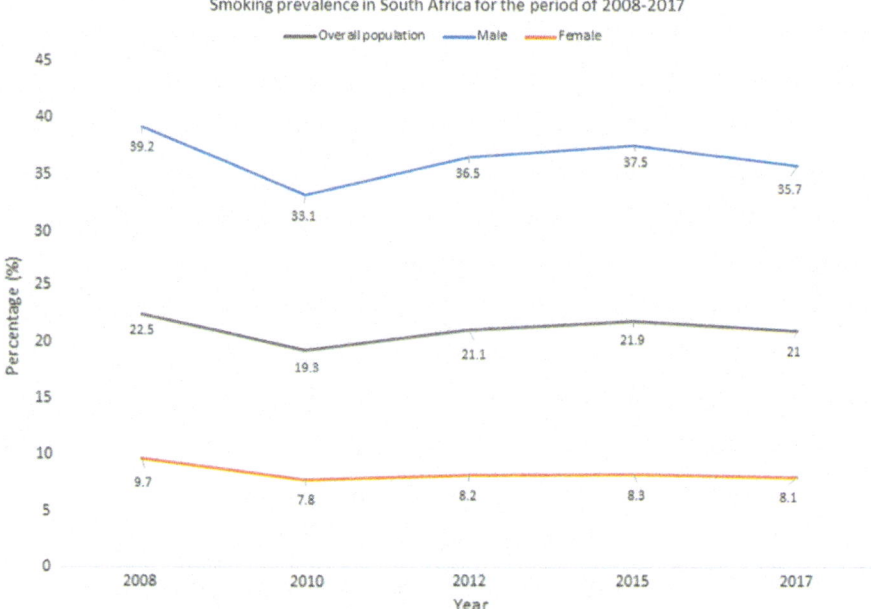

Fig. 3.45 Prevalence of smoking in South Africa, 2008–2017. (*Data Source* World Bank. *Graph Source* Funani Mpande)

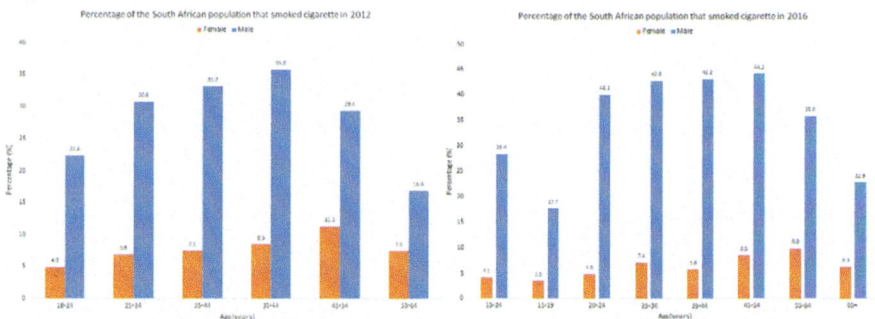

Fig. 3.46 Percentage of South Africans who smokes cigarettes, 2012 versus 2016. (*Data Source* World Bank. *Graph Source* Funani Mpande)

The cigarette tax has increased over the past three years to R2.13 (0.15 US$; 0.12 Euro exchange rates as of May 7, 2021) for a pack of 20 cigarettes and R14.44 (1.02 US$; 0.84 Euro exchange rate) for cigars (Fig. 3.50).

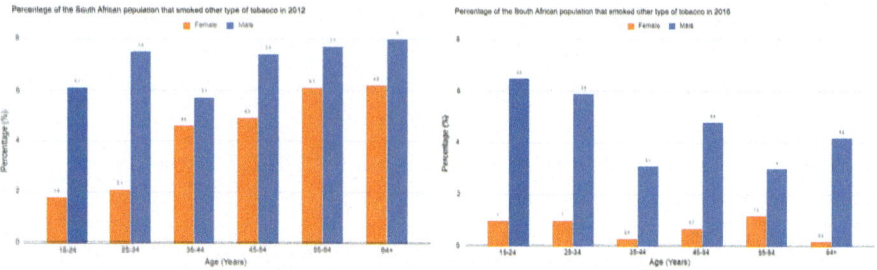

Fig. 3.47 Percentage of South Africans who smoked other types of tobacco, 2012 and 2016. (*Data Source* World Bank. *Graph Source* Funani Mpande)

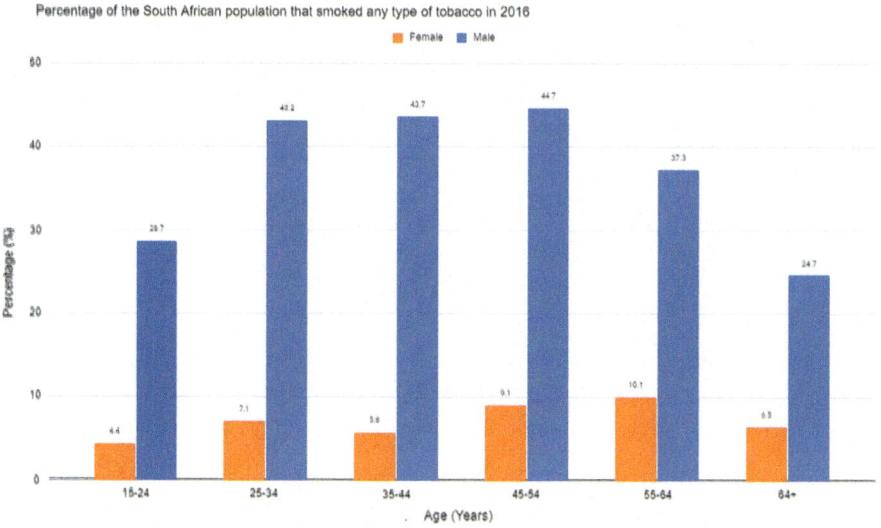

Fig. 3.48 Percentage of South Africans who smoked any type of tobacco, 2016. (*Data Source* World Bank. *Graph Source* Funani Mpande)

3.3.2 Alcohol Consumption

Alcohol consumption in Algeria, unlike many other sampled countries, has been decreasing since 1961 (Fig. 3.51).

In Nigeria, alcohol per capita consumption increased from 2010 to 2016 by an overall rate of 1.91% (3.21% for men and 0.61% for women). There is no policy on alcohol sales in Nigeria, and age restrictions are not effective, even with a 20% excise duty tax on alcohol. Alcohol is banned in some northern parts of Nigeria due to its Muslim-dominated population (Fig. 3.52).

In South Africa, per capita alcohol consumption decreased for all from 2005 to 2016. For men, alcohol consumption decreased by 23.41%, and for women by

3.3 Substance Consumption

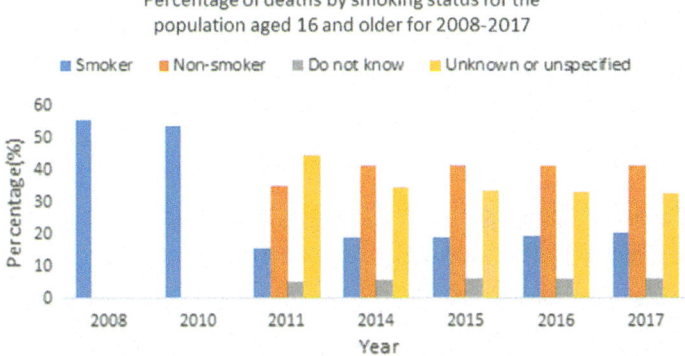

Fig. 3.49 Percentage of deaths among people aged 16 and older, by smoking status, 2008–2017. (*Data Source* World Bank. *Graph Source* Funani Mpande)

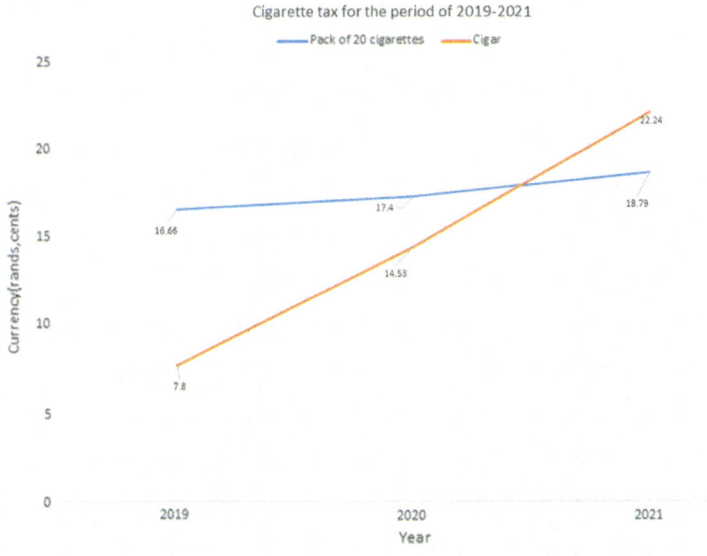

Fig. 3.50 Cigarette taxes, 2019–2021. (*Data Source* World Bank. *Graph Source* Funani Mpande)

21.11%, contributing to an overall reduction of 25.61% (Fig. 3.53). According to the 2016 South Africa Demographic and Health Survey, men in South Africa tend to drink more alcohol than women in every age group. Women tend to be judged or shamed for consuming large volumes of alcohol or drinking in social spaces, for instance. Most beer brands in South Africa are associated with masculinity.

From 2010 to 2016, beer consumption increased by 7.9% but decreased by 9.6% for other alcohols (sorghum, millet, maize beers, cider, fortified wine, fermented wheat, rice, and other beverages). Wine and spirit consumption increased slightly by 2%, according to the WHO Global Status Report on Alcohol and Health.

Recorded alcohol per capita (15+) consumption, 1961–2016

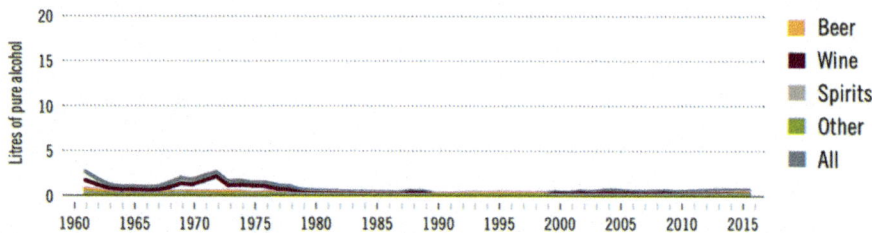

Fig. 3.51 Alcohol consumption, 1961–2016. (*Data Source* World Health Organization. *Graph Source* World Health Organization)

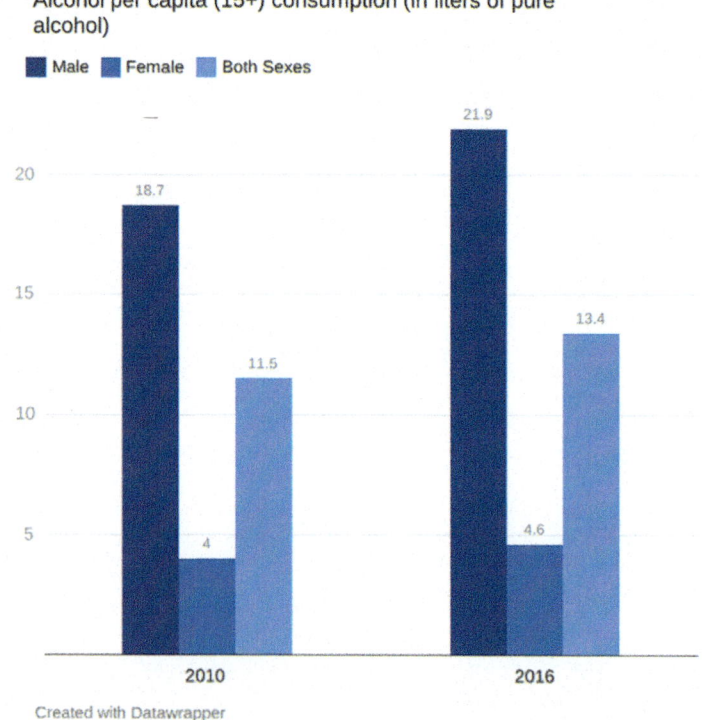

Fig. 3.52 Alcohol use per capita among those aged 15 and older. (*Data Source* World Bank. *Graph Source* Ademola Olokun)

The CAGE questionnaire is used to check whether an individual has an alcohol addiction. More than 20% of men, mainly those aged 20–34, tested high on this questionnaire, compared to less than 4% of women (South Africa Demographic and Health Survey 2016; Figs. 3.54 and 3.55).

3.3 Substance Consumption

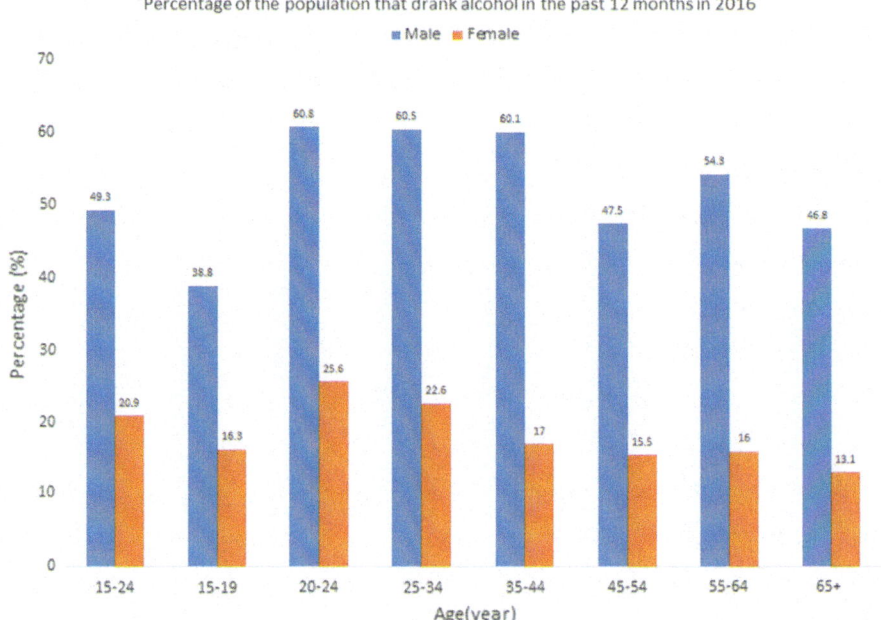

Fig. 3.53 Percentage of men and women who used alcohol in South Africa, 2016. (*Data Source* World Health Organization. *Graph Source* Funani Mpande)

Alcohol taxation increases every year, and the most taxed products are spirits and sparkling wine. The spirit increased R8.39 (US$0.60 or 0.49 Euro, exchange rate on May 7, 2021) between 2019 and 2021, and sparkling wine increased R1.14 (US$0.081 or 0.067 Euro). (National Treasury 2021).

Recorded alcohol per capita consumption is the number of liters of alcohol consumed by those aged 15 and older per capita over a calendar year in a country. This indicator accounts for consumption using data from production, import, export, and sales data via taxation (Fig. 3.56).[12]

---

[12] To convert into liters, the percentage of alcohol by volume is as follows: 40% for distilled spirits; 30% for spirit-like beverages; 18% for fermented wheat; 17% for fortified wine; 16% for vermouth; 12% for grape wine; 9% for grape must and fermented beverages; and 5% for sorghum, millet, maize, barley beers, and cider.

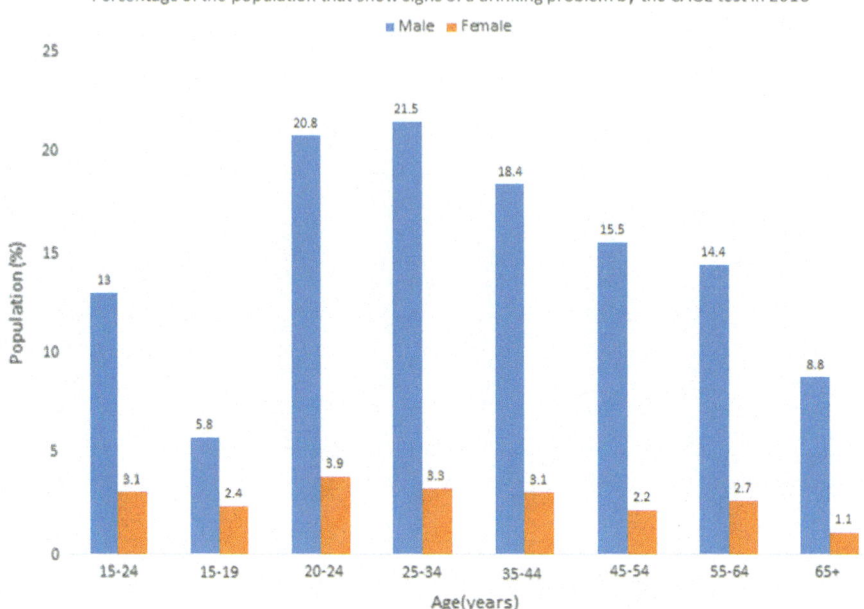

Fig. 3.54 CAGE results. (*Data Source* Department of Statistics South Africa. *Graph Source* Funani Mpande)

3.4 Nutrition

3.4.1 Nutrition

In Ghana, the calorie and protein availability per capita per day has increased since 1984. However, the amount of animal, fish, and seafood protein has not changed much (Fig. 3.57).

According to the Food and Agriculture Organization of the United Nations, the average food intake in Kenya is 2,155 kcal/person/day. Of this, 1,183 (55%) kilocalories come from maize, wheat, beans, potatoes, plantains, and rice. Maize is the most important cereal crop and main staple food, providing more than one-third of the caloric intake, and it accounts for about 56% of cultivated land in Kenya. Most Kenyans prefer white corn flour to produce *ugali*, a thick porridge of maize meal that is usually eaten daily with vegetables, meat, or fermented milk. On average, a Kenyan consumes 88 kg of maize products per year, followed by wheat (17% of staple food consumption) and beans (9% of food calories and 5% of total food calories in the national diet; Fig. 3.58).

Kenya produces potatoes, plantains, and rice but needs to import wheat and more rice due to food shortages. Nevertheless, Kenya is on track to meet four maternal, infant, and young child nutrition targets. Some progress has been made to reduce

3.4 Nutrition

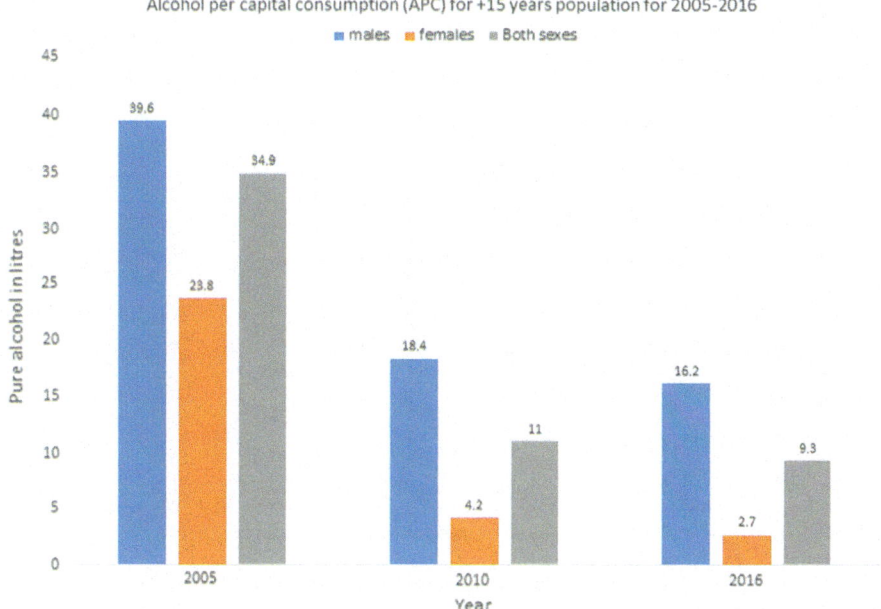

Fig. 3.55 Alcohol use per capita in South Africa for people aged 15 and older, 2005–2016. (*Data Source* Department of Statistics South Africa. *Graph Source* Funani Mpande)

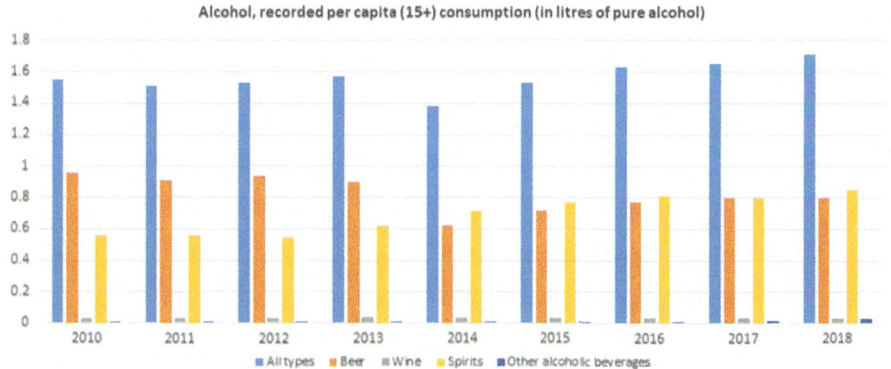

Fig. 3.56 Alcohol consumption per capita among those aged 15 and older. (*Data Source* Department of Statistics South Africa. *Graph Source* Funani Mpande)

anemia among women, which affects 27.2% of women aged 15–49. Progress also has been made toward achieving low birthweight targets, as 11.5% of infants are born with a low weight. Kenya has shown limited progress toward NCD targets and no progress toward obesity targets (11.1% of adult women and over 2.8% of adult

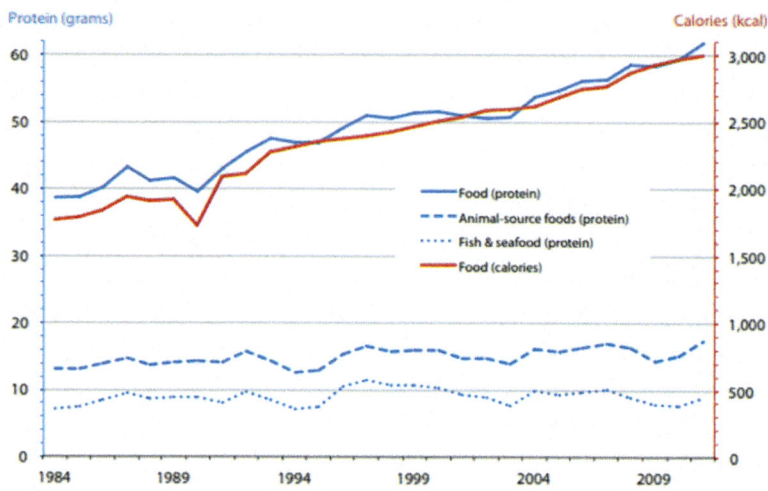

Fig. 3.57 Calorie and protein availability per capita in Ghana, 1984–2011. (*Data Source* International Food Policy Research Institute. *Graph Source* International Food Policy Research Institute)

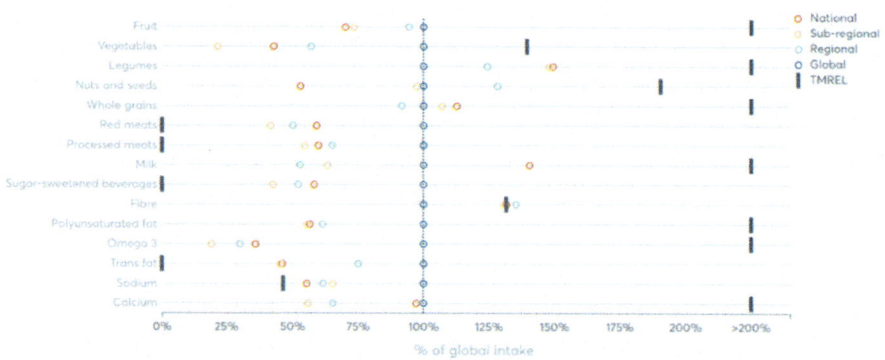

Fig. 3.58 Dietary intake of essential foods and nutrients among Kenyans aged 25 and over. (*Data source* Global Nutrition Report. *Graph source* Global Nutrition Report)

men are obese). Kenya's obesity prevalence is lower than the regional average of 18.4% for women and 7.8% for men.

According to the UN Food and Agriculture Organization, South Africans have increased their fat intake to 13.93 g/day from 1992 to 2018 and decreased their protein intake by 1.05 g/day. According to Steyn et al. (2006), the South African population is increasingly consuming a typical Western diet with higher calories, saturated fat, animal protein, sodium, and sugar. Fruit and vegetable intake also is low (Fig. 3.59).

3.4 Nutrition

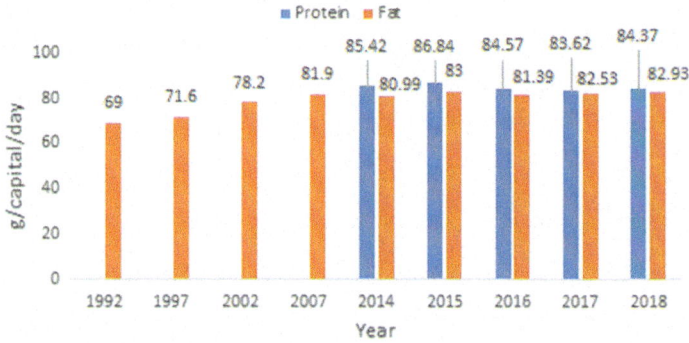

Fig. 3.59 Fat and protein intake in South Africa, 1992–2018. (*Data Source* UN Food and Agriculture Organization. *Graph Source* Funani Mpande)

3.4.2 Malnutrition

Malnutrition includes undernutrition (wasting, stunting, underweight), inadequate supply of vitamins or minerals, excess weight, and obesity. Malnutrition can result in diet-related NCDs. The body mass index (weight in kilograms divided by the square of height in meters, kg/m^2) is a commonly used index to classify weight in adults. According to WHO classifications, for individuals aged 20 and older, a BMI less than 18.5 is considered underweight, 18.5 to 24.9 is normal weight, 25 to 29.9 is overweight, and 30 or more is obese.

3.4.3 Undernutrition

The three sub-forms of undernutrition are wasting (too thin concerning height), stunting (too short concerning age), and underweight. Wasting may be due to food insufficiency or infectious disease (e.g. diarrhea). In 2020, 149 million children under five years old were stunted, 45 million were wasted, and 38.9 million were overweight or obese. Undernutrition is linked to 45% of deaths among these children. Stunting is the moderate and severe percentage of children aged 0–59 months below two standard deviations from the median height for age set by the WHO child growth standards. It may result from chronic or recurrent undernutrition, often linked to poor socioeconomic status, poor maternal health and nutrition, frequent illness, and inappropriate infant and toddler feeding. Underweight is determined if the BMI of a child falls under the fifth percentile compared to other children the same age. Children who are underweight may be stunted, wasted, or both.

In Algeria between 2004 and 2018, the prevalence of undernourishment as a percentage of the population declined at a moderate rate from 7 to 2.8%. The prevalence of underweight children under five was at 2.7% in 2019, down from 3% in 2012 (Fig. 3.60).

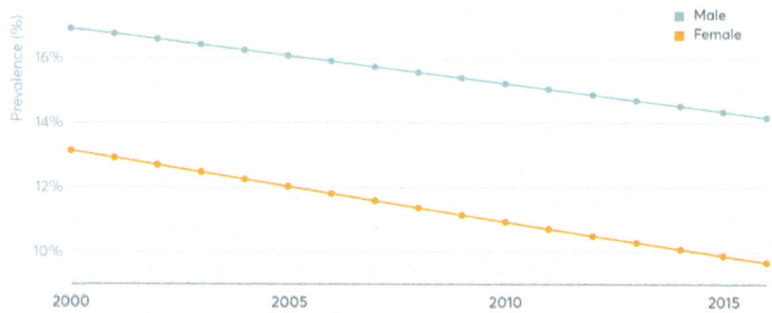

Fig. 3.60 Prevalence of undernourishment in Algeria. (*Data source* Global Nutrition Report. *Graph source* Global Nutrition Report)

In Côte d'Ivoire, the undernourished population reached almost 20% in 2018, which is slightly higher than in 2016 and lower than in 2014 by just more than 0.4%. Food insecurity due to the inaccessibility and instability of food production is widespread in the country, affecting 12.8% of the population (Fig. 3.61).

Kenya is on track to meet its target for reducing stunting. Its rate is 26.2% of children under age five affected, which is lower than the average of 29.1% across Africa. Kenya also is on track to reducing waste among children under five. Only 4.2% of children are affected, compared to 6.4% in Africa (Fig. 3.62).

According to the Global Hunger Index 2020, Nigeria ranks 98th out of 107 countries (the higher the number, the worse the situation). As shown in Fig. 3.63, the prevalence of undernourishment as a percentage of the total population increased from 2010 to 2018. The increase was a direct or underlying cause of 45% of all deaths of children under five. Inequality plays a significant role in these statistics, as the northern region is considerably less wealthy than the southern region. Recent terrorist attacks in some states in the northern region also contribute to this disparity.

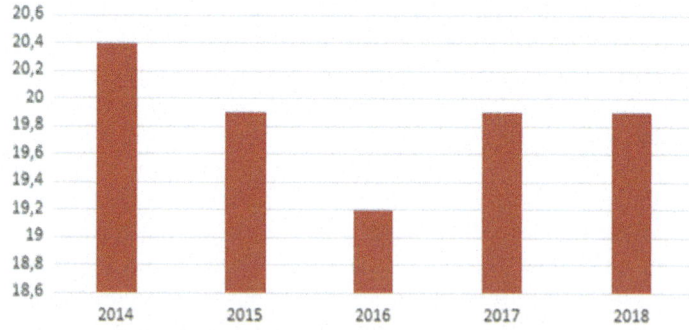

Fig. 3.61 Prevalence of undernourishment in Côte d'Ivoire (percentage of population). (*Data Source* World Bank. *Graph Source* Fofana Daouda)

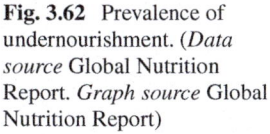

Fig. 3.62 Prevalence of undernourishment. (*Data source* Global Nutrition Report. *Graph source* Global Nutrition Report)

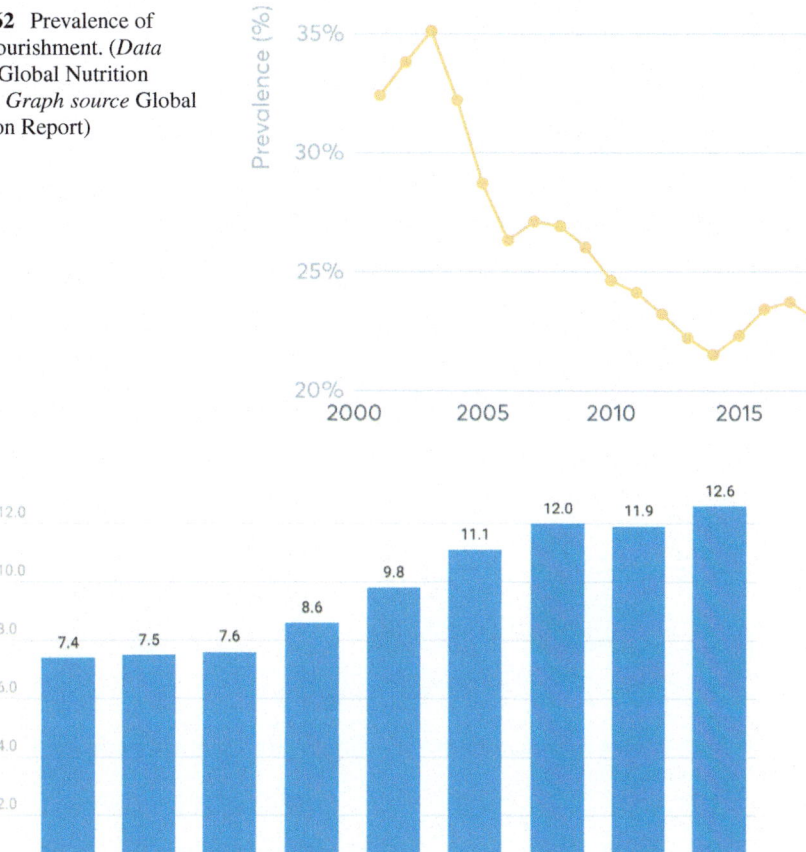

Fig. 3.63 Prevalence of undernourishment as a percentage of the population. (*Data source* Global Hunger Index. *Graph source* Ademola Olokun)

In South Africa, the estimated stunting proportions declined by 0.9% from 2010 to 2020, according to UNICEF/WHO/World Bank (2017). See Figs. 3.64, 3.65, and 3.66.

According to the Global Nutrition Report (2021), both wasting and stunting declined from 2004–2016. Boys tend to have higher occurrences than girls, but wasting among boys declined by 6.9%, compared to 3.9% among girls after a temporary increase in 2012. Stunting declined by 11.5% for boys and 5.3% for girls. The prevalence of underweight adults in South Africa declined from 2007 to 2016 (Fig. 3.67). Males are more likely to be underweight than females: the percentage change for males is 1.8% and 0.6% for females.

In South Africa, undernutrition most affects young people aged 15 to 24 years. Among underweight South Africans, males have higher BMIs than females

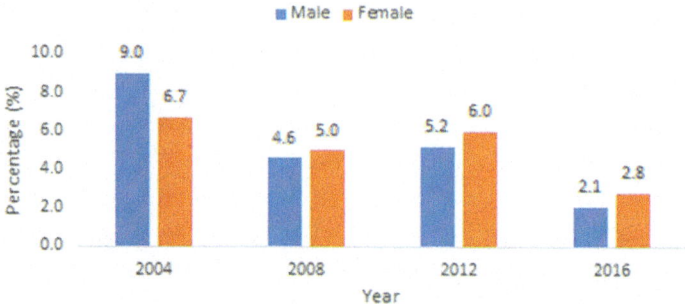

Fig. 3.64 Prevalence of wasting in children under five in South Africa. (*Data Source* World Bank. *Graph Source* Funani Mpande)

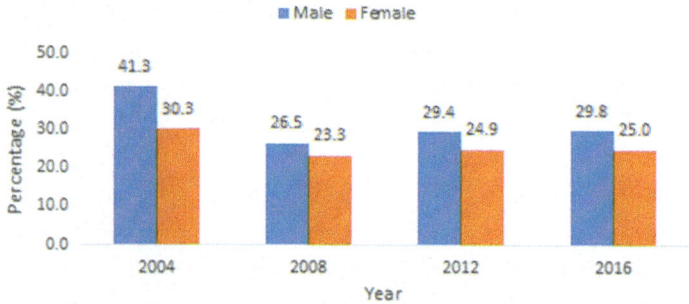

Fig. 3.65 Prevalence of stunting in children under five in South Africa. (*Data Source* World Bank. *Graph Source* Funani Mpande)

Fig. 3.66 Stunting proportions in South Africa, 2010–2020. (*Data Source* UNICEF. *Graph Source* Funani Mpande)

3.5 Urbanization

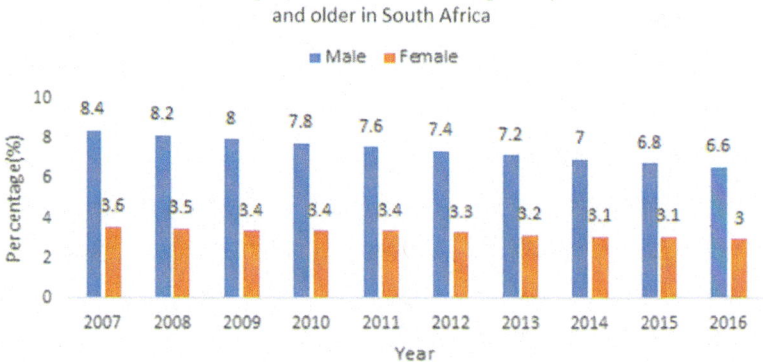

Fig. 3.67 Underweight prevalence among adults aged 18 years and older in South Africa. (*Data source* Global Nutrition Report. *Graph source* Funani Mpande)

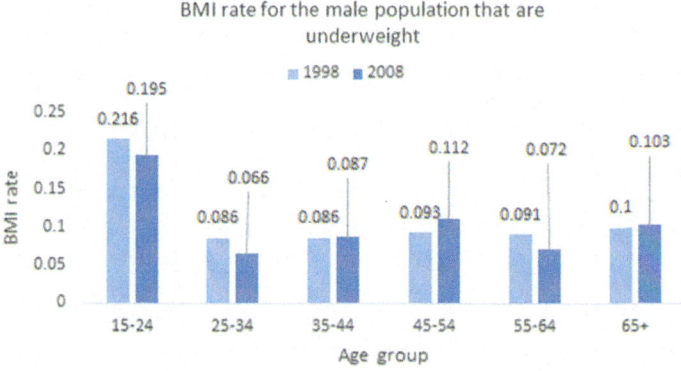

Fig. 3.68 BMI among underweight men. (*Data source* Global Nutrition Report. *Graph source* Funani Mpande)

(Figs. 3.68 and 3.69). For most age groups, undernutrition has declined marginally with time except among 35–44 year-olds, for whom it increased by 0.001. Underweight men aged 45–54 years increased by 0.019% in 2008, and women aged 55–64 years increased by 0.004 in 2008.

3.5 Urbanization

Urbanization refers to the percentage of a population living in cities. It signifies a demographic transition from an agriculture-based economy to an industrial, technological, and service-based economy. In principle, cities offer more favorable settings

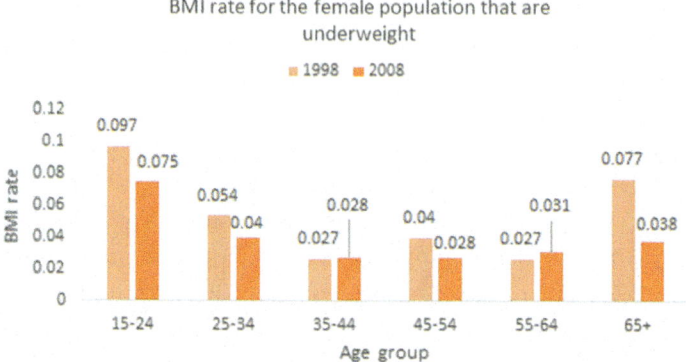

Fig. 3.69 BMI among underweight women. (*Data source* Global Nutrition Report. *Graph source* Funani Mpande)

for addressing social and environmental problems than rural areas. As such, urbanization can help measure the degree of development of a country, as cities provide better jobs, education opportunities, income, healthcare, and other services. However, it may also imply an increase in office jobs, which requires less physical work and is likely to be a risk factor for weight- and heart-related diseases, such as hypertension and obesity.

The urban population in Algeria has also increased by 6.3% from 2009 to 2019 (Fig. 3.70) A similar trend is observed in Côte d'Ivoire (Fig. 3.71).

The total percentage of South Africans living in urban areas has continuously increased over the past decade by 4.11% from 2011 to 2019 (Fig. 3.72). Urbanization is common in major cities as people migrate for better employment and living conditions.

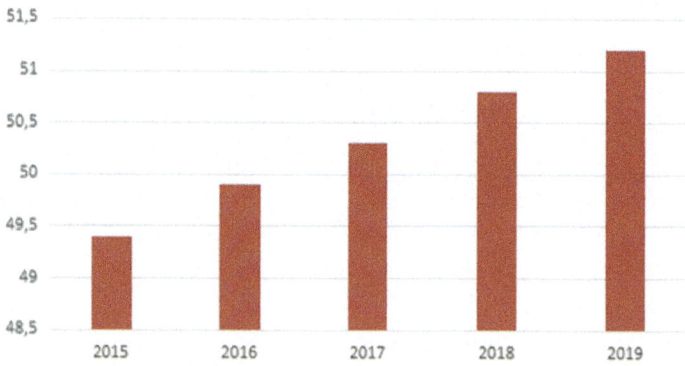

Fig. 3.70 Urban population (%). (*Data source* World Bank. *Graph source* Abdelkader Bouregag)

3.6 Physical Activity

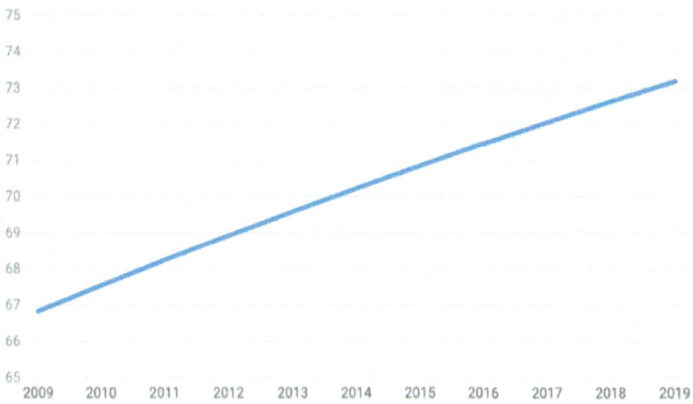

Fig. 3.71 Share (%) of urban population in total population. (*Data source* World Bank. *Graph source* Fofana Daouda)

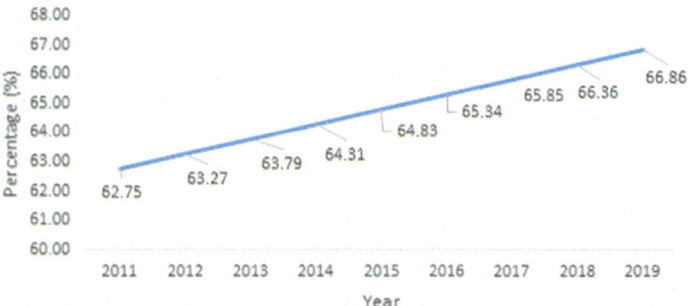

Fig. 3.72 Percentage of South Africans living in urban areas. (*Data source* World Bank. *Graph source* Funani Mpande)

3.6 Physical Activity

Physical activity is a key risk factor for obesity. Decreasing physical activity is observed in many developing countries, mainly due to job structure changes caused by urbanization. A 2018 study by *BMC Public Health* reported the country-wide prevalence of physical inactivity among adults aged 18–64 years in Kenya and identified the following populations to be targeted for interventions: women, middle-aged people (40–65), middle-class people, and post-secondary students. Physical activity in Kenya is mostly associated with work rather than health. This self-report should be considered with caution, however, as answers might be subjective. Among the four

Country	Year	Prevalence of insufficient physical activity among school going adolescents aged 11-17 (crude estimate)[f]		
		Both sexes	Male	Female
Kenya	2016	86.8 [84.2-89.1]	84.9 [82.0-87.4]	88.9 [86.4-90.9]
	2015	86.9 [84.2-89.1]	84.9 [82.0-87.4]	88.8 [86.4-90.9]
	2014	86.9 [84.3-89.1]	84.9 [82.1-87.4]	88.8 [86.4-90.8]
	2013	86.9 [84.3-89.1]	84.9 [82.2-87.4]	88.8 [86.4-90.8]
	2012	86.9 [84.3-89.1]	85.0 [82.2-87.4]	88.8 [86.4-90.8]
	2011	86.9 [84.3-89.1]	85.0 [82.3-87.4]	88.8 [86.4-90.8]
	2010	86.9 [84.3-89.1]	85.0 [82.3-87.4]	88.7 [86.4-90.7]
	2009	86.9 [84.4-89.1]	85.1 [82.4-87.4]	88.7 [86.4-90.7]
	2008	86.9 [84.4-89.1]	85.1 [82.4-87.5]	88.7 [86.4-90.7]
	2007	86.9 [84.4-89.1]	85.1 [82.4-87.5]	88.7 [86.3-90.7]
	2006	86.9 [84.4-89.1]	85.2 [82.5-87.5]	88.7 [86.3-90.7]
	2005	86.9 [84.4-89.1]	85.2 [82.5-87.5]	88.7 [86.3-90.7]
	2004	86.9 [84.4-89.1]	85.2 [82.5-87.6]	88.6 [86.2-90.7]
	2003	86.9 [84.4-89.1]	85.3 [82.5-87.6]	88.6 [86.2-90.7]
	2002	86.9 [84.3-89.2]	85.3 [82.6-87.7]	88.6 [86.2-90.7]
	2001	86.9 [84.3-89.2]	85.3 [82.6-87.7]	88.6 [86.1-90.7]

Fig. 3.73 Prevalence of insufficient physical activity among adolescents in school-aged 11–17 in Kenya, 2001–2016. (*Data source* BMC Public Health. *Table source* BMC Public Health)

Country	Year	Age Group	Prevalence of insufficient physical activity among adults aged 18+ years (age-standardized estimate) (%)[f]			Prevalence of insufficient physical activity among adults aged 18+ years (crude estimate) (%)[f]		
			Both sexes	Male	Female	Both sexes	Male	Female
Kenya	2016	18+ years	15.4 [13.1-17.8]	13.9 [11.8-16.0]	16.9 [14.3-19.5]	14.2 [12.0-16.4]	12.7 [10.8-14.6]	15.7 [13.3-18.2]

Fig. 3.74 Prevalence of insufficient physical activity among adults in Kenya. (*Data source* BMC Public Health. *Table source* BMC Public Health)

major risk factors for NCDs, physical inactivity is the only one with no associated policy (Figs. 3.73 and 3.74).[13]

Culture may contribute to physical activity preferences. For example, in some rural areas in Nigeria and South Africa, people view voluptuousness as a symbol of wealth and health. They believe fat provides resistance to diseases like HIV. Women tend to have lower physical levels, as many work as stay-at-home housewives. South Africa has high levels of physical inactivity, and women tend to be more physically inactive than men across all age groups. School and sports activities provide physical activities for younger populations aged 15–24 (Figs. 3.75 and 3.76).

---

[13] Estimates are based on self-reported physical activity captured using the Global Physical Activity Questionnaire, the International Physical Activity Questionnaire, or similar questionnaire on physical activity. Where necessary, adjustments were made if the reported definition differed from the indicator definition, if survey coverage was limited to urban areas, and if age coverage was narrower than 18+ years. No estimates were produced for countries with no data.

3.7 Overweight

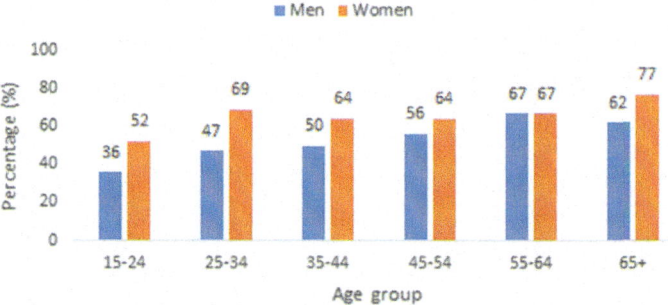

Fig. 3.75 Percentage of South Africans that were physically inactive in 2003, by gender. (*Data source* World Bank. *Graph source* Funani Mpande)

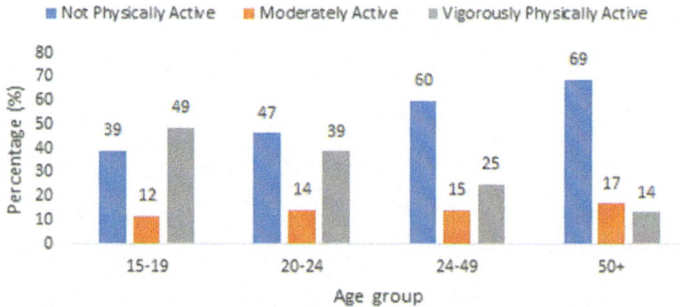

Fig. 3.76 Percentage of South Africans that were physically inactive in 2012, by age. (*Data source* World Bank. *Graph source* Funani Mpande)

According to Mlangeni et al. (2018), a 2012 population-based household survey elicited factors that influence physical inactivity in South Africa and found that individuals who reported physical inactivity had higher educations (i.e. higher socioeconomic status), which increased the likelihood of moderate physical activity. Females living in urban areas tend to be moderately more physically active as they age, whereas married females living in rural areas and with poorer self-rated health tend to engage less in physical activity (Figs. 3.77 and 3.78).

3.7 Overweight

Excess weight and obesity reflect abnormal or excessive fat accumulation that may impair health. For adults, being overweight is defined as a BMI between 25.0 and 30.0. For children under five, it is a weight-for-height greater than two standard deviations above the WHO Child Growth Standard, or above the 85th percentile in BMI compared to similarly aged children. For children between 5 and 19, overweight

Fig. 3.77 Average BMI of men in South Africa. (*Data source* Global Nutrition Report. *Graph source* Funani Mpande)

Fig. 3.78 Average BMI of women in South Africa. (*Data source* Global Nutrition Report. *Graph source* Funani Mpande)

is defined by a BMI-for-age greater than one standard deviation above the WHO Growth Reference median. In 2016, more than 1.9 billion adults aged 18+ were overweight.

The prevalence of overweight people in Algeria increased from 47.1% in 1997 to 62% in 2016, growing at an average annual rate of 1.46%. Similar patterns occur in Kenya. The 2008 Kenya Demographic Health Survey finds that 25% of women in Kenya are overweight or obese and in urban areas, such as Nairobi, 41% of women are overweight or obese women. The prevalence of overweight children under five years old is 4.1%. However, Kenya is on track to prevent the figure from increasing (Fig. 3.79).

In South Africa, the BMI index among overweight people is similar for both genders in the urban areas and exceeded 0.2 in both 1998 and 2008 (Fig. 3.80). Males in rural areas tend to have a rate that is below 0.2, whereas females in rural areas have higher BMIs than those in urban areas.

3.7 Overweight

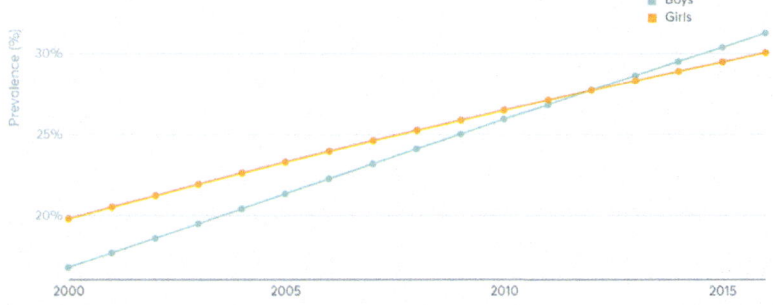

Fig. 3.79 Prevalence of overweight children under five in Kenya, 2000–2015. (*Data source* Global Nutrition Report. *Graph source* Global Nutrition Report)

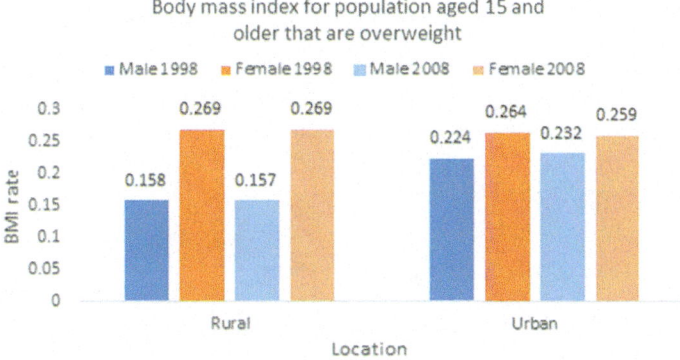

Fig. 3.80 BMI of men and women in South African aged 15 and older, 1998 and 2008. (*Data source* Global Nutrition Report. *Graph source* Funani Mpande)

More than 70% of women over 35 years old in South Africa were obese in both 1998 and 2008. Men's BMI increased by about 5% for each age group from 1998 to 2008 (Fig. 3.81).

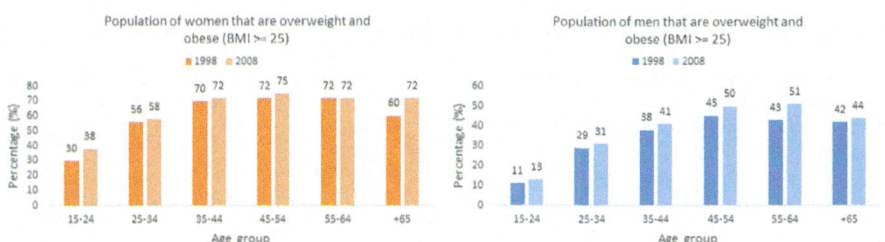

Fig. 3.81 Percentages of overweight or obese men and women in South Africa, 1998 and 2008. (*Data source* Global Nutrition Report. *Graph source* Funani Mpande)

3.7.1 Obesity

In Algeria, male obesity prevalence in 2016 was 19.9%, and female obesity prevalence was 34.9%. Between 1997 and 2016, it grew substantially among men from 9 to 19.9%, an increasing annual rate that peaked 5.32% in 1999 and then decreased to 3.65% in 2016. Obesity prevalence among women increased from 22.4% in 1997 to 34.9% in 2016, growing at an average annual rate of 2.36%.

In Ghana, the prevalence of obesity among all adults increased between 2009 and 2016. Like all other samples, women tend to have a higher prevalence of obesity than males (Fig. 3.82).

Kenya has shown limited progress toward achieving diet-related NCD targets. The country has shown no progress toward achieving obesity targets, with an estimated 11.1% of women and 2.8% of men aged 18 years and over living with obesity. Kenya's obesity prevalence is lower than the regional average of 18.4% for women and 7.8% for men. At the same time, diabetes is estimated to affect 6.2% of adult women and 5.8% of adult men (Figs. 3.83, 3.84, 3.85, and 3.86).

In South Africa, obesity is ranked fifth as a risk factor for early death or disability. Urban populations tend to have higher BMIs than rural ones. The BMI rate, measured using the post-stratification weights, exceeded 0.2 for women in 1998 and 2008 in both locations (Figs. 3.85, 3.86, and 3.87).

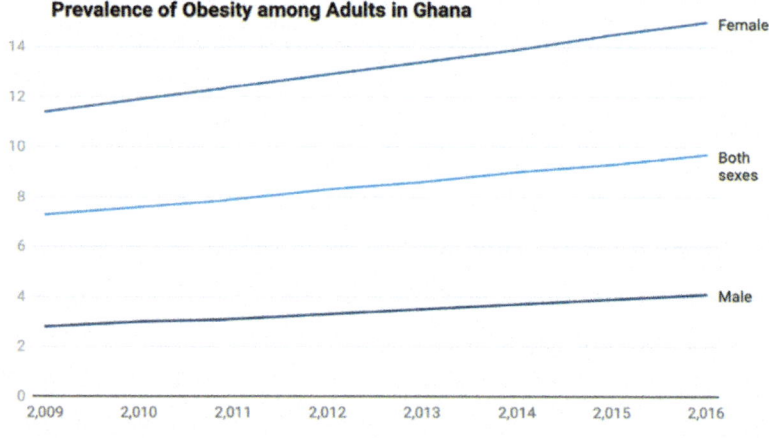

Fig. 3.82 The prevalence of obesity among adults in Ghana. (*Data source* World Bank. *Graph source* Gilbert Gadzekpo)

3.8 Summary

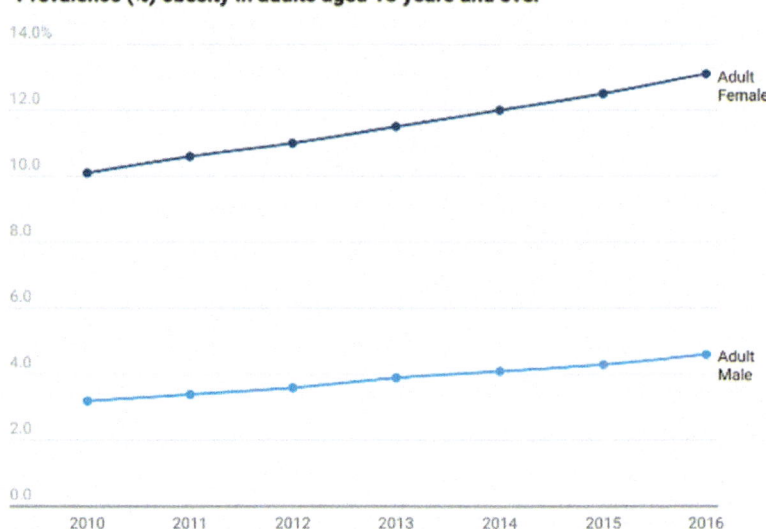

Fig. 3.83 Prevalence of obesity in adults. (*Data source* World Bank. *Graph source* Beatrice Birir)

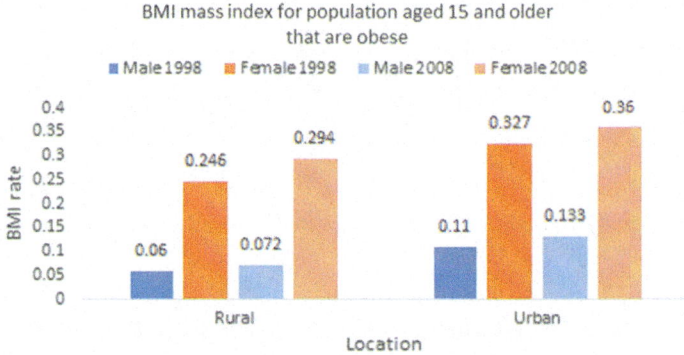

Fig. 3.84 BMI for those aged 15 and older. (*Data source* Global Nutrition Report. *Graph source* Beatrice Birir)

3.8 Summary

In the past years, infectious diseases (e.g. HIV, malaria, and TB) have been major concerns in Africa. As a result of financial and medical resources invested in controlling the spread and influence, especially preventive care, death rates from all three studied infectious diseases have either declined or remained low in all samples in the past decade. Education, prompt screening and diagnosis, and affordable, accessible, and effective treatment are key contributors to this success.

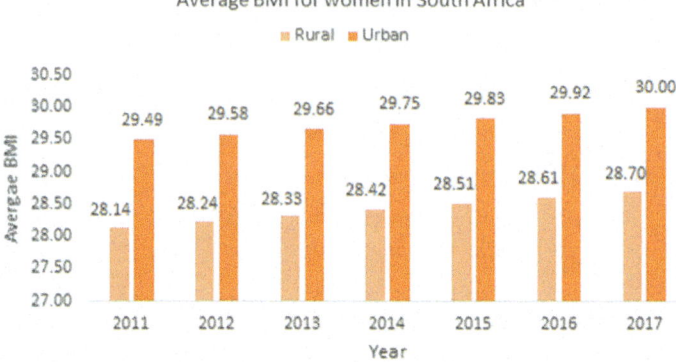

Fig. 3.85 Average BMI for women in South Africa. (*Data source* Global Nutrition Report. *Graph source* Funani Mpande)

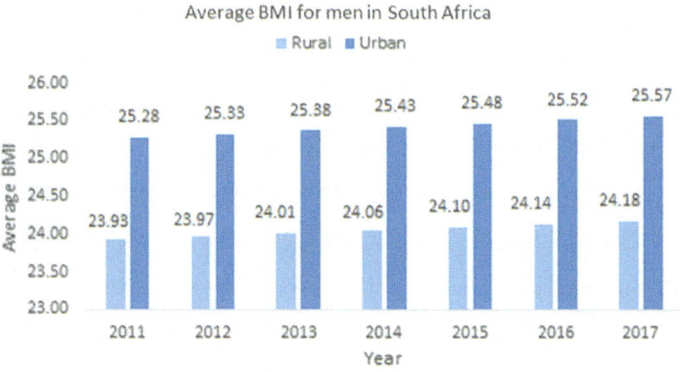

Fig. 3.86 Average BMI for men in South Africa. (*Data source* Global Nutrition Report. *Graph source* Funani Mpande)

Attention now is slowly shifting toward NCDs, which are on the rise in many parts of Africa due to pollution, Westernized diets, reduced physical activity levels, urbanization, and increased tobacco and alcohol consumption, to name a few. These increases are expected as a country develops. However, because Africa has committed most of its health resources to infectious diseases, it has a severe scarcity of resources, staff, and facilities to treat NCDs and related social issues, such as preventative care (e.g. education, screenings), treatment compliance, and social stigma.

Identifying, monitoring, and reducing risk factors can be a cost-effective way to reduce death from NCDs like cardiovascular disease and diabetes. Proper education and advocacy are key elements of this effort. Considering the lack of financial capacity in most African countries, reducing the incidence of NCDs should cost much less than treating them. For example, the government can increase taxes on cigarettes, tobacco, and alcohol to reduce consumption, which is essential to prevent

3.8 Summary

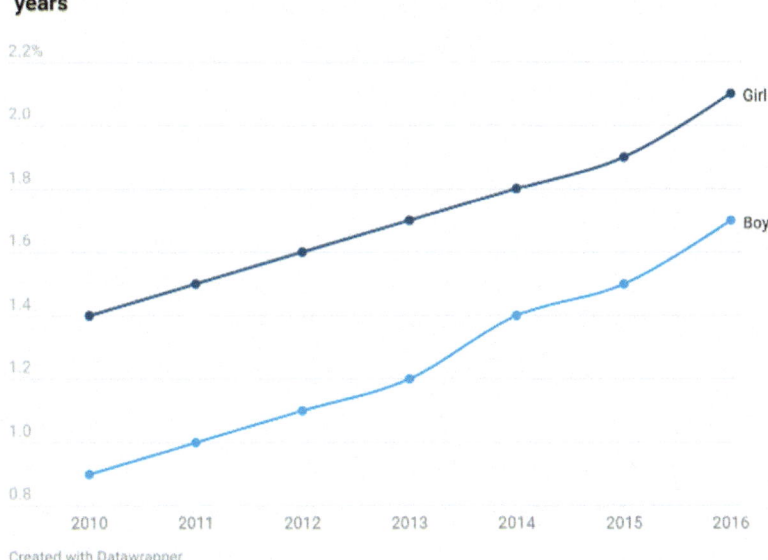

Fig. 3.87 Prevalence of obesity in children aged 5–19. (*Data source* World Bank. *Graph source* Funani Mpande)

lung and other cancers. Paying attention to NCDs does not mean infectious diseases are no longer the priority, as the two are often interrelated. For example, HIV patients are more vulnerable to cancer. Therefore, maintaining expertise in infectious diseases is still necessary.

Open Access This chapter is licensed under the terms of the Creative Commons Attribution 4.0 International License (http://creativecommons.org/licenses/by/4.0/), which permits use, sharing, adaptation, distribution and reproduction in any medium or format, as long as you give appropriate credit to the original author(s) and the source, provide a link to the Creative Commons license and indicate if changes were made.

The images or other third party material in this chapter are included in the chapter's Creative Commons license, unless indicated otherwise in a credit line to the material. If material is not included in the chapter's Creative Commons license and your intended use is not permitted by statutory regulation or exceeds the permitted use, you will need to obtain permission directly from the copyright holder.

Chapter 4
Health Resources

Health resources (hospitals, doctors nurses, and other health professionals) are in noticeable scarcity in African countries. According to the target set by the World Health Organization (WHO), there should be at least two hospitals per 100,000 inhabitants, and 20 doctors per 100,000 inhabitants. Most countries studied in this book achieve the target of having at least two hospitals per 100,000 population, but only nationally not regionally. Most health resources are concentrated in the urban areas, leaving the rural areas less accessible to the resources. Furthermore, healthcare in most countries is divided into private and public. Public healthcare is often funded by the government and offered to all citizens, and private healthcare facilities are used mostly by people with more access to funds. In countries in North Africa, where the government provides a stronger healthcare budget, the healthcare facilities are mainly run publicly rendering less financial burden on patients. While in other countries, public hospitals are often less funded and more crowded, many patients with more sufficient financial ability would seek treatment through private hospitals. The loss of healthcare professional personnel is also a crucial issue existing in the healthcare system in Africa. South Africa reported an increasing resignation trend in the medical professions between 2011 and 2015 due to unsatisfactory salary and working conditions in the public hospitals, where they received their medical training after graduation. After resignation, these professionals often relocate themselves to private sectors, other provinces, or abroad, causing a lack of providers in the public sector. This chapter aims at investigating this phenomenon, as well as the reasons behind it, such as the lack of medical students, brain drain in the health professions, and the lack of resources to support people receiving higher education.

4.1 Hospital Distribution

Health center density reflects the number of health centers relative to population size. It is an effective indicator of patients' physical accessibility to outpatient healthcare services. The target set by WHO is two health facilities per 100,000 inhabitants. The countries studied in this report have achieved this target nationally or at least regionally. Hospital distribution is often correlated with regional population density and urbanization, which means cities with more resources tend to have more healthcare facilities and more complete healthcare systems. Therefore, hospital distribution also identifies the key healthcare regions of countries.

Côte d'Ivoire measures its health system capacity using the hospital distribution (Fig. 4.1) or the number of energy-saving performance contracts (ESPCs) of healthcare facilities per 10,000 population, rather than the density of facilities (Fig. 4.2).

The data collected considers primary healthcare or first-contact healthcare facilities as level-2 facilities. The target proposed by WHO is one ESPC per 10,000 people. Côte d'Ivoire had 2,479 ESPCs in 2018. Despite a 10.08% increase of 227 ESPCs in 2017, its national ratio of one ESPC per 10,164 inhabitants remains below the WHO target (Fig. 4.2).

The national ratio of level-2 hospitals reached 0.7 in 2018, which is also below the WHO target of one ESPC per 10,000 population (Fig. 4.3).

In Ghana, the healthcare system comprises about 60% public facilities (1,625 of which are run by the government) and 40% private facilities. The Christian Health Association of Ghana has 928 private hospitals and 220 private health facilities. The Ashanti region has the most health facilities in Ghana, followed by the Greater Accra and eastern regions. The two northern regions have the least (Figs. 4.4 and 4.5).

Kenya achieved the WHO goal on a national level in 2018, when health facility density reached 2.2 per 100,000 population. However, many countries are still below this target, especially in the eastern part of the country (Fig. 4.6).

In Nigeria, healthcare services were delivered at over 40,110 health centers included on the Federal Ministry of Health's master facility list in 2020. Two-thirds of the services were publicly administered; the remaining third was run by private firms. Of the total, 88.15% were primary facilities, 11.6% offered secondary services, and 0.25% engaged in tertiary care (Fig. 4.7).

Around 73% of Nigerian hospitals and clinics are in the public sector, and 27% are private. Many have long wait times, old facilities, antiquated equipment, and shortages of health workers. Private healthcare, although more expensive, offers shorter wait times, better facilities, and superior care in terms of service delivery (Fig. 4.8).

South Africa has over 3,000 public clinics and over 470 public hospitals, as well as over 1,500 private clinics and over 260 private hospitals. Among all the provinces, Gauteng has the most healthcare facilities due to its large population and major economic activity (Fig. 4.9).

4.2 Health Provider Distribution

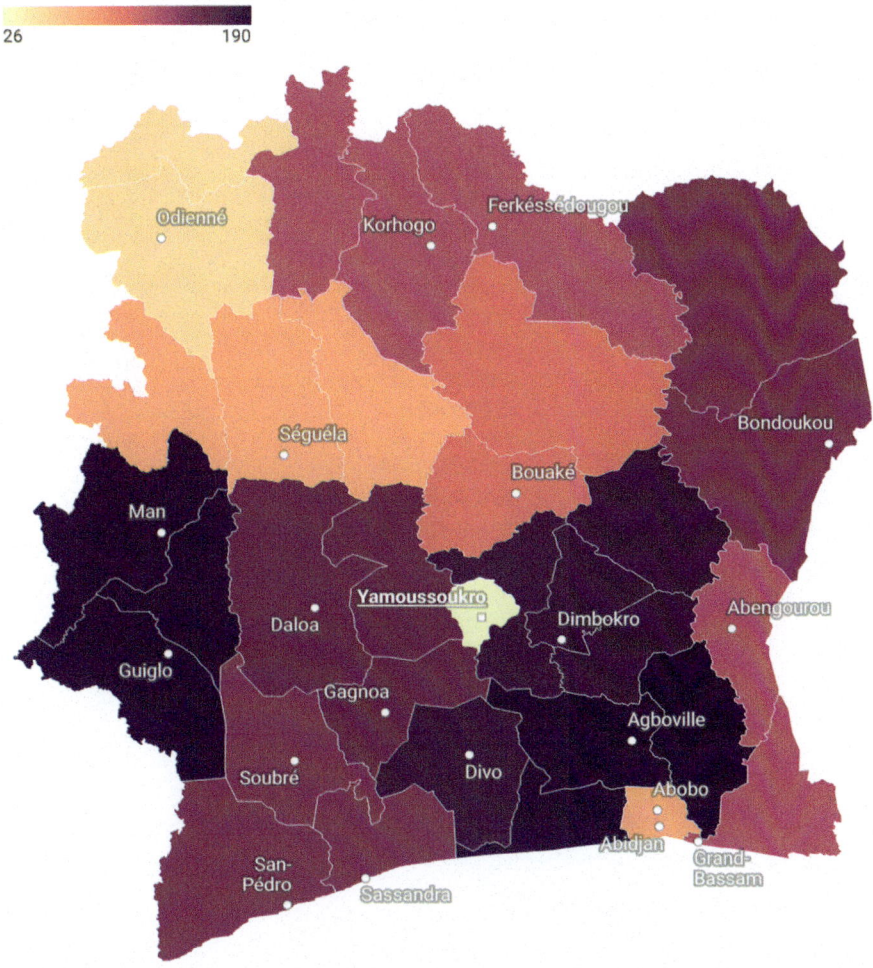

Fig. 4.1 Hospital distribution in Côte d'Ivoire, by district (2018) (*Data source* Syndicat National des Médecins Privés de Côte d'ivoire. *Map source* the author)

4.2 Health Provider Distribution

Health provider density reflects the number of health centers relative to a population size of 100,000. Countries with fewer than 10 doctors or 40 nurses and midwives for every 10,000 people are considered underserved.[1] As of 2020, over 55% of WHO Member States reported having less than 20 medical doctors per 10,000 inhabitants

---

[1] https://apps.who.int/iris/bitstream/handle/10665/311696/WHO-DAD-2019.1-eng.pdf?ua=1.

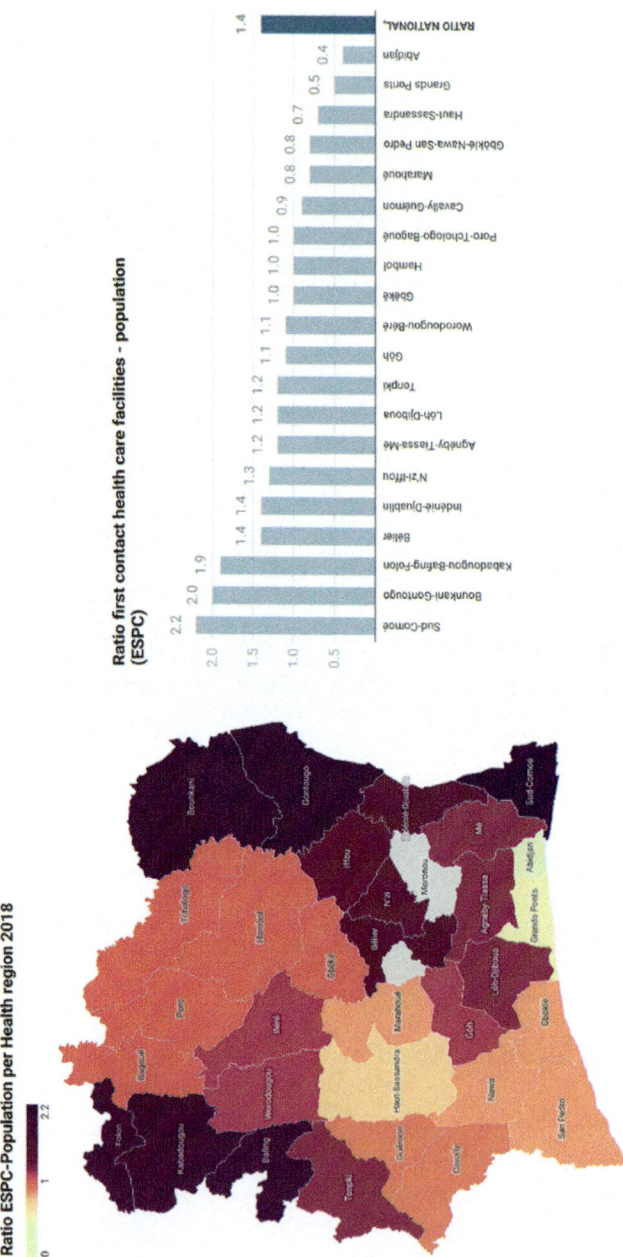

Fig. 4.2 Ratio of ESPCs in Côte d'Ivoire (2018) and the ratio of first-line health facilities in Côte d'Ivoire (2018) (*Data source* Syndicat National des Médecins Privés de Côte d'ivoire. *Map source* (left) the author and *Table source* (right) Syndicat National des Médecins Privés de Côte d'ivoire)

4.2 Health Provider Distribution

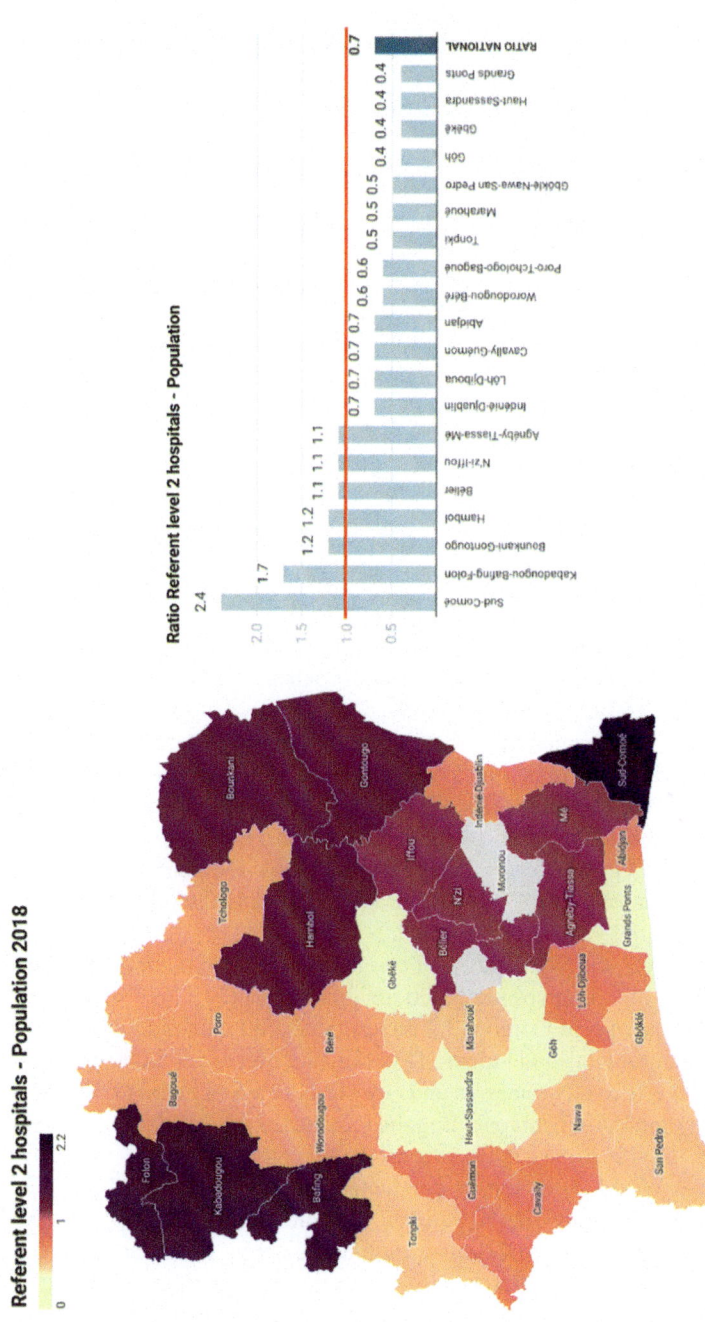

Fig. 4.3 Level-2 hospitals in Côte d'Ivoire (2018) and Level-2 hospitals in Côte d'Ivoire, by population (2018) (*Data source* Syndicat National des Médecins Privés de Côte d'ivoire). *Map source* (left) the author (right) Syndicat National des Médecins Privés de Côte d'ivoire)

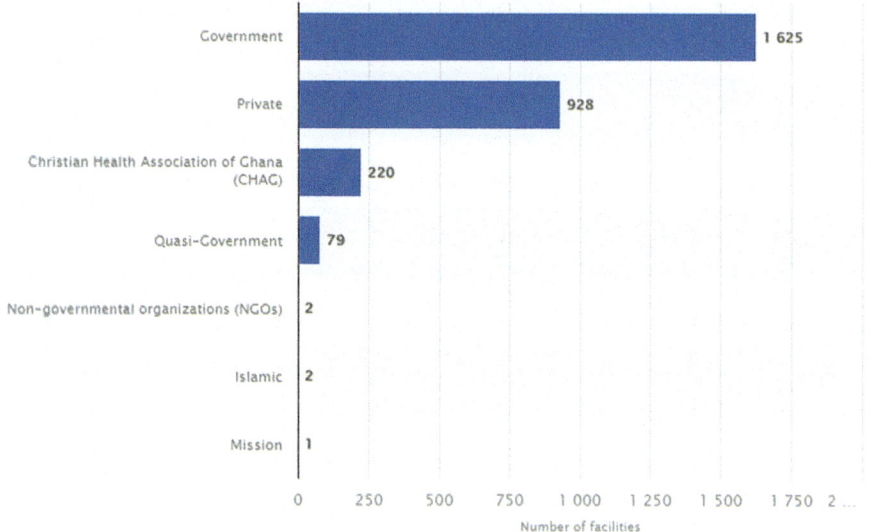

Fig. 4.4 Number of health facilities in Ghana in 2020, by type of ownership (*Data source* Ghana Statistical Service. *Graph source* Statista)

(almost 40 countries in the WHO African region). Africa has access to only 3% of health workers, a crucial issue in this region.

In Côte d'Ivoire, the national ratio was one healthcare provider per 7,354 inhabitants (1.4 doctors per 10,000 inhabitants) in 2018. Eight health regions (40%) reached the WHO target of one doctor per 10,000 inhabitants. Abidjan had 2.1 doctors per 10,000 inhabitants, Sud Comoé had 1.8, and Aries had 1.6 for two consecutive years. Cavally-Guémon and Gboklè-Nawa San-Pédro fell below the goal with 0.5 doctors per 10,000 inhabitants, and Poro-Tchologo-Bagoue had only 0.6 doctors per 10,000 inhabitants (Fig. 4.10).

At the national level, the WHO target of one nurse per 5,000 inhabitants has been reached with a ratio of 2.3 nurses per 5,000 inhabitants (Fig. 4.11).

The health regions of Sud Comoé (3.2 nurses per 5,000 inhabitants), Bélier (3.0 nurses per 5,000 inhabitants), and Indenie-Djuablin (2.9 nurses per 5,000 inhabitants) had the highest ratios. Cavally-Guémon and Gboklè-Nawa-San Pedro (1.3 nurses per 5,000 inhabitants) and Poro-Tchologo-Bagoue (1.4 nurses per 5,000 inhabitants) had the lowest ratios.

According to a World Bank survey conducted between 2015 and 2017, Ghana had only one doctor for every 10,450 patients, far below the WHO goal of 1:1,320. As shown in Fig. 4.12, doctors in Ghana are spread far across different regions, with much less dense coverage in the Greater Accra and Ashanti regions.

The current nurse-to-patient ratio according to the same report stands at 2.352, which exceeds the WHO's recommended one nurse-to-1,000 ratio. Figure 4.12 shows

4.2 Health Provider Distribution

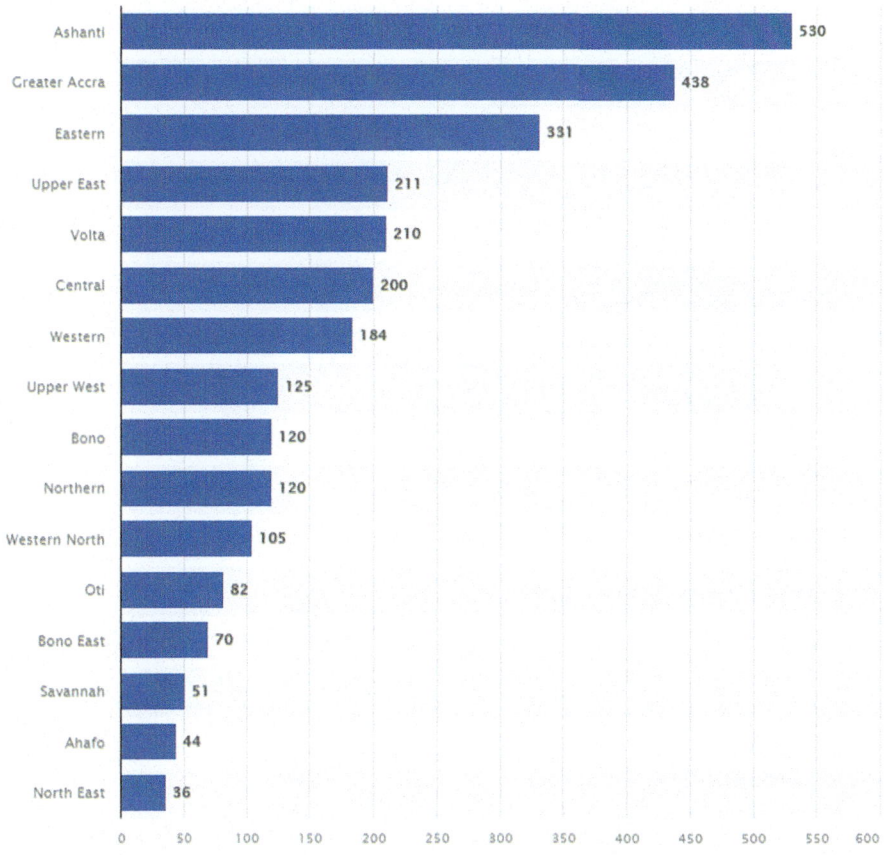

Fig. 4.5 Number of health facilities in Ghana in 2020, by region (*Data source* Ghana Statistical Service. *Graph source* Statista)

the distribution of nurses across Ghana, showing highly concentrated Volta, Eastern, Ashanti, and Western regions and less concentrated Upper East and Upper West regions.

According to a 2016 report by the Ghana Health Service, healthcare providers largely consist of nurses (37,582), physicians (3,527), and dentists (573; Fig. 4.13).

In Kenya, the physician density per 10,000 population is 0.2, nursing and midwifery personnel density is 0.8, pharmaceutical personnel density is 0.2, and other health workers' density is 0.1 (Figs. 4.14 and 4.15).

The specific density heat map is shown below.

In Nigeria, there were 75,000 doctors licensed by the Medical and Dental Council of Nigeria in 2018, but only 42,000 were practicing, leaving only one doctor for

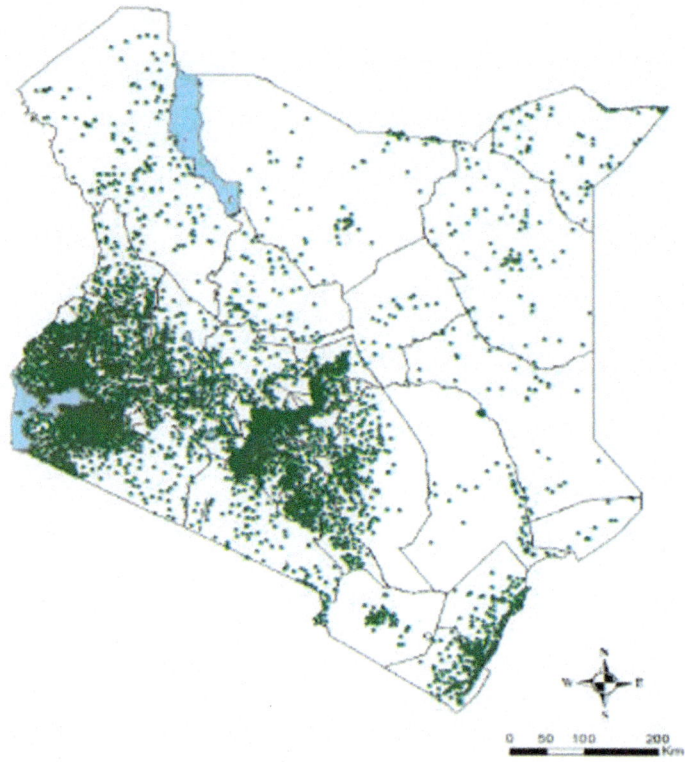

Fig. 4.6 Hospital distribution in Kenya (*Data source* Ministry of Health, Kenya. *Map source* Ministry of Health, Kenya)

every 4,800 people. The large discrepancy between licensed and practicing doctors is predominantly because most health professionals choose to work in Lagos and other urban areas in the south, leaving an acute shortage of health professionals in the northern part of the country. Of the country's 164 universities, only 41 are accredited to teach medicine, and they cannot train personnel quickly enough to replace those that emigrate. Statistics show that approximately 2,300 medical doctors graduate each year.

The Health Professions Council of South Africa has 72,207 registered professionals on the Medical and Dental Board. Most medical officers in 2015 were men, and most of them were based in Gauteng province, with a few in the Northern Cape province (Fig. 4.16). South Africa has one public health doctor for every 2,457 people and one private-sector doctor for every 429–571 people (Fig. 4.17). Because 48% of registered nurses are over 50 years old and only 5% are under 30, South Africa may encounter a resource drain as older nurses retire (Fig. 4.18).

4.2 Health Provider Distribution

Region	Public Primary	Public Secondary	Public Tertiary	Private Primary	Private Secondary	Private Tertiary	Total
North Central	6,468	235	18	1,870	578	10	9,179
North East	4,261	155	13	382	162	1	4,974
North West	7,243	214	24	493	313	18	8,305
South East	3,289	135	15	828	994	6	5,267
South South	3,373	278	11	614	607	14	4,897
South West	3,730	205	19	1,950	1,577	7	7,488
	28,364	1,222	100	6,137	4,231	56	40,110

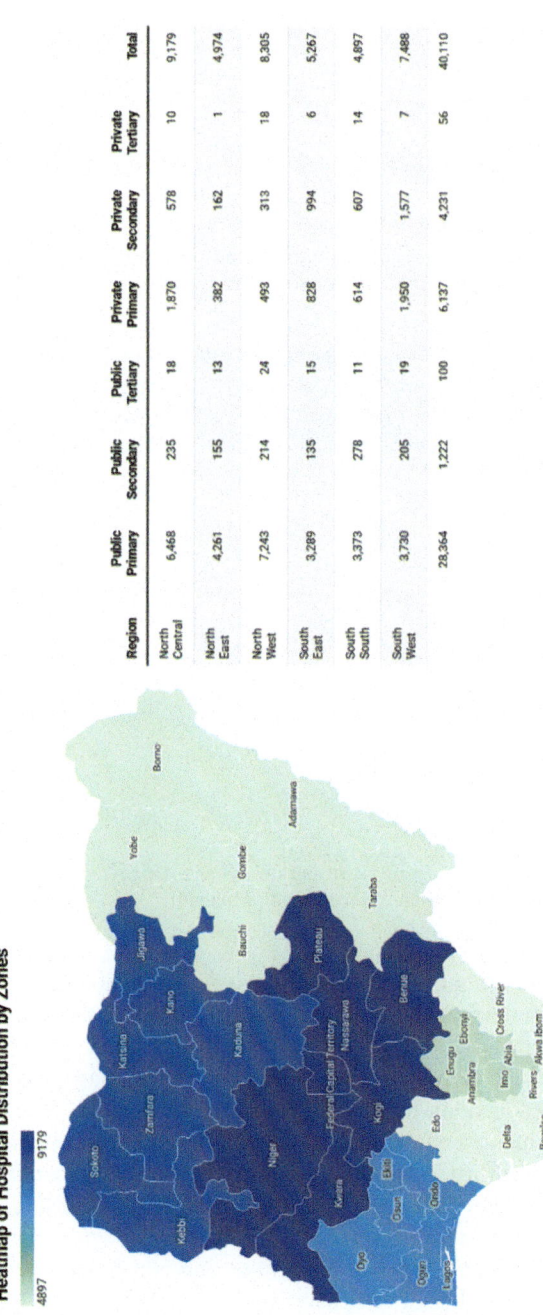

Fig. 4.7 Heatmap of hospital distribution in Nigeria, by zone and Distribution of healthcare facilities in Nigeria, by zone (*Data source* Federal Ministry of Health in Nigeria. *Table source* (left) the author (right) Ademola Olokun)

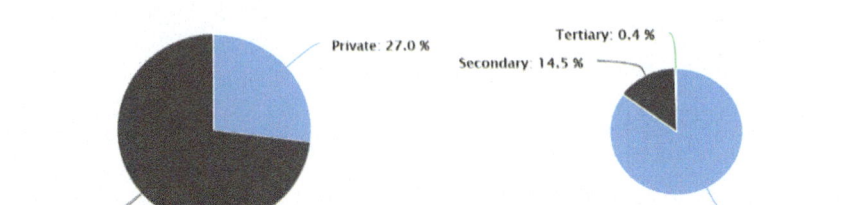

Fig. 4.8 Hospitals and clinics in Nigeria, by ownership and by the level of care (*Data source* Federal Ministry of Health in Nigeria. *Table source* Ademola Olokun)

Province	Public clinic	Public hospital	Private clinic	Private hospital	Community Health Centre	Total
Gauteng	329	44	657	95	32	1157
Eastern Cape	732	101	102	22	37	994
KwaZulu-Natal	609	79	233	46	22	989
Western Cape	194	77	347	42	9	669
Limpopo	453	42	90	14	26	625
Mpumalanga	232	32	70	13	57	404
North West	256	31	56	16	45	404
Free State	209	34	64	18	9	334
Northern Cape	127	38	26	10	32	233
South Africa	3141	478	1645	276	269	5809

Fig. 4.9 Public and private healthcare facility distribution in South Africa (*Data source* Department of Health, Republic of South Africa. *Table source* Funani Mpande)

The resignation trend among medical officers is also a major concern in South Africa, especially in Western Cape. In 2015, Western Cape had the highest number (729) of medical officer resignations, loosely followed by Eastern Cape (342). Among the 729 resignations in Western Cape, most are young people aged 40 and below, intensifying the severity of brain drain in the medical professions. The resignation of the younger staff is due to a number of reasons. In South Africa, medical training is conducted at public facilities. After training, many of the younger staff relocate to other provinces, to the private sector, or abroad. The trend of resignation, however, is insufficient to prove an increase or decrease in the number of resignations. According to the trend of resignations in Limpopo, Free State, and North West, which are the provinces with the least number of resignations, only Limpopo shows an increase between 2013 and 2015, while the other two stayed steady. (African Institute for Health and Leadership Development 2017; Figs. 4.19 and 4.20).

4.2 Health Provider Distribution

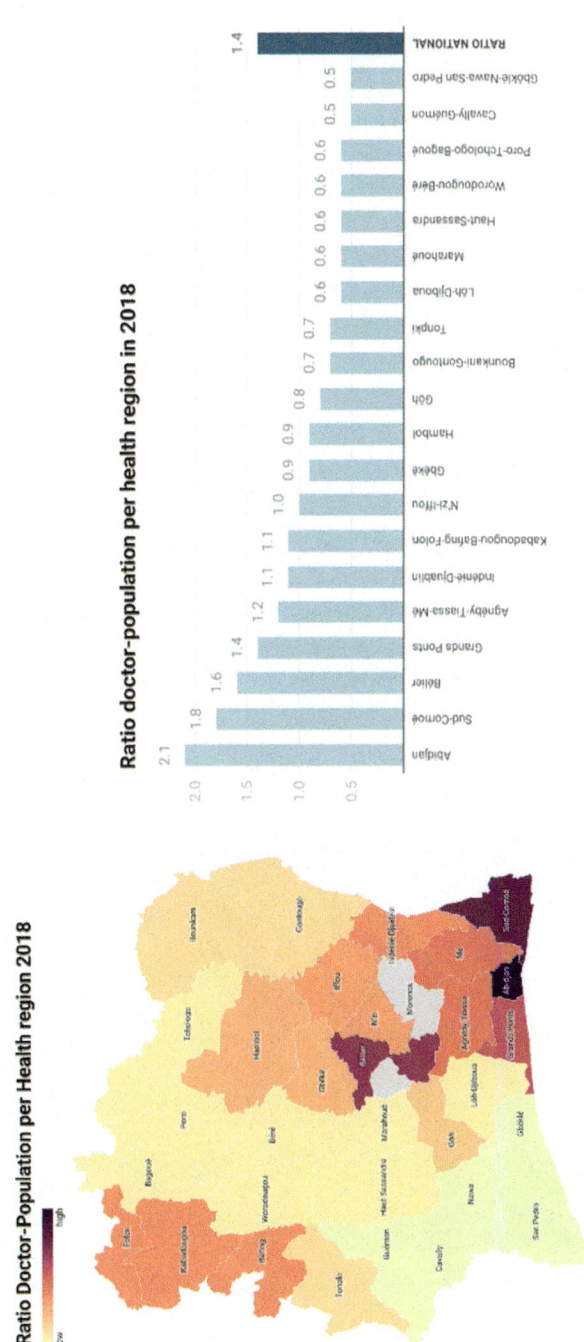

Fig. 4.10 Ratio of doctors to population in Côte d'Ivoire, 2018 (*Data source* Syndicat National des Médecins Privés de Côte d'ivoire. *Map source* (left) the author (right) Syndicat National des Médecins Privés de Côte d'ivoire)

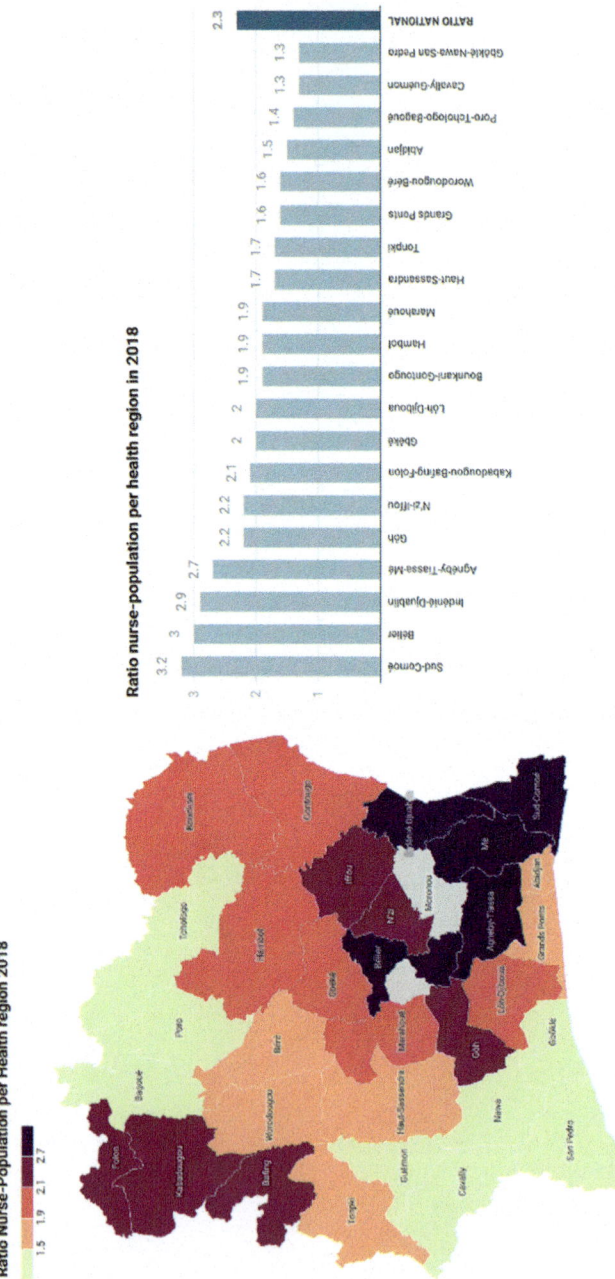

Fig. 4.11 The ratio of nurses to the population in Côte d'Ivoire, 2018 (*Data source* Syndicat National des Médecins Privés de Côte d'ivoire. *Map source* (left) the author (right) Syndicat National des Médecins Privésde Côte d'ivoire)

4.2 Health Provider Distribution

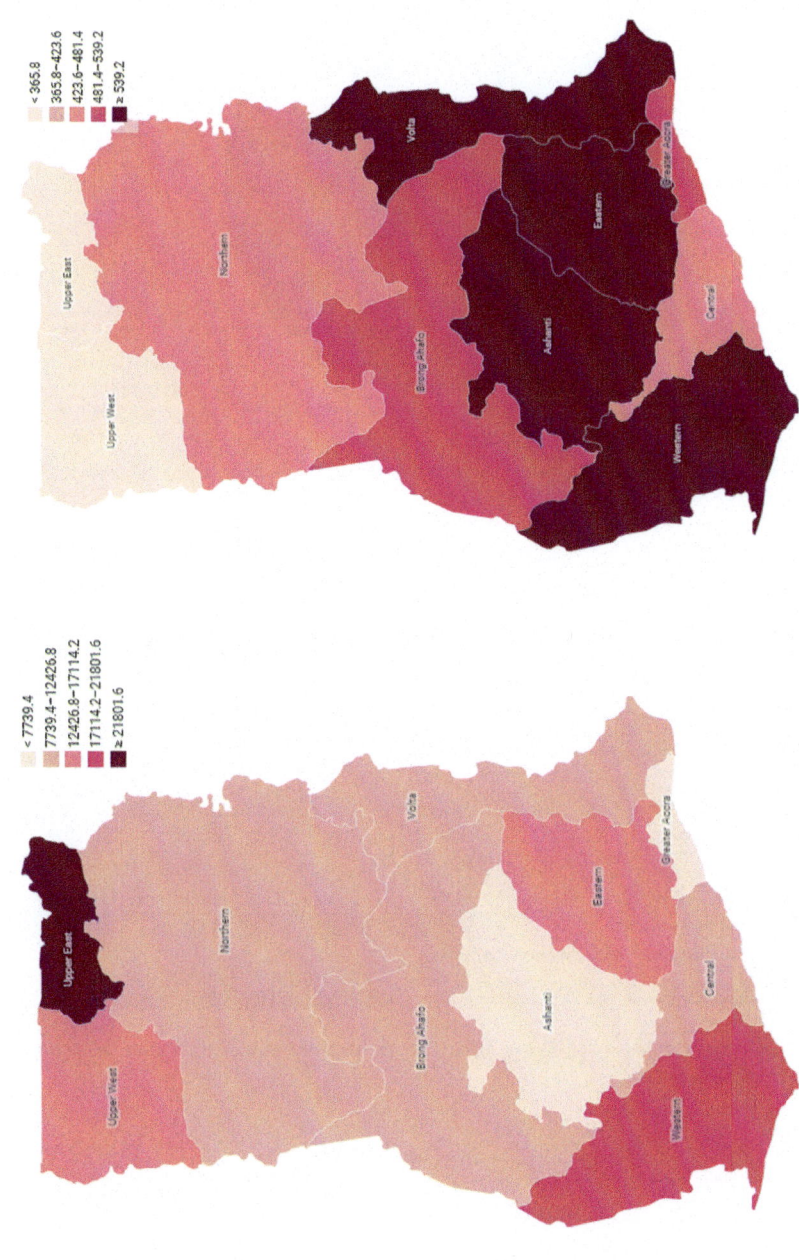

Fig. 4.12 Distribution of doctor (left) and nurse (right) coverage in Ghana (2017) (*Data source* World Bank. *Map source* the author)

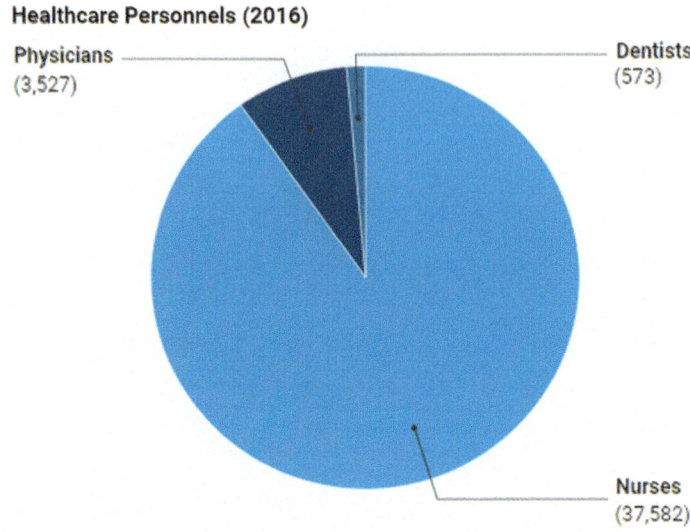

Fig. 4.13 Healthcare personnel in Ghana (*Data source* World Bank. *Map source* The author)

	Annual Output	Total # Registered	Total # Retained	Ratio per 10,000 pop	Density 1: N pop	Density 1: N pop
				Pop estimate: The 2009 Kenya Population and Housing Census	Pop estimate: The 2009 Kenya Population and Housing Census	*Population in "Worldometers"
Medical Officers	611	9,497	5,660	1.5	1: 6,822	1: 7,516
Dentists	52	1,066	603	0.2	1: 64,030	1: 70,548
Pharmacists	330	2,377	1,971	0.5	1: 19,530	1: 21,518
Pharm Technologists	994	7,243	4,671	1.2	1: 8,266	1: 9,107
Clinical Officers	1,642	13,913	10,562	2.7	1: 3,656	1: 4,028
ML Technologists	1,236	6,626	5,203	1.3	1: 7,421	1: 8,177
ML Technicians	326	4,445	3,213	0.8	1: 12,017	1: 13,241
Nurses and Midwives	6,326	63,113	31,896	8.3	1: 1,211	1: 1,334
Total (All cadres retained)			63,785	16.5	1: 605	1: 667
Total Active Doctors, Clinical Officers, Nurses/Midwives			53,118	13.8	1:727	1: 801
WHO estimates for the number of physicians, nurses, and midwives per 1,000 population needed to meet the SDGs by 2030				44.5		

Fig. 4.14 Health worker density in Kenya (*Data source* Ministry of Health, Kenya. *Map source* Ministry of Health, Kenya)

4.2 Health Provider Distribution

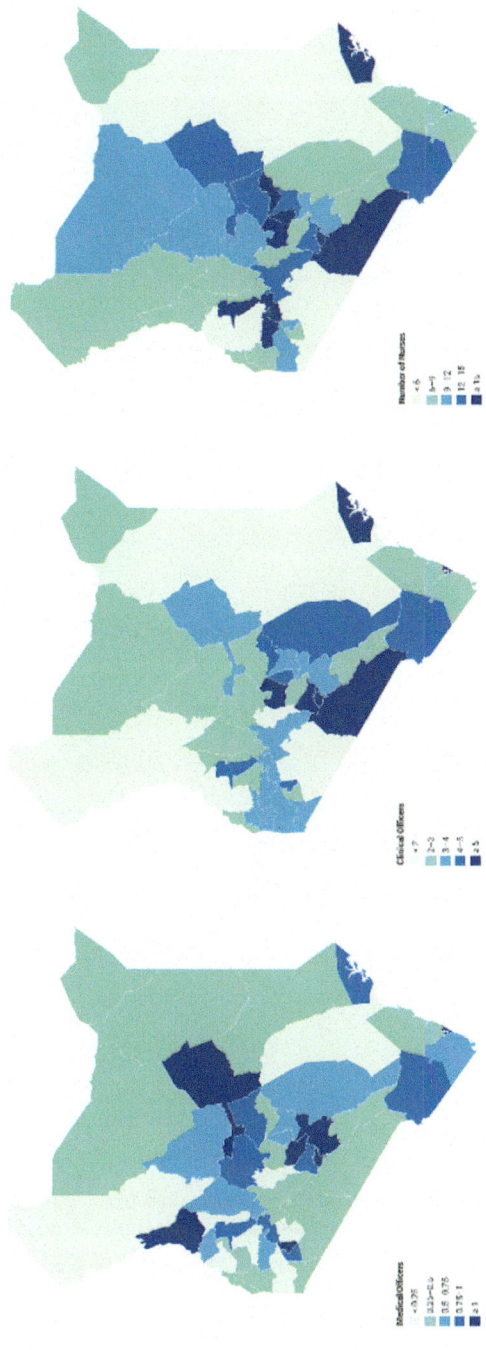

Fig. 4.15 Heat map of health worker density in Kenya (*Data source* Ministry of Health, Kenya. *Map source* The author)

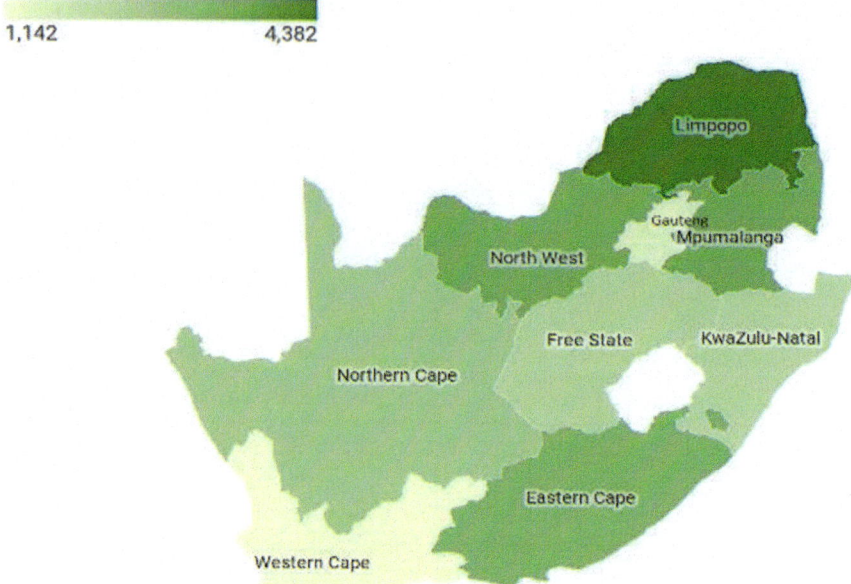

Fig. 4.16 Doctors per person in South Africa, 2015 (*Data source* Health Professions Council. *Map source* Funani Mpande)

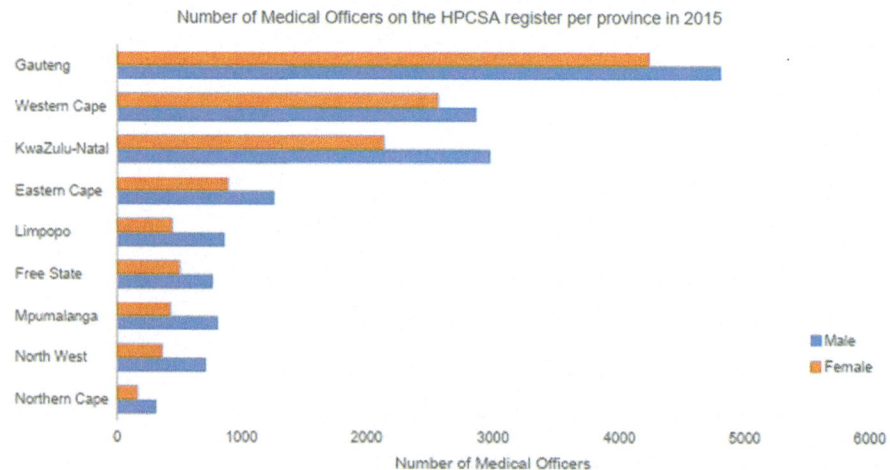

Fig. 4.17 Number of medical officers on the Health Professions Council of South Africa register in 2015, by province (*Data source* Health Professions Council. *Graph source* Funani Mpande)

4.3 Summary

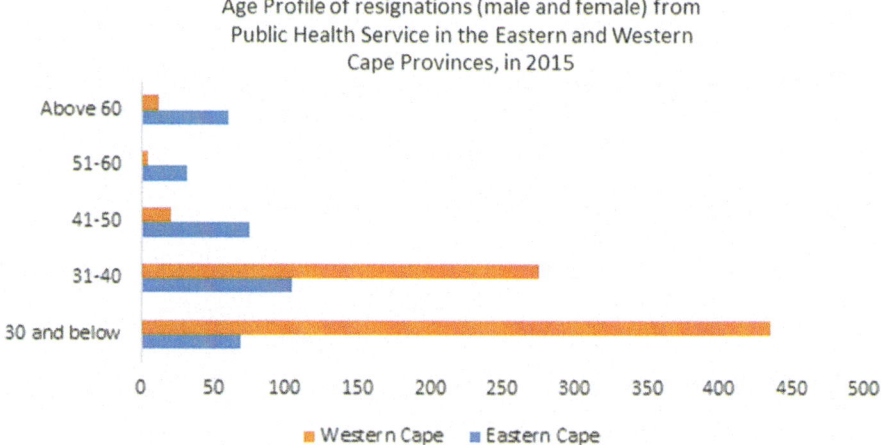

Fig. 4.18 The age profile of resignations from public health service in eastern and western Cape provinces, 2015 y(*Data source* African Institute for Health and Leadership Development. *Graph source* Funani Mpande)

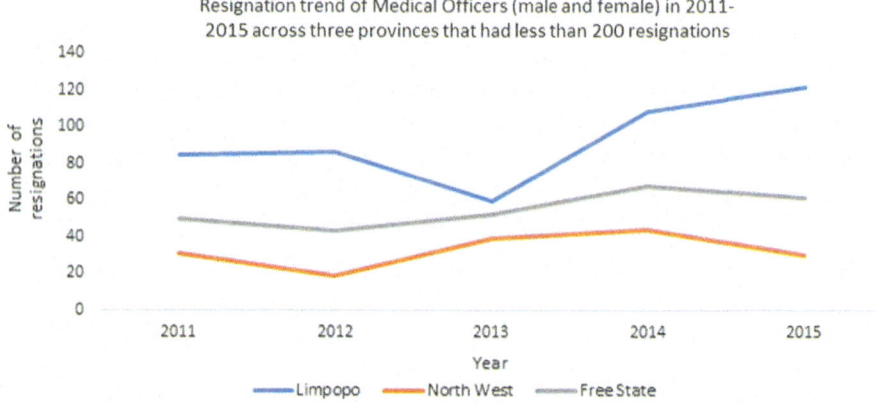

Fig. 4.19 Resignation trend among medical officers in three provinces in South Africa with less than 200 resignations, 2011–2015 (*Data source* Health Professions Council. *Graph source* Funani Mpande)

4.3 Summary

Algeria, Kenya, Côte d'Ivoire, Ghana, and Nigeria meet the WHO's target of hospital-to-patient ratio on the national level, but not necessarily on the regional level. All of them are lacking doctors, nurses, and other health professionals. Health resources are mostly concentrated in urban areas, especially major cities. However, even in cities

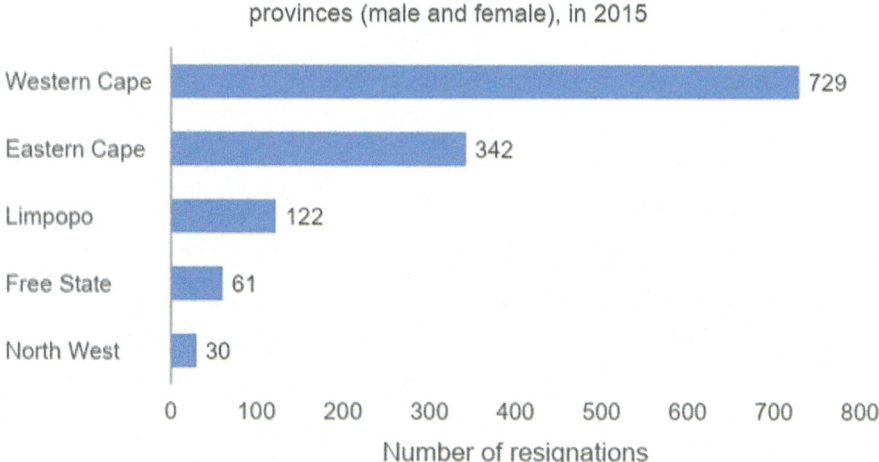

Fig. 4.20 Medical officer resignations across five provinces in South Africa, 2015 (*Data source* Health Professions Council. *Graph source* Funani Mpande)

with the most abundant healthcare resources, the standard doctor-to-patient, nurse-to-patient, and hospital-to-patient ratios set by WHO are not met. Apart from not having enough medical students, brain drain in the health professions is also a major issue. Many professionals choose to go to other countries, especially Europe and North America, for better income. Some resign early due to difficult working conditions. Unfortunately, due to data limitations, any recent changes in these numbers are not addressed in this paper. However, resources and personnel are expected to increase as local economies grow and more people receive higher education.

Open Access This chapter is licensed under the terms of the Creative Commons Attribution 4.0 International License (http://creativecommons.org/licenses/by/4.0/), which permits use, sharing, adaptation, distribution and reproduction in any medium or format, as long as you give appropriate credit to the original author(s) and the source, provide a link to the Creative Commons license and indicate if changes were made.

The images or other third party material in this chapter are included in the chapter's Creative Commons license, unless indicated otherwise in a credit line to the material. If material is not included in the chapter's Creative Commons license and your intended use is not permitted by statutory regulation or exceeds the permitted use, you will need to obtain permission directly from the copyright holder.

Chapter 5
Healthcare Affordability

To determine the affordability of healthcare, understanding the healthcare financial system is essential. Hospital bills are usually paid by insurance companies, by patients, and by governments. Therefore, this section investigates current insurance plans in each of the studied countries, admission fees for hospitals, and government health expenditures.

5.1 Insurance Coverage

Universal health coverage refers to a government system that ensures all people have access to necessary and high-quality health services (i.e., essential medicines, vaccines, preventive care) without causing financial hardship. Universal health coverage aims at removing financial barriers to accessing primary health care, particularly for the poor and vulnerable. Healthcare insurance covers all or part of the risk incurred by medical expenses by funding health services. Health insurance coverage is often proportional to government healthcare expenditure. For example, in 2017, South Africa, Kenya, and Nigeria had a coverage rate of 17%, 10%, and 3%, respectively, and their health expenditure was 4.35%, 2.05%, and 0.53%, respectively.[1] Kenya and Nigeria's community health insurance has a flatter structure of payment that is independent of income and poorly developed; thus health insurance coverage is low.

Citizens in Algeria are insured by the Caisse Nationale de la Sécurité Sociale des Travailleurs Salariés (National Fund for Employed Workers' Insurances), which covers salaried employees and their dependents, or by the Caisse Nationale de Sécurité Sociale des Non-salariés (National Social Security Fund for Workers and Self-Employed Persons), which covers independent workers and their dependents. Both funds cover healthcare provided through state-run facilities or the transfer-abroad

---

[1] https://sph.umich.edu/pursuit/2021posts/future-of-universal-health-coverage-in-africa.html.

program. Even though insurance agreements can be made in some cases between public and private treatment centers, 85% of Algerians are covered by public schemes.

Côte d'Ivoire established a compulsory national system of coverage, *couverture maladie universelle* ("universal health coverage") in October 2019. The system is regulated by the National Health Insurance Fund of Côte d'Ivoire. Its objective is to guarantee all residents access to high-quality, low-cost healthcare, including 85% of global drugs. It has two plans: a contributory scheme known as the Régime Générale de Base (Basic General Scheme) that costs 1,000 francs per person per month and a non-contributory scheme known as the Régime d'Assurance Médicale (Medical Assistance Regime) that is targeted at low-income beneficiaries. Other health insurance, such as Mutuelle de Crédit et d'Epargne pour les Fonctionnaires de Côte d'Ivoire and Caisse Nationale de Prévoyance Sociale, are complementary. By the end of June 2020, almost 300,000 beneficiaries had universal health coverage; 102,231 were treated, and 174,165 had consultations.

Ghana practices a graded premium payment method. The premium is calculated according to earnings, and an exemption is provided for extremely low-income beneficiaries. The government of Ghana introduced the National Health Insurance Scheme in 2005, with the goal of removing financial barriers to healthcare and protecting all citizens from financial burdens. It covers 95% of the medicines in the Essential Medicines List for about 30% of Ghanaians. It includes a nationally standardized package intended to cover 95% of disease conditions and includes primary, tertiary, and pharmaceutical goods and services. It also provides access benefits to accredited public and private providers. It does not cover some treatments, such as cancer treatment other than breast and cervical cancers, dialysis for chronic renal failure, organ transplant, and services provided under government vertical programs (ARV treatment for HIV/AIDS, immunizations, and family planning). However, the government is planning to include and moderately increase its investment in breast, childhood, cervical, and other cancers, as well as renal disease. Ghana still reports poor patient experiences and increased cost of care. Most Ghanaians still pay out-of-pocket for healthcare. Exemptions from co-payments or fees at the point of service are mandated by law but not enforced, so patients are charged co-payments for services that should be fully subsidized. Ghana also has private healthcare, which is necessary for those who want shorter wait times, modern equipment, and high-quality medication, though private facility standards vary. For example, those in areas with big expat communities are well equipped. Private health insurance coverage has stalled due to risk aversion related to oncology and other high-risk care, though some providers offer limited coverage of chronic illnesses as part of their marketing strategies.

In Kenya, less than 20% of the population has medical insurance, though it is targeting universal coverage by 2022. Kenya has three types of insurance: the National Health Insurance Fund, private insurance, and community-based healthcare insurance schemes. The National Health Insurance Fund is supported by the government and covers a large portion of Kenya's population. It costs approximately US$5 per month, covers the principal member and beneficiaries, and includes some inpatient and outpatient services in various hospitals. It is mandatory for all formal-sector employees (public and private) and voluntary for those in the informal sector. As part of the universal health coverage target, the government hopes to expand coverage of the National Health Insurance Fund with significant reforms aimed at enrolling more people and expanding the range of services. Kenya's private health insurance is mainly purchased by wealthier citizens, such as employed and urban residents who tend to be better educated than rural residents and have access to more information on private health insurance. Kenya has 22 private insurers mostly in urban areas, each with different packages at different prices. Patients can use both the National Health Insurance Fund and private insurance. Finally, community-based health insurance schemes are suitable alternatives to the more expensive conventional ones. These schemes are mainly initiated and managed by community members to ensure access to healthcare with minimal financial burden. The schemes generally follow the primary healthcare model by providing curative (e.g. illness and injury) treatment and preventive (e.g. education, immunization, and well-child) health services. Costs vary from community to community, but most have a one-time lifetime fee of $2 or a set contribution per month. Overall, Kenya shows some geographic disparities in health insurance coverage. Nearly 30% of people in urban areas have some form of health insurance, whereas coverage is only about 14% in rural areas (KNBS 2018). This disparity may reflect the higher levels of informal sector employment in rural areas and less awareness of insurance options.

In Nigeria, health insurance is mostly available to civil servants and private employees. New polls by private institutions suggest that about 15% of Nigerians have either private or social health insurance, which is more than the 5% previously thought. That means about 83% of Nigerians pay medical bills out-of-pocket, and the remaining 2% get support from family and friends. Further, cancer care is excluded from the National Health Insurance Scheme. Private healthcare is relatively expensive, as all equipment and supplies must be imported and are subject to customs duties. The National Health Insurance Scheme provides social (compulsory) health insurance. Private health maintenance organizations (HMOs) also provide voluntary health insurance. The Formal Sector Social Health Insurance Programme provides insurance through accredited HMOs. Public employees contribute 5.25% of their salary, and private employees contribute 15% of their basic salary to health insurance. The Vital Contributors Social Health Insurance Program is voluntary with a premium rate of approximately US$403 annually per person. For private insurance by HMOs, plans start at US$92 per person. The government recently launched a new insurance scheme, the Group Individual and Family Social Health Insurance Programme, which targets more individuals.

South Africa has large private insurance companies and different medical schemes that are highly fragmented. However, the government is currently developing a National Health Insurance system to provide access to affordable, high-quality personal health services for all South Africans, irrespective of socio-economic status. Since 2012, the system has been implemented in phases and is primarily funded by general taxes.

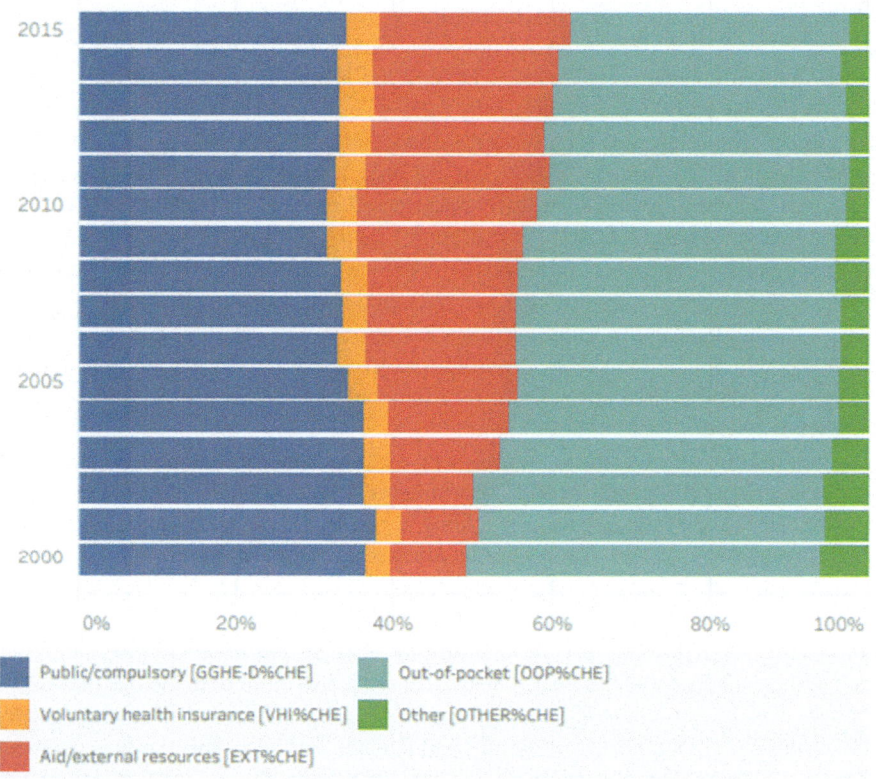

Fig. 5.1 Structure of health expenditure in sub-Saharan Africa, by financing source (*Data source* World Health Organization. *Graph source* World Health Organization)

5.2 Government Health Expenditure

Government health spending should be the primary source of funding in the health sector, but only a third of total health expenditure was sourced from the government in sub-Saharan Africa in 2015,[2] as confirmed by a WHO dashboard report.[3] As Fig. 5.1 illustrates, insurance covers a small portion of the total health expenditure. Around one-third is paid out-of-pocket by patients.

Among the eight countries studied in this report, South Africa has the highest health expenditure as a share of GDP. Nigeria used to have the lowest share but was replaced by Ghana when it decreased its government healthcare expenditure (Fig. 5.2).

---

[2] https://gh.bmj.com/content/4/1/e001159.

[3] https://www.who.int/health_financing/topics/resource-tracking/African-Regional-Health-Expenditure-Dashboard.pdf.

5.2 Government Health Expenditure

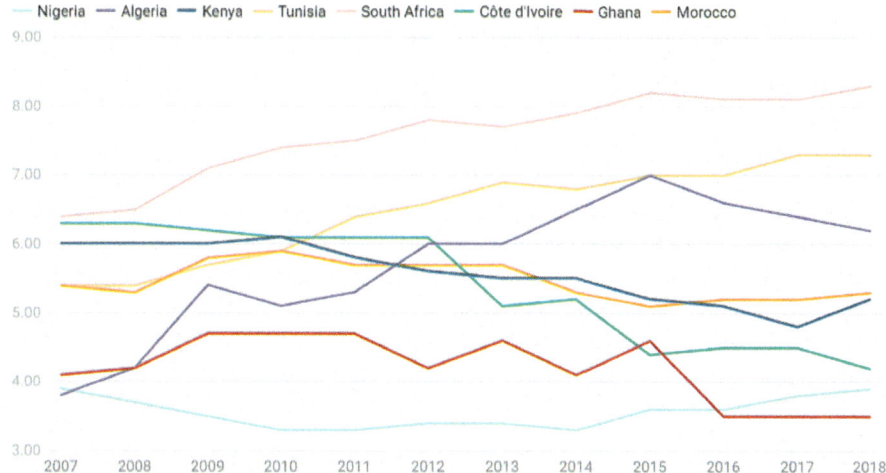

Fig. 5.2 Government health expenditure in the eight studied countries as a share of GDP (*Data source* World Bank. *Graph source* the author)

Kenya's health expenditure as a share of GDP was 5.2% in 2018, up from 4.8% in the previous year. Health expenditure per capita in Kenya increased from US$27 in 2004 to US$88 in 2018, an average annual growth of 9.21% (Fig. 5.3).

The 2012–2013 Kenya Health Accounts provide some fascinating insights. Kenya spent KES 234 billion (US$2,743 million) on health-related expenditures, which is equivalent to 7% of the country's GDP or the total value of Kenya's production in agriculture plus revenue from tourism and other sectors. In concrete terms, that is

Indicators	FY 2001/02	FY 2005/06	FY 2009/10	FY 2012/13	FY 2015/16
Total population, 2009 population census	31,190,843	35,638,694	38,610,097	41,193,418	44,200,000
Exchange rate, Kenya National Bureau of Statistics	78.60	73.40	75.82	85.30	99.48
Total GDP at current prices (Ksh)	2,483,087,895,837	3,372,242,485,458	3,502,864,214,981	3,986,072,438,769	6,709,670,650,000
Total government expenditure (Ksh)	469,454,107,719	891,152,529,242	1,173,991,183,006	1,485,559,882,940	2,271,729,850,000
Total government expenditure (USD)	5,972,698,571	12,141,042,633	15,483,924,862	17,415,707,889	22,836,045,939
Total health expenditure (THE) (Ksh)	125,436,833,424	155,556,805,311	200,622,887,192	281,216,602,402	345,746,685,197
Current health expenditure (Ksh)	Breakdown not available	Breakdown not available	193,858,239,565	261,901,511,259	325,690,079,566
Capital formation (Ksh)	Breakdown not available*	Breakdown not available*	6,764,647,627	19,315,091,143	20,056,605,631
THE (USD)	1,595,888,466	2,119,302,525	2,558,675,964	3,188,401,852	3,475,539,658
THE per capita (Ksh)	4,022	4,365	5,025	6,602	7,822
THE per capita (USD)	51.17	59.47	66.27	77.4	78.6
THE as a percent of nominal GDP	5.1%	4.6%	5.5%	6.8%	5.2%
Government health expenditure as a percent of total government expenditure	7.9%	5.1%	4.8%	6.1%	6.7%

Fig. 5.3 Health expenditure in Kenya; THE: total health expenditure (*Data source* Kenya Health Accounts. *Graph source* Kenya Health Accounts)

seven times the cost of the Thika Superhighway, "our national pride," as President Kibaki called it in 2012. Most of Kenya's health expenditure was spent on salaries, allowances, drug supplies, and other regular costs. Only 7% went to building new facilities or purchasing equipment. Kenya spent 60% of recurrent expenditures on curative care, but only 16% on vaccination, HIV/TB prevention, insecticide-treated nets, and epidemic preparedness. As a country, Kenya devotes a higher share of health expenditure (20%) on governance, such as the health system and financing administration; in other words, it spends more on salaries for people in the ministries of health who do not see any patient than it does on disease prevention or health promotion. Kenya's recurrent healthcare is funded almost equally by direct, out-of-pocket payments from households (32%) and taxes (31%), followed by donor contributions (26%), and finally health insurance (13%). See Figs. 5.4 and 5.5.

The Nigerian government allocated 4.42% (NGN 600.52 billion) of its NGN 13.58 trillion total budget to the health sector, which falls short of the 15% benchmark in the 2014 National Health Act. Health expenditure as a share of GDP has been mostly stable from 2006 to 2018, with a 4% share of health expenditure in 2006.

Based on the Health Budget Brief South Africa report, the consolidated national and provincial health allocations and estimates are indicated in Fig. 5.6.

According to the Health Budget Brief South Africa report of 2019/2020, the National Department of Health projected to spend R216 billion for the nine provincial health departments. This constituted 11.8% of government resources and 4% of the country's GDP in 2019 (Figs. 5.7 and 5.8).

Indicators	FY 2001/02	FY 2005/06	FY 2009/10	FY 2012/13	FY 2015/16
Public	29.6%	29.3%	28.8%	33.5%	37.0%
Private	54.0%	39.3%	36.7%	40.6%	39.6%
Donors	16.4%	31.0%	34.5%	24.7%	23.4%
Other	0.1%	0.4%	0.0%	1.1%	0.0%

Fig. 5.4 Health financing sources in Kenya as a percentage of total health expenditure (*Data source* Kenya Health Accounts. *Graph source* Kenya Health Accounts)

Indicators	FY 2001/02	FY 2005/06	FY 2009/10	FY 2012/13	FY 2015/16
Government schemes and compulsory contributory healthcare financing schemes	n/a	n/a	32.0%	40.6%	42.8%
Household out-of-pocket payment	n/a	n/a	25.1%	26.6%	26.1%
Donor financing schemes (non-resident)	n/a	n/a	30.4%	20.9%	17.9%
Voluntary healthcare payment schemes	n/a	n/a	12.5%	12.0%	13.2%

Fig. 5.5 Health financing schemes in Kenya as a percentage of total health expenditure (*Data source* Kenya Health Accounts. *Graph source* Kenya Health Accounts)

5.2 Government Health Expenditure

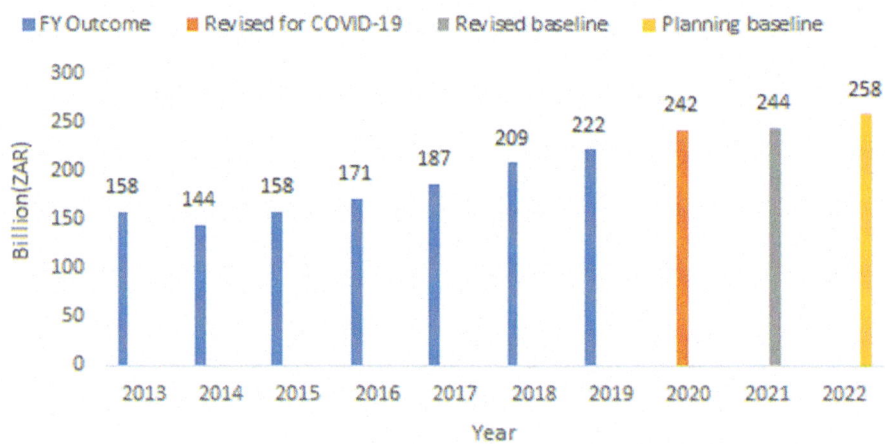

Fig. 5.6 Consolidated national and provincial health allocation in South Africa (*Data source* UNICEF. *Graph source* Funani Mpande)

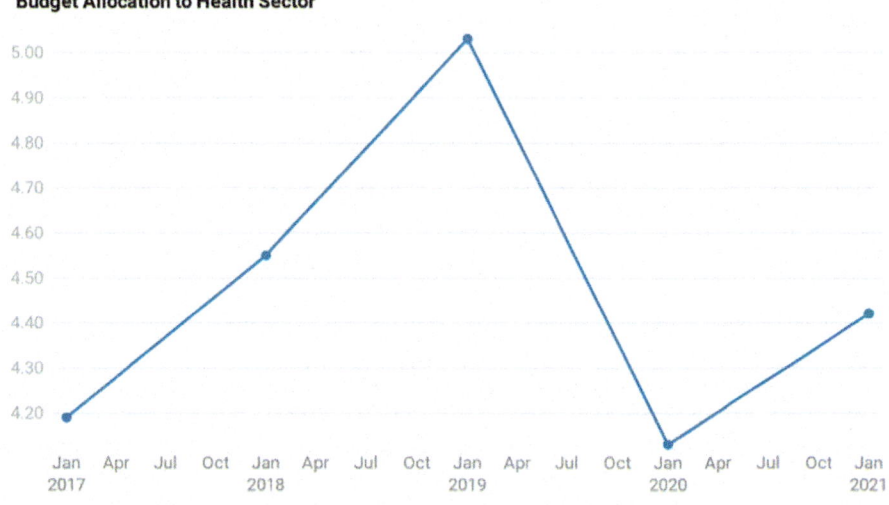

Fig. 5.7 Budget allocation to the health sector (*Data source* National Department of Health, South Africa. *Graph source* Funani Mpande)

Health Spending	National (R billion)	Provincial (R billion)	Percentage of total	Provincial population (million)
Nationa Department of Health	51.5			
Of which transfers to provincial health departments	-45			
Net NDoH spending	6.5		3	
Combined provincial health budgets		209.5	97	
Gauteng		50.8	24	13.5
KwaZulu-Natal		45	21	10.8
Eastern Cape		25.2	12	6.7
Western Cape		24.8	11	6.4
Limpopo		20.8	10	5.7
Mpumalanga		14.4	7	4.3
North West		12.3	6	3.8
Free State		11.1	5	2.8
Northern Cape		5.2	2	1.2

Fig. 5.8 Health spending in South Africa (*Data source* National Department of Health, South Africa. *Table source* Funani Mpande)

5.3 Individual Healthcare Affordability

This section assesses the individual affordability of hospital costs based on average and minimum income and poverty level.

5.3.1 Hospital Costs

The hospital costs in this report mainly involve the cost per bed per day and the cost per outpatient visit by hospital level based on average and minimum income. This approach helps assess the financial burden on patients paying out-of-pocket. Table 5.1 presents estimated costs in Kenya for public hospitals with an occupancy rate of 80%. Costs include personnel and food costs but not drug and diagnostic test fees. The results are presented in USD in 2000 and 2015.

In Nigeria, consultation with a general practitioner or private specialist costs between 10,000 and 40,000 Naira (£22–£87 or US$27.5–$110) in 2018, depending on the doctor and institution. This cost excludes treatment and medical examination fees. A one-night hospital stay in a single room costs between 30,000 and 100,000 Naira (£65–£218 or US$82–$275) but includes treatment and medical examinations.[4] According to a study done at a public Nigerian hospital in 2012, the cost of stay per patient ranged from 12,745 to 238,123 Naira (US$82.23–$1536.28), depending on the medical severity. The average cost per day was 19,506 Naira (US$125.85). In comparison, a study conducted by the Hospital Association of South Africa in 2013 to compare the cost of hospital services indicated that patients at public facilities do not pay a value-added tax. The average difference per day was 122.97 Euros (Fig. 5.9).

---

[4] https://pubmed.ncbi.nlm.nih.gov/23301452/.

5.3 Individual Healthcare Affordability

Table 5.1 Hospital costs in Kenya, 2000–2015

Hospital costs		
Cost per bed per day by hospital level (USD)[a]		
	2000	2015
Primary	14.62	19.64
Secondary	19.08	25.62
Tertiary	26.06	34.99
Cost per outpatient visit by hospital level[a]		
	2000	2015
Primary	3.93	5.55
Secondary	5.58	7.88
Tertiary	8.25	11.65
Health Center Costs		
Cost per 20-min health center visit by population coverage (USD)[b]		
	2000	2015
50%	6.42	7.29
80%	6.42	8.59
95%	6.97	13.04

[a] Public facility, 80% occupancy rate, excludes drugs and diagnostics;

[b] public facility, by different population coverage, excludes drugs and diagnostics

(*Data source* Ministry of Health, Kenya. *Map source* Beatrice Birir)

Type of care	Base scenario (2010/2011)	Cost in rands	US$	Euro
Public	Average cost per patient-day equivalent for district hospital	1543	108.21	90.7
	Average cost per patient day equivalent for all hospitals	2237	156.87	131.49
	Average cost per admission	**8775**	**615.37**	**515.79**
Private	Average cost per day	4329	303.58	254.46
	Average cost per day (excluding VAT)	3797	266.27	223.19
	Averge cost per admission	**9284**	**651.06**	**545.71**

Fig. 5.9 Hospital Association of South Africa 2013 costs (*Data source* National Department of Health, South Africa. *Table source* Funani Mpande)

The cost of hospitals is generally understudied, as prices vary between private institutions and public institutions, hospital to hospital, and region to region. However, according to data collected from Nigeria and South Africa, the average cost per patient is approximately US$100–$200 per day. The average GDP per capita in 2018 in the eight studied countries was US$2,717. Even without accounting for inflation, these data indicate most patients would incur financial hardship from healthcare expenses.

5.3.2 Income

This section looks at average and minimum incomes in the eight studied countries. Overall, average and minimum incomes have increased in the past 50 years along with rapid economic growth. However, a huge gap remains between income and expenditure, especially for healthcare products.

Minimum wages in Kenya remained unchanged at 13,572 KES/month in 2019 and 2020 (Figs. 5.10 and 5.11).

In Nigeria, salaries range from a minimum of 85,700 NGN (US$209) per month to 1,510,000 NGN (US$3,680) per month maximum average salary (the actual maximum is higher). The minimum wage has undergone a two-fold increase since 2004. As of 2021, the current monthly minimum wage is NGN30,000 (US$73 at the official rate in 2021, US$62 at the parallel rate in 2021). Some states in Nigeria have yet to implement this wage and still pay NGN18,000 (US$44 at the official

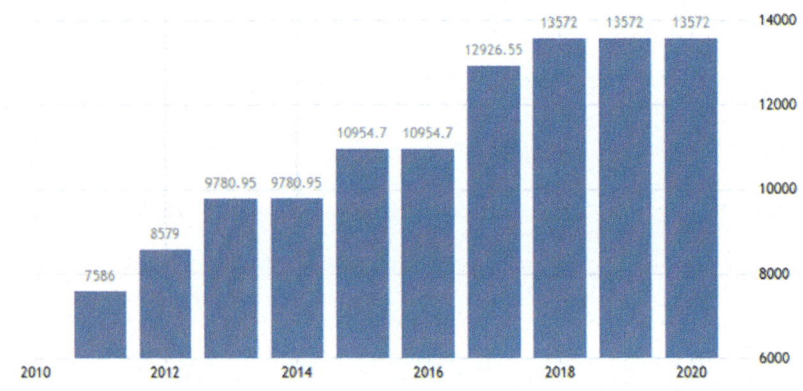

Actual	Previous	Highest	Lowest	Dates	Unit	Frequency
13572.00	13572.00	13572.00	1700.00	1994 - 2020	KES/Month	Yearly

Fig. 5.10 Wages in Kenya, 1994–2020 (*Data source* National Bureau of Statistics, Kenya. *Graph by* Beatrice Birir)

Wages

	2019	2011	2004
NGN	30,000	18,000	5,500
USD	98	115	42
Euro	87	89	30

Fig. 5.11 Wages in Kenya, 2004–2019 (*Data source* National Bureau of Statistics, Kenya. *Graph by* Beatrice Birir)

5.3 Individual Healthcare Affordability

rate in 2021, and US$37 at the parallel rate in 2021). As of May 2020, 40% of Nigerians lived below the poverty line (the only data ever published on this issue). However, poverty levels may be overestimated due to a lack of information on the large, informal sector of the economy.

Due to the inequality in South Africa, the average monthly household income varies by race. Black South African household income is eight times less than that of White South African households. During 2006–2008, Black South African household income increased slightly (exchange rate for June 28, 2021, R1 = US$0.070 or 0.059 Euro) but decreased in White households (Finn, Leibbrandt, and Woolard 2009). Annual income increased from 2006 to 2015 to US$265.45 or 222.17 Euro (Statistics South Africa 2019). The Minister of Employment and Labour announced a national minimum wage increase from R20.69 to R21.69, effective March 2021. Currently, the hourly wage is US$1.52 or 1.28 Euros (Figs. 5.12 and 5.13).

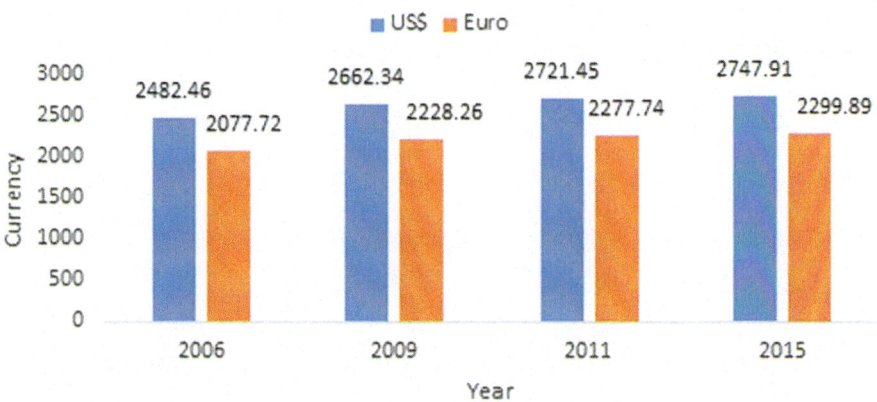

Fig. 5.12 Average annual labor market income in South Africa, 2006–2015 (*Data source* Minister of Employment and Labour, South Africa. *Graph source* Funani Mpande)

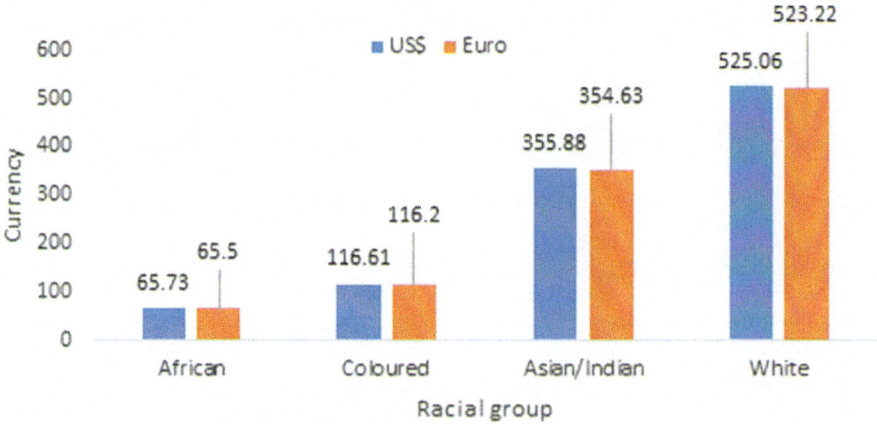

Fig. 5.13 Average household per capita monthly income per racial group in South Africa, 2008 (*Data source* Minister of Employment and Labour, South Africa. *Graph source* Funani Mpande)

5.3.3 Poverty

Chronic poverty refers to those who are likely to remain poor. Transitory refers to those who are more likely to move to the middle class. Vulnerable refers to those who are currently in the middle class but are likely to become poor (Fig. 5.14). Extreme poverty is defined as living on less than US$1.90 per day.

In 2018, 40% of the population in Africa lived in extreme poverty, accounting for two-thirds of the globe. The percentage has decreased by 1.6% since 2015, which is not fast enough to keep up with population growth. If the specified number of extreme poverty populations is inspected, the number of people in poverty in Africa actually increased (Figs. 5.15, 5.16 and 5.17).[5]

Extreme poverty will become the most predominant problem in Africa in the coming decades, as half of the countries had an extreme poverty rate higher than 35% in 2017. Nigeria has the largest poor population in sub-Saharan Africa, where 79 million people are extremely poor, followed by Kenya (17 million), South Africa (11 million), Côte d'Ivoire (6 million), and Ghana (4 million).[6]

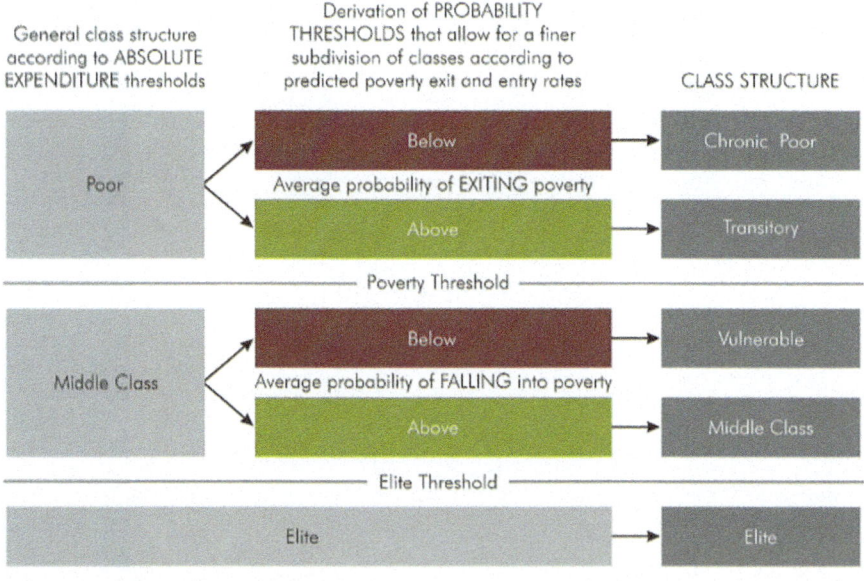

Source: Schotte et al. (2018)

Fig. 5.14 Schema of social stratification: a poverty dynamics approach to structured inequality (*Source* Schotte et al. (2018))

---

[5] https://blogs.worldbank.org/opendata/number-poor-people-continues-rise-sub-saharan-africa-despite-slow-decline-poverty-rate.

[6] https://blogs.worldbank.org/opendata/african-countries-show-mixed-progress-towards-poverty-reduction-and-half-them-have-extreme.

5.3 Individual Healthcare Affordability

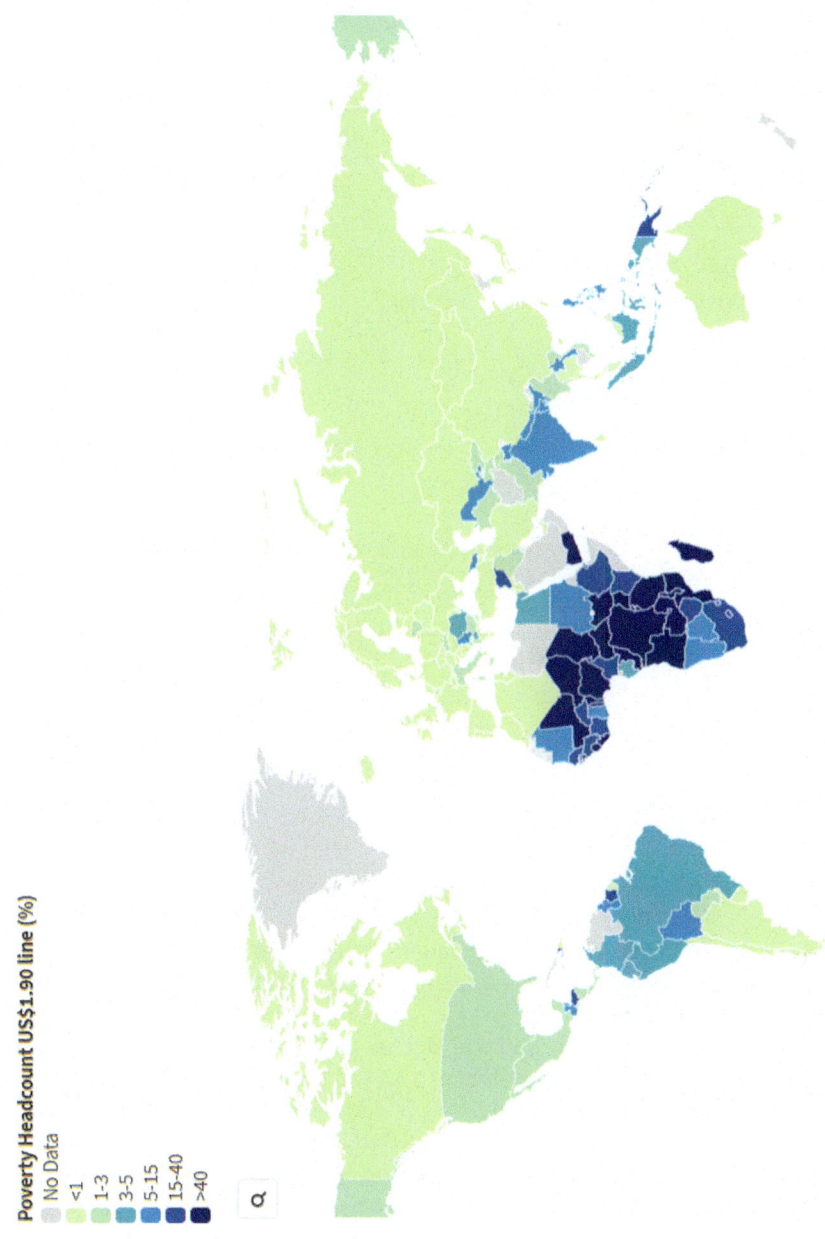

Fig. 5.15 Those living in poverty around the world (*Source* World Bank)

Fig. 5.16 The poverty rate in Africa (*Source* World Bank)

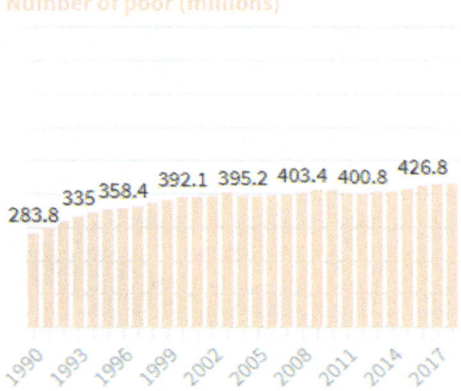

Fig. 5.17 The number of poor in Africa (*Source* World Bank)

Kenya's poverty level has decreased since 2005. The ratio at the national poverty line was 36.1% in 2015, down by 22.86% from 2005. The national poverty headcount ratio refers to the percentage of the population living below the national poverty line. National estimates are based on population-weighted subgroup estimates from household surveys (Fig. 5.18).

Based on a 2019 report by the National Bureau of Statistics in Nigeria, 40% of its population lived below the poverty line of 137,430 Naira per year (US$381.75), and 25% were vulnerable to falling below the poverty line. Figure 5.19 shows how the poverty level decreased by 26.56% from 2010 to 2018 (although there is no data for 2015–2018). With the recent COVID-19 outbreak and fall in global oil prices, which Nigeria heavily relies on for its revenue, there is a strong chance that these numbers might increase.

5.4 Summary

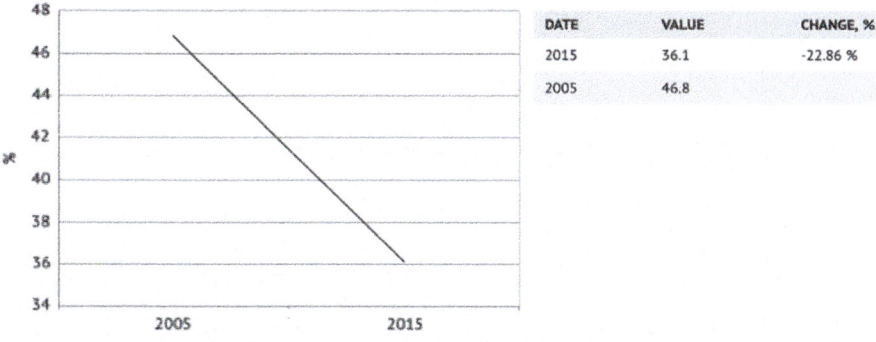

Fig. 5.18 Poverty in Kenya (*Source* Poverty and Equity Database)

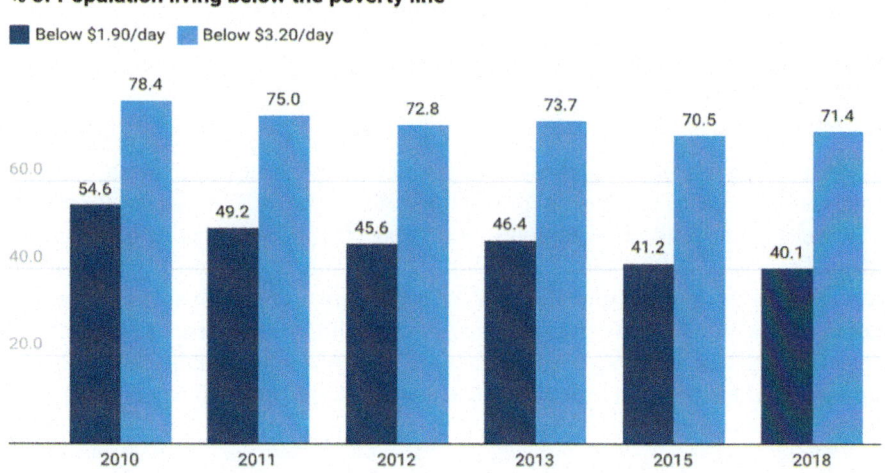

Fig. 5.19 Poverty in Nigeria (*Data source* World Bank. *Graph source* Abdelkader Bouregag)

The population that is chronically poor in South Africa has declined by 10% from 2008 to 2017. The number in transitory poverty has been fairly consistent, whereas those vulnerable to poverty have increased by 5.8% (Statistics South Africa 2019; Fig. 5.20).

5.4 Summary

The cost of healthcare is an enormous financial burden for the government, families, and individuals. Data from Nigeria, South Africa, and Kenya show that out-of-pocket healthcare fees are not affordable for most. For example, the average cost per day in a

Fig. 5.20 Socio-economic classes in South Africa, 2008–2017 (*Data source* Statistics South Africa. *Graph source* Funani Mpande)

Nigerian hospital is almost equivalent to a month's worth of income if the patient earns minimum wage. The average monthly income of South Africa, which has the highest GDP per capita in all eight samples, is around US$500, but the average cost per hospital visit is US$100–200. Most countries have some form of health insurance, and governments are trying to provide universal healthcare to reduce financial burdens for patients. However, budget constraints mean that health insurance is not as effective as expected. Thus far, only Algeria has managed to provide free healthcare to everyone through insurance. In other samples, such as Ghana, patients still pay out-of-pocket before their insurance covers the claims.

Open Access This chapter is licensed under the terms of the Creative Commons Attribution 4.0 International License (http://creativecommons.org/licenses/by/4.0/), which permits use, sharing, adaptation, distribution and reproduction in any medium or format, as long as you give appropriate credit to the original author(s) and the source, provide a link to the Creative Commons license and indicate if changes were made.

The images or other third party material in this chapter are included in the chapter's Creative Commons license, unless indicated otherwise in a credit line to the material. If material is not included in the chapter's Creative Commons license and your intended use is not permitted by statutory regulation or exceeds the permitted use, you will need to obtain permission directly from the copyright holder.

Chapter 6
Social Media and Technology Use

Geographic disparity in the allocation of healthcare resources can be identified in many African countries. Rural communities across the continent typically have restricted access to fewer resources. Not only are these regions faced with a limited supply of medical facilities, services, and healthcare professionals, but they are also more likely to be at a social, educational, and financial disadvantage. In addition, resources are unevenly distributed between urban and rural areas. Members of rural communities often have to travel long distances to urban areas to seek medical treatment or assistance. In addition, poverty and education levels may also affect patients' ability to access, communicate, and understand medical information. Given all the barriers and inequalities in real life, the internet and social media serve as critical alternative avenues for people to access basic healthcare services regardless of their physical location. A survey conducted by the Pew Research Center in 2017 indicated that 41% of respondents in sub-Saharan Africa used the Internet to access health and medical information. The percentage of online engagement is significant and demonstrates the enormous potential of online platforms in providing equitable access to information and ease of communication. Hence, understanding Internet use can tremendously benefit the development of telemedicine and health monitoring applications in Africa.

This chapter explores the most recent data on internet coverage, mobile phone use coverage, and social media coverage. It also reviews the specific social media platforms people use for work, school, social connections, and healthcare services. The impact of COVID-19 on the use of the internet is also examined briefly. A discussion of the possible opportunities of using digital platforms and media in the healthcare field is also concluded in the end.

6.1 Internet and Social Media Coverage

Internet and social media use has grown vigorously in Africa. Between 2008 and 2012, internet bandwidth availability has grown 20-fold. By the end of 2015, 46% of the overall population in Africa had access to mobile services. However, only 22% of the population has access to the internet (World Bank, 2017). North Africa has the highest internet penetration at 56%, followed by South Africa at 45%, Western Africa at 16%, Eastern Africa at 10%, and Central Africa at 8% (Statistia, 2022). However, Nigeria has the highest number of internet users (109.2 million), followed by Egypt and South Africa (Statistia, 2022). This section reviews the internet and mobile coverage and its trend in Algeria, Côte d'Ivoire, Ghana, Kenya, and Nigeria. It also explores the social media tools used by people for school, work, social connection, and healthcare.

Algeria reported 25 million social media users as of January 2021, an increase of 3 million (14%) between 2020 and 2021, which now covers 56.5% of the total population (Fig. 6.1).

In Côte d'Ivoire, between January 2020 to January 2021, mobile connections increased by 8.5% (2.9 million), internet users by 2.5% (0.31 million), and active social media users by 20.4% (1.0 million). Total internet users reached 12.50 million, or 46.8% of the total population, and are expected to increase by 2.5% (0.31 million) annually. The vast majority (5.82 million or 98.6%) of internet users access the internet via mobile devices. The top three websites are Google.com, Youtube.com, and Jumia.ci, and the top four social media platforms are Facebook, Instagram, Twitter, and LinkedIn (Fig. 6.2 and Table 6.1).

The total number of internet users in Ghana is 15.70 million, or 50% of the total population. Internet users increased by 6.4% (943,000) between 2020 and 2021. Among all the internet users, 92.3% of whom access the internet through

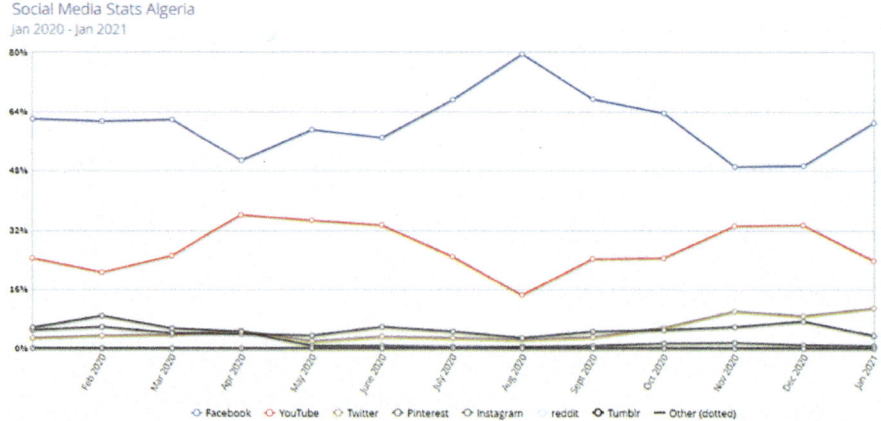

Fig. 6.1 Social media use in Algeria. (*Source* Statcounter)

6.1 Internet and Social Media Coverage

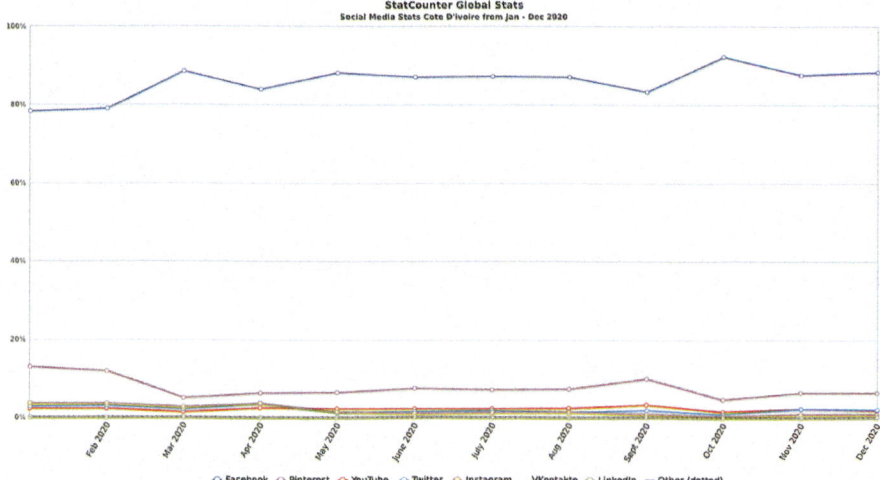

Fig. 6.2 Social media use in Côte d'Ivoire. (*Source* Statcounter)

Table 6.1 The number of people who can be reached with online advertising. (*Data source* Datareportal. *Table source* Fofana Daouda)

Platform	Number of people who can be reached with adverts 2021	2020	2019	2018
Facebook	5.4 million (64.2% male)	4.50 million (66.7% male)	4.70 million (67% male)	4.3 million (67% male)
Instagram	950 thousand (66% male)	620 thousand (66.1% male)	720 thousand (68% male)	640 thousand (68% male)
Twitter	148.4 thousand (87% male)	147.5 thousand (76.5% male)	92.5 thousand (77% male)	–
LinkedIn	850 thousand (63.6% male)	740 thousand (63.3% male)	610 thousand (63% male)	–

mobile devices. The mobile device user population in 2021, was approximately 14.47 million. On average, users aged 16–64 spend 4 h and 20 min on the internet per day. The top three visited websites are Google.com, Betway.com.gh, and Youtube.com. The total number of active social media users in Ghana is 8.20 million (26.1% of the total population), which is a 36.7% increase. Eight million (98.2%) of them access social media via mobile devices (Figs. 6.3, 6.4, 6.5, 6.6, and 6.7).

Ghana Health Service mostly uses print media for health information dissemination (e.g. leaflets, posters, and billboards). Many people also receive information through interpersonal channels (e.g. doctors, community health workers, family, and friends). MoTech is a mobile technology for community health and telehealth that is being piloted in rural communities. In this way, social media offers effective tools for health-related messaging while the functionality of traditional media dwindles.

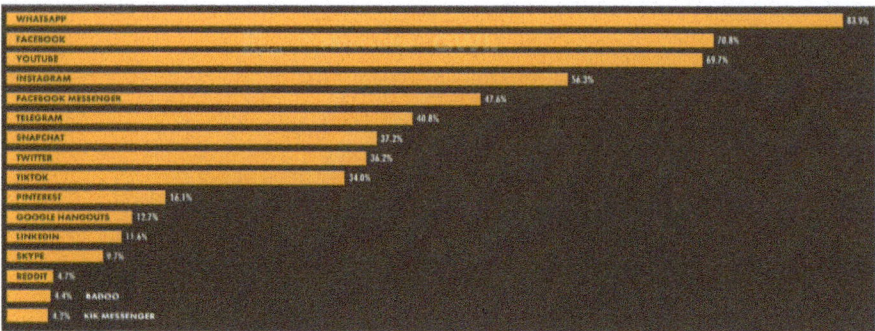

Fig. 6.3 Popular social media platforms in Ghana. (*Data source* Datareportal)

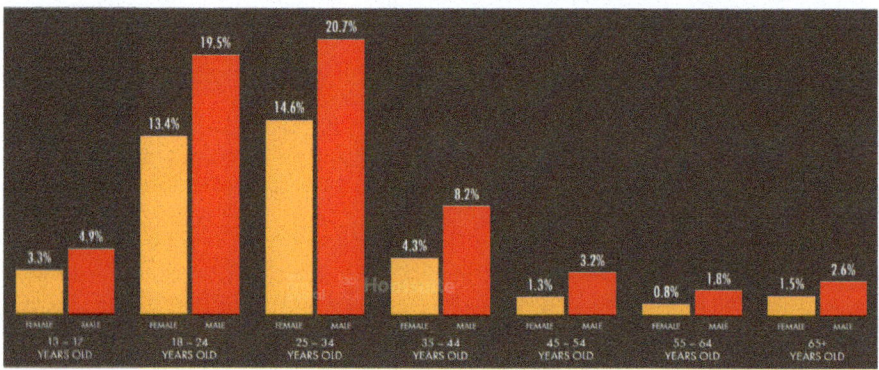

Fig. 6.4 Social media users in Ghana. (*Data source* Datareportal)

In Kenya, 28.2% of its population lives in urban centers, and 71.8% live in rural areas. In January 2021, 21.75 million people were recorded as internet users, with 40% internet coverage. The number of social media users increased by 25% (2.2 million) from 2020, totaling 11 million, or 20.2% of the total population. Most Kenyans access social media using mobile apps, but they increasingly use mobile browsers, which are presumed to offer more privacy than standalone mobile apps. There were 59.24 million mobile connections in Kenya in January 2021, an increase of 11% (5.9 million) from January 2020. The number of mobile connections in Kenya in January 2021 was equivalent to 108.9% of the total population, indicating that some people had more than one mobile connection.

Few Kenyans use Microsoft Teams or Zoom outside the corporate setting. However, with the COVID-19 pandemic, the use of video conferencing and web conferencing platforms has become more common (Fig. 6.7).

Nigeria has a population of 208 million people, 52% of whom live in urban areas. According to DataReportal, in 2021, 90% of Nigerians have mobile phones, 99.2% of people aged 16–64 use smartphones, and 14.6% use non-smartphones. Around

6.1 Internet and Social Media Coverage

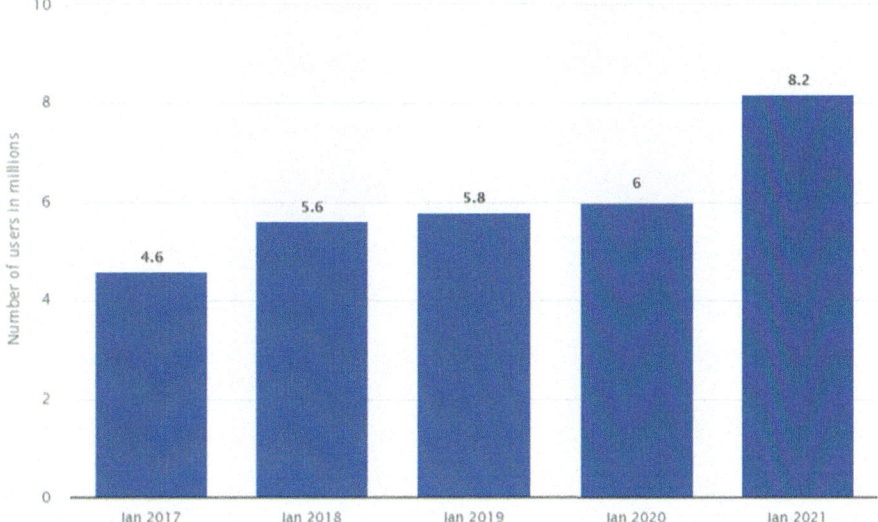

Fig. 6.5 Social Media Usage over the Years in Ghana. (*Data source* Datareportal. *Graph source* Gilbert Gadzekpo)

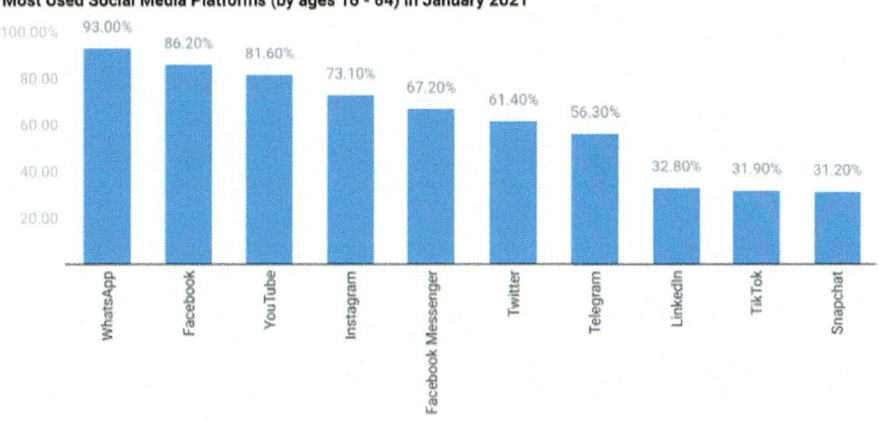

Fig. 6.6 Most used social media platforms in Kenya. (*Data source* Datareportal. *Graph source* Beatrice Birir)

50% of the total population are internet users, and 15.8% are active social media users. The top three most used social media platforms are WhatsApp, Facebook, and YouTube. Social media use increased substantially between 2018 and 2019 and continues to grow. However, social media platforms focusing on professional development, networking, and communication, such as LinkedIn, WhatsApp, and Facebook, experienced declines in use between 2020 to 2021, whereas those focused

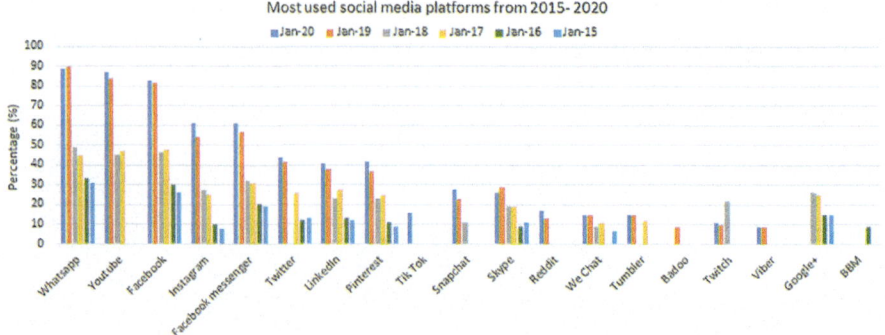

Fig. 6.7 Most popular social media platforms in Nigeria. (*Data source* Datareportal. *Graph source* Ademola Olokun)

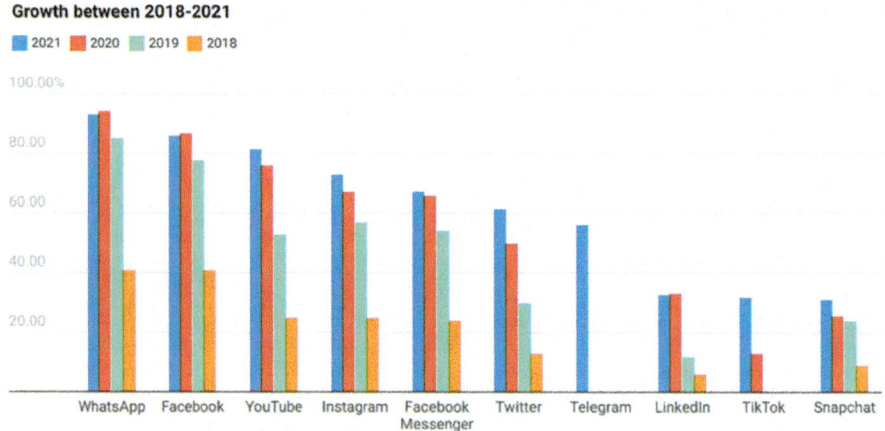

Fig. 6.8 The growth of social media use in Nigeria. (*Data source* Datareportal. *Graph source* Ademola Olokun)

on entertainment and videos, such as YouTube and Instagram, continue to increase (Fig. 6.8). This change may be due to the impact of COVID-19.

Nigeria mainly uses uLesson, Pass.ng, Gradely.ng, Zoom, Google Meet, LinkedIn Learning, and YouTube for educational purposes. The uLesson app offers junior and senior secondary school students a holistic learning experience in mathematics, English, science, technology, business, physics, chemistry, and biology while also preparing senior school students for the West African Senior School Certificate Examination, the Joint Admissions and Matriculation Board exam, and the General Certificate of Education exam. Pass.ng is a web, desktop, and mobile examination preparatory and testing platform that helps users excel in all major Nigerian Examinations and tests. Gradely offers personalized learning resources for parents to help

6.1 Internet and Social Media Coverage

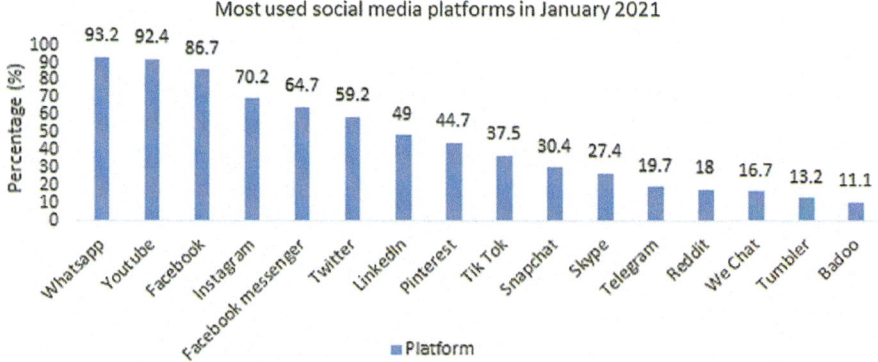

Fig. 6.9 Most popular social media platforms in South Africa. (*Data source*: HelloYes. *Graph source*: Funani Mpande)

their children progress and succeed in school and in life. Zoom, Google Workspace, Microsoft 365, LinkedIn, Slack, and YouTube are also used for work.

Nigeria also has some unique platforms for patient-doctor and healthcare-related communication. OTRAC is an e-learning platform that provides tailored training and courses for public and general health practitioners. 247Medic is an online (subscription-based) medical care consultation and advisory service providing patients the ability to call or chat with a doctor, request onsite laboratory services, and have medications delivered. Mamalette provides first-time African parents with information on fertility, pregnancy, birth, and babies with online courses, expert advice, active online forums, live events, and other useful tools. Babymigo is a parenting community, and OMOMI provides mothers and pregnant women with lifesaving maternal and child health information while connecting them to doctors in real time. MyPaddi gives young people access to much-needed sexual and reproductive health information and products while ensuring complete anonymity.

In South Africa, the most used platform is Whatsapp, which is used to make voice calls, video calls, share media, and send messages. The five most popular social media networks in South Africa are Whatsapp, YouTube, Facebook, Facebook Messenger, and Instagram (HelloYes Marketing 2020; Fig. 6.9).

Facebook, Twitter, Skype, Microsoft Teams, and Google Meet are used for educational purposes, and Skype, Google Meet, Microsoft Teams, LinkedIn, YouTube, Twitter, Instagram, Pinterest, Quora, Facebook, and WhatsApp are used for work purposes. People tend to use Twitter, LinkedIn, Instagram, and Facebook for medical and health-related communication.

6.2 Impact of COVID-19

The COVID-19 pandemic has boosted the use of the internet globally. During lockdowns, some governments developed their own applications and software to share COVID information, and others use existing platforms, such as Twitter. Survey data show that Kenyans, Nigerians, and South Africans got much of their news and information about COVID-19 from social media, with 47% of respondents saying that social media was a primary source of information about the coronavirus. South Africa developed a free exposure notification app called COVID Alert South Africa to let people know when they have been in close contact with someone who tested positive. Tik Tok, Twitter, and Telegram trended during the pandemic. Twitter is mostly used by the government to share information about COVID cases. Some social media platforms (e.g. TikTok, IMO, Likee, Vskit, Telegram, and Vimeo) gained significant popularity during 2020, leading to a surge in penetration and acceptance of other lesser-known social media sites and apps. Youths especially used TikTok to interact with others and complete online challenges. Telegram users increased as people grew concerned about the WhatsApp privacy policy (Fig. 6.10).

This boost in social media usage has had some troubling outcomes, such as a rise in "fake" news containing incorrect, biased, and deliberately misleading information. As this misinformation is shared online, many people can be exposed to it. For example, misinformation around COVID-19 included inaccuracies about how the disease spreads, vaccination safety, and ineffective and dangerous "cures." Vaccine misinformation in particular has led to fears and anti-vaccination movements promoting misperceptions and unsafe behaviors. Online harassment is also common and causes emotional distress.

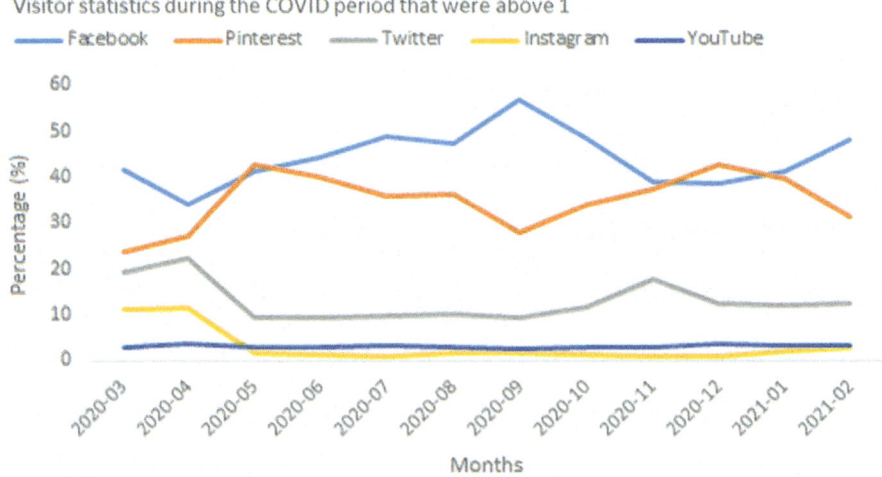

Fig. 6.10 Social media use during the coronavirus pandemic in South Africa. (*Data source* HelloYes. *Graph source* Funani Mpande)

6.3 Summary

The number of mobile users reached 46% by the end of 2015 in Africa. However, only 22% of the population has the access to the internet in 2018. The high coverage of mobile phones and the gap between mobile coverage and internet coverage imply that text messages may be a more suitable communication medium now. However, there is a growth in internet coverage, indicating that in the future there will be more opportunities to share information through online platforms. The COVID-19 pandemic boosted the use of online platforms and the internet in Africa. Internet users are more familiar and comfortable using online tools such as zoom and google meetings for work and school, Facebook, WhatsApp, and Twitter for social networking, and Youtube, and TikTok for videos and entertainment. A number of online healthcare platforms have also been built for providing patient-doctor communication, health-related courses, and between-patient help groups.

The use of social media remains an under-studied topic with huge potential to affect healthcare. Africa has substantial geographic disparity and inequality in the distribution of medical resources. Social media can improve accessibility to healthcare by minimizing the need to travel a long distance for costly hospital visits. Currently, the use of the internet and social media in healthcare in Africa is limited due to low coverage of the internet, and the lack of information collection systems. Information collection systems such as electronic health records are still at their initial stage. Up to this time most hospitals use hand-written paperwork to keep their patient's records, which is causing difficulties in storing patients' information as well as transferring them to other healthcare providers. The high mobile coverage helps health providers to connect the patients regardless of the geographic distance. However, the low-literacy rate in some countries limits the method of communication further and demands that health providers connect with their patients via phone calls.

As internet and mobile coverage becomes increasingly available in Africa, it introduces more flexible forms of healthcare, such as virtual meetings and online information portals. The use of pictures and videos can make healthcare information more vivid and simple to understand. It can also increase the accessibility of low-literacy populations, which is essential in countries like Cote d'Ivoire, where the literacy rate is below 50%. Along with the growth of internet usage, the spread of fake news and misleading information, such as vaccine misinformation, will also become a concern for users.

Open Access This chapter is licensed under the terms of the Creative Commons Attribution 4.0 International License (http://creativecommons.org/licenses/by/4.0/), which permits use, sharing, adaptation, distribution and reproduction in any medium or format, as long as you give appropriate credit to the original author(s) and the source, provide a link to the Creative Commons license and indicate if changes were made.

The images or other third party material in this chapter are included in the chapter's Creative Commons license, unless indicated otherwise in a credit line to the material. If material is not included in the chapter's Creative Commons license and your intended use is not permitted by statutory regulation or exceeds the permitted use, you will need to obtain permission directly from the copyright holder.

Chapter 7
Conclusion

In general, the healthcare systems in all eight studied countries are working toward a more positive future. This report confirms some challenges they face and discusses the future directions of these governments. Overall, the incidence, prevalence, and death rates of infectious diseases like TB, HIV, and malaria are decreasing, but NCDs are increasing in incidence due to increased tobacco and alcohol consumption, rising obesity levels, decreases in physical activity, urbanization, education access, and poverty. As education and literacy rates increase, so does poverty, though slower than expected. All eight countries have decent hospital distribution and are working toward the goal of 2.2 hospitals per 10,000 inhabitants. Healthcare providers remain scarce, possibly because governments have prioritized funding tertiary facilities and services, rather than primary care coverage and healthcare providers' benefits.

Many research studies show that healthcare systems in Africa are underfunded and under-resourced, and our data confirm this finding. However, although we tried to use the most recent data for all eight samples, most are from 2016 or earlier, and not all countries had data for all the sections covered here. Data came from websites covering demographics, prevalence, incidence, and death rates of diseases, as well as education, economy, and finance-related information (e.g. World Bank, Knoema, and Statistics). Although not always current, these sites accurately depict trends for each indicator. In addition to surveys and censuses, data projections also provide insight. The exact values of some indicators may differ, but general trends should be reliable.

Country-specific data, such as hospital distribution and insurance information, is scattered and difficult to find. Most countries' health departments publish annual reports, but that is not always the case for governments in Africa. Some governments do not have an official website. Some departments did not start publishing reports until 2017, for example, and some of those have missing or incomplete years. It is therefore difficult to obtain the most recent data or depict trends. Moreover, academic articles and news articles often do not publish data annually.

Data that are qualitative, less useful for budgeting, and less essential to the government are the most challenging to find. These data include patterns and trends related to nutrition, physical activity, social media use, and insurance coverage. Even if they are not directly related to disease, this information often provides important information about key health risk factors. Understanding changes in these indicators can generate predictions of future health trends, especially if that knowledge can be used to benefit patients in the long term.

Complete List of Data Sources

Accueil

Cancer Association of South Africa

Central Intelligence Agency World Factbook

Cleiss

Department of Health, Republic of South Africa

Food and Agriculture Organization of the United Nations

Global Health Data Exchange

Global Nutrition Report

Health Data

Jeune Afrique

Journal du Net

Knoema

La Presse Médicale

National Treasury, Republic of South Africa

NCD Risk Factor Collaboration

Pan African Medical Journal

Portail Officiel du Gouvernement de Côte d'Ivoire

Revue Médicale Suisse

Statistia

Statistics South Africa

UN Sustainable Development

UNICEF

United Nations International Children's Emergency Fund

US Agency for International Development

World Bank

World Health Organization

World Population Review

Complete List of Works Cited

1. Bigna JJ, Noubiap JJ (2019) The rising burden of non-communicable diseases in sub-Saharan Africa. Lancet Glob Health 7(10):E1295–E1296. https://doi.org/10.1016/S2214-109X(19)30370-5
2. Dwyer-Lindgren L, Cork MA, Sligar A et al (2019) Mapping HIV prevalence in sub-Saharan Africa between 2000 and 2017. Nature 570:189–193. https://doi.org/10.1038/s41586-019-1200-9
3. Goliber T (2002) The status of the HIV/AIDS epidemic in Sub-Saharan Africa https://www.prb.org/resources/the-status-of-the-hiv-aids-epidemic-in-sub-saharan-africa/. Accessed 3 Nov 2021
4. Rao C, Lopez AD, Hemed Y (2006) Causes of Death. In: Jamison DT, Feachem RG, Makgoba MW, et al (2006) Disease and mortality in Sub-Saharan Africa, 2nd edn. The International Bank for Reconstruction and Development/The World Bank, Washington (DC). Chapter 5
5. World Bank (2013) The global burden of disease: main findings for sub-Saharan Africa. https://www.worldbank.org/en/region/afr/publication/global-burden-of-disease-findings-for-sub-saharan-africa. Accessed 3 Nov 2021
6. Grosse R, Auffrey C (1989) Literacy and health status in developing countries. Annu Rev Public Health 10:281–297. https://doi.org/10.1146/annurev.pu.10.050189.001433
7. Kanj M, Mitic W (2009) Health literacy final. https://www.who.int/healthpromotion/conferences/7gchp/Track1_Inner.pdf. Accessed 3 Nov 2021
8. Healthy People (2020) Health literacy. https://www.healthypeople.gov/2020/topics-objectives/topic/social-determinants-health/interventions-resources/health-literacy. Accessed 3 Nov 2021
9. World Health Organization, (2015) Global reference list of 100 core health indicators. https://apps.who.int/iris/bitstream/handle/10665/173589/WHO_HIS_HSI_2015.3_eng.pdf?sequence=1 Accessed 3 Nov 2021
10. Kuznets S (1960) Population change and aggregate output. In: Universities-National Bureau. (1960) Demographic and economic change in developed countries. Columbia University Press. pp 324–351 https://www.nber.org/system/files/chapters/c2392/c2392.pdf. Accessed 3 Nov 2021
11. Deffner D, McElreath R (2020) The importance of life history and population regulation for the evolution of social learning. Philos Trans R Soc B: Biol Sci 375(1803) https://doi.org/10.1098/rstb.2019.0492
12. Götmark F, Andersson M (2020) Human fertility in relation to education, economy, religion, contraception, and family planning programs. BMC Public Health 20:265. https://doi.org/10.1186/s12889-020-8331-7
13. Walls HL, Vearey J, Modisenyane M, Chetty-Makkan CM, Charalambous S, Smith RD, Hanefeld J (2016) Understanding healthcare and population mobility in southern Africa: The case of South Africa. S Afr Med J 106(1):14–15. https://doi.org/10.7196/SAMJ.2016.v106i1.10210. PMID: 26792300
14. Dubale, BW, Friedman, LE, Chemali Z, et al (2019) Systematic review of burnout among healthcare providers in sub-Saharan Africa. BMC Public Health 19:1247https://doi.org/10.1186/s12889-019-7566-7
15. Delobelle P, Rawlinson JL, Ntuli S, Malatsi I, Decock R, Depoorter AM (2011) Job satisfaction and turnover intent of primary healthcare nurses in rural South Africa: a questionnaire survey. J Adv Nurs 67(2):371–383. https://doi.org/10.1111/j.1365-2648.2010.05496.x

16. Young F, Critchley JA, Johnstone LK, Unwin NC (2009) A review of co-morbidity between infectious and chronic disease in Sub Saharan Africa: TB and diabetes mellitus, HIV and metabolic syndrome, and the impact of globalization. Glob Health 5:9. https://doi.org/10.1186/1744-8603-5-9
17. Vorobiof D, Abratt R (2007) The cancer burden in Africa. S Afr Med J 97(10):937. https://doi.org/10.7196/SAMJ.569
18. Selgelid MJ (2005) Ethics and infectious disease. Bioethics 19(3):272–289. https://doi.org/10.1111/j.1467-8519.2005.00441.x
19. Schneider M, Norman R, Parry C, Bradshaw D, Pluddemann A, & Assessment Collaborating Group, a. (2007). Estimating the burden of disease attributable to alcohol use in South Africa in 2000. S Af Med J 97(8):664https://doi.org/10.7196/SAMJ.658
20. Searchinger T, Craig H, Waite R, Lipinski B, Leeson G. (2013) Achieving Replacement Level Fertility https://files.wri.org/d8/s3fs-public/achieving_replacement_level_fertility_0.pdf Accessed November 3, 2021
21. Odimegwu C, Adedini S (2014) Gender equity and fertility intention in selected sub-Saharan African countries. Gend Behav 12
22. Sanders DM, Todd C, Chopra M (2005) Confronting Africa's health crisis: more of the same will not be enough. BMJ (Clinical Research Ed.) 331(7519):755–758. https://doi.org/10.1136/bmj.331.7519.755
23. UNICE (2004) Strategies for girls' education. Author, New York, NY. Retrieved from https://www.unicef.org/sowc06/pdfs/sge_English_Version_B.pdf. Accessed 3 Nov 2021
24. Social Progress Imperative https://www.socialprogress.org/index/global/results. Accessed 3 Nov 2021
25. Masekela R, Gray C, Green R, Manjra A, Kritzinger F, Levin M, Za H (2018) The increasing burden of asthma in South African children: a call to action. S Afr Med J 108(7):537–539. https://doi.org/10.7196/SAMJ.2018.v108i7.13162
26. Sitas F, Parkin M, Chirenje Z, et al. Cancers. In: Jamison DT, Feachem RG, Makgoba MW, et al (eds) (2006) Disease and mortality in sub-Saharan Africa, 2nd edn. The International Bank for Reconstruction and Development/The World Bank, Washington (DC). Chapter 20. https://www.ncbi.nlm.nih.gov/books/NBK2293/
27. World Bank (2019) World Health Statistics Overview 2019: Monitoring health for the SDGs. https://apps.who.int/iris/bitstream/handle/10665/311696/WHO-DAD-2019.1-eng.pdf?ua=1. Accessed 3 Nov 2021
28. Bahnassy AA, Abdellateif MS, Zekri AN. (2020) Cancer in Africa: is it a genetic or environmental health problem? Front Oncol 10.https://doi.org/10.3389/fonc.2020.604214
29. Ferlay J, Ervik M, Lam F, et al (2018) Global cancer observatory: cancer today. Int Agency Res Cancer, Lyon. https://gco.iarc.fr/today
30. Micah AE, Chen CS, Zlavog BS (2019) Trends and drivers of government health spending in sub-Saharan Africa, 1995–2015 BMJ Global Health 4:e001159
31. World Health Organiztaion (2016) African regional health expenditure dashboard https://www.who.int/health_financing/topics/resource-tracking/African-Regional-Health-Expenditure-Dashboard.pdf. Accessed 3 Nov 2021
32. Uche EO, Ezomike UO, Chukwu JC, Ituen MA (2012) Intensive care unit admissions in Federal Medical Centre Umuahia south east Nigeria. Niger J Med: J Natl Assoc Resid Dr Niger 21(1):70–73
33. Schoch M, Lankner C (2020) The number of poor people continues to rise in Sub-Saharan Africa, despite a slow decline in the poverty rate. World Bank https://blogs.worldbank.org/opendata/number-poor-people-continues-rise-sub-saharan-africa-despite-slow-decline-poverty-rate. Accessed 3 Nov 2021
34. Schoch M, Lankner C (2020). African countries show mixed progress towards poverty reduction and half of them have an extreme poverty rate above 35%. World Bank https://blogs.worldbank.org/opendata/african-countries-show-mixed-progress-towards-poverty-reduction-and-half-them-have-extreme. Accessed 3 Nov 2021

35. Mash R, Howe A, Olayemi O (2018) Reflections on family medicine and primary healthcare in sub-Saharan AfricaBMJ. Global Health 3:e000662
36. Marquez P, Farrington J (2013) The challenge of non-communicable diseases and road traffic injuries in sub-Saharan Africa: an overview
37. Linard C, Tatem AJ (2012) Large-scale spatial population databases in infectious disease research. Int J Health Geogr 11:7. https://doi.org/10.1186/1476-072X-11-7
38. Levitt NS (2008) Diabetes in Africa: epidemiology, management and healthcare challenges. Heart (British Cardiac Society) 94(11):1376–1382. https://doi.org/10.1136/hrt.2008.147306
39. Jemal A, Bray F, Forman D, O'Brien M, Ferlay J, Center M, Parkin DM (2012) Cancer burden in Africa and opportunities for prevention. Cancer 118(18):4372–4384. https://doi.org/10.1002/cncr.27410
40. Buonsenso D, Cinicola B, Kallon MN, Iodice F (2020) Child healthcare and immunizations in sub-Saharan Africa during the COVID-19 pandemic. Front Pediatr 6(8):517. https://doi.org/10.3389/fped.2020.00517.PMID:32850565;PMCID:PMC7424001
41. Hotez PJ, Kamath A (2009) Neglected tropical diseases in sub-saharan Africa: review of their prevalence, distribution, and disease burden. PLoS Negl Trop Dis 3(8):e412. https://doi.org/10.1371/journal.pntd.0000412
42. Hay SI, Guerra CA, Tatem AJ, Atkinson PM, Snow RW (2005) Urbanization, malaria transmission and disease burden in Africa. Nat Rev Microbiol 3(1):81–90. https://doi.org/10.1038/nrmicro1069
43. Claassens MM, van Schalkwyk C, du Toit E, Roest E, Lombard CJ, Enarson DA, Beyers N, Borgdorff MW (2013) Tuberculosis in healthcare workers and infection control measures at primary healthcare facilities in South Africa. PLoS One 8(10):e76272. https://doi.org/10.1371/journal.pone.0076272. PMID: 24098461; PMCID: PMC3788748
44. Cappuccio FP, Miller MA (2016) Cardiovascular disease and hypertension in sub-Saharan Africa: burden, risk and interventions. Intern Emerg Med 11(3):299–305. https://doi.org/10.1007/s11739-016-1423-9
45. Boum Y, Mburu Y (2020) Burden of disease in francophone Africa 1990–2017: the triple penalty? Lancet Glob Health 8(3):e306–e307. https://doi.org/10.1016/S2214-109X(20)30040-1
46. Barnes KI, Chanda P, Ab Barnabas G (2009) Impact of the large-scale deployment of artemether/lumefantrine on the malaria disease burden in Africa: case studies of South Africa Zambia and Ethiopia. Malar J 8:S8. https://doi.org/10.1186/1475-2875-8-S1-S8
47. De-Graft Aikins A, Unwin N, Agyemang C, Allotey P, Campbell C, Arhinful D (2010) Tackling Africa's chronic disease burden: from the local to the global. Glob Health 6:5. https://doi.org/10.1186/1744-8603-6-5
48. De-Graft Aikins A, Marks DF (2007) Health, disease and healthcare in Africa. J Health Psychol 12(3):387–402. https://doi.org/10.1177/1359105307076228
49. Ongole JJ, Rossouw TM, Fourie PB, Stoltz AC, Hugo J, Marcus TS (2020) Sustaining essential healthcare in Africa during the COVID-19 pandemic. Int J Tuberc Lung Dis: Off J Int Union Tuberc Lung Dis 24(6):643–645. https://doi.org/10.5588/ijtld.20.0214
50. Owoyemi A, Owoyemi J, Osiyemi A, Boyd A (2020) Artificial Intelligence for Healthcare in Africa. Frontiers in digital health 2:6. https://doi.org/10.3389/fdgth.2020.00006
51. Ssozi J, Amlani S (2015) The effectiveness of health expenditure on the proximate and ultimate goals of healthcare in sub-Saharan Africa. World Dev 76:165–179. https://doi.org/10.1016/j.worlddev.2015.07.010
52. Meyer JC, Schellack N, Stokes J, Lancaster R, Zeeman H, Defty D, Godman B, Steel G (2017) Ongoing initiatives to improve the quality and efficiency of medicine use within the public healthcare system in South Africa a preliminary study. Front Pharmacol 8:751. https://doi.org/10.3389/fphar.2017.00751
53. Montgomery Y (2016) Private vs. public healthcare in South Africa. Honors Theses:2741. https://scholarworks.wmich.edu/honors_theses/2741
54. Pillai G, Davies G, Denti P, Steimer JL, McIlleron H, Zvada S, Chigutsa E, Ngaimisi E, Mirza F, Tadmor B, Holford NH (2013) Pharmacometrics: opportunity for reducing disease burden in

the developing world: the case of Africa. CPT: Pharmacomet Syst Pharmacol 2(8):e69. https://doi.org/10.1038/psp.2013.45
55. Hsiao A, Vogt V, Quentin W (2019) Effect of corruption on perceived difficulties in healthcare access in sub-Saharan Africa. PLoS ONE 14(8):e0220583. https://doi.org/10.1371/journal.pone.0220583
56. Oleribe OO, Momoh J, Uzochukwu BS, Mbofana F, Adebiyi A, Barbera T, Williams R, Taylor-Robinson SD (2019) Identifying Key Challenges Facing Healthcare Systems In Africa And Potential Solutions. Int J Gen Med 12:395–403. https://doi.org/10.2147/IJGM.S223882
57. Bonfrer I, van de Poel E, Grimm M, Van Doorslaer E (2014) Does the distribution of healthcare utilization match needs in Africa? Health Policy Plan 29(7):921–937. https://doi.org/10.1093/heapol/czt074
58. Stuckler D, King L, Robinson H, McKee M (2008) WHO's budgetary allocations and burden of disease: a comparative analysis. Lancet (London, England) 372(9649):1563–1569. https://doi.org/10.1016/S0140-6736(08)61656-6
59. Bailey C, Blake C, Schriver M, Cubaka VK, Thomas T, Martin Hilber A (2016) A systematic review of supportive supervision as a strategy to improve primary healthcare services in Sub-Saharan Africa. Int J Gynaecol Obstet: Off Organ Int Fed Gynaecol Obstet 132(1):117–125. https://doi.org/10.1016/j.ijgo.2015.10.004
60. Ruxwana NL, Herselman ME, Conradie DP (2010) ICT applications as e-health solutions in rural healthcare in the Eastern Cape Province of South Africa. Health Inf Manag: J Health Inf Manag Assoc Aust 39(1):17–26. https://doi.org/10.1177/183335831003900104
61. Mars M (2013) Telemedicine and advances in urban and rural healthcare delivery in Africa. Prog Cardiovasc Dis 56(3):326–335. https://doi.org/10.1016/j.pcad.2013.10.006
62. Hampshire K, Porter G, Owusu SA, Mariwah S, Abane A, Robson E, Munthali A, DeLannoy A, Bango A, Gunguluza N, Milner J (2015) Informal m-health: How are young people using mobile phones to bridge healthcare gaps in Sub-Saharan Africa? Soc Sci Med 1982(142):90–99. https://doi.org/10.1016/j.socscimed.2015.07.033
63. Forland F, Rohwer AC, Klatser P, Boer K, Mayanja-Kizza H (2013) Strengthening evidence-based healthcare in Africa. Evid Based Med 18(6):204–206. https://doi.org/10.1136/eb-2012-101143
64. Chersich MF, Gray G, Fairlie L (2020) COVID-19 in Africa: care and protection for frontline healthcare workers. Global Health 16:46. https://doi.org/10.1186/s12992-020-00574-3

Open Access This chapter is licensed under the terms of the Creative Commons Attribution 4.0 International License (http://creativecommons.org/licenses/by/4.0/), which permits use, sharing, adaptation, distribution and reproduction in any medium or format, as long as you give appropriate credit to the original author(s) and the source, provide a link to the Creative Commons license and indicate if changes were made.

The images or other third party material in this chapter are included in the chapter's Creative Commons license, unless indicated otherwise in a credit line to the material. If material is not included in the chapter's Creative Commons license and your intended use is not permitted by statutory regulation or exceeds the permitted use, you will need to obtain permission directly from the copyright holder.

The manufacturer's authorised representative in the EU is Springer Nature Customer Service Centre GmbH, Europaplatz 3, 69115 Heidelberg, Germany. If you have any concerns regarding our products, please contact ProductSafety@springernature.com

Printed and bound by CPI Group (UK) Ltd, Croydon, CR0 4YY
27/03/2026
02079484-0001